The Battle of Killiekrankie: The First Jacobite Campaign, 1689–1691

Jonathan D. Oates

'This Is the Century of the Soldier', Falvio Testir, Poet, 1641

I0894063

Helion & Company

Helion & Company Limited
Unit 8 Amherst Business Centre
Budbrooke Road
Warwick
CV34 5WE
England
Tel. 01926 499 619
Fax 0121 711 4075
Email: info@helion.co.uk
Website: www.helion.co.uk
Twitter: @helionbooks
Visit our blog http://blog.helion.co.uk/

Published by Helion & Company 2018
Designed and typeset by Mach 3 Solutions Ltd (www.mach3solutions.co.uk)
Cover designed by Paul Hewitt, Battlefield Design (www.battlefield-design.co.uk)
Printed by Henry Ling Limited, Dorchester, Dorset

Text © Jonathan Oates 2018

Images within text© as individually credited
Colour plates by Mark Allen © Helion & Company 2018
Maps drawn by George Anderson © Helion & Company 2018

Every reasonable effort has been made to trace copyright holders and to obtain their permission for the use of copyright material. The author and publisher apologize for any errors or omissions in this work, and would be grateful if notified of any corrections that should be incorporated in future reprints or editions of this book.

ISBN 978-1-912390-98-4

British Library Cataloguing-in-Publication Data.
A catalogue record for this book is available from the British Library.

All rights reserved. No part of this publication may be reproduced, stored in a retrieval system, or transmitted, in any form, or by any means, electronic, mechanical, photocopying, recording or otherwise, without the express written consent of Helion & Company Limited.

For details of other military history titles published by Helion & Company Limited contact the above address, or visit our website: http://www.helion.co.uk.

We always welcome receiving book proposals from prospective authors.

Contents

List of Illustrations

List of Maps

Acknowledgements

I would like to thank all those who have contributed towards the book. Firstly there are the staffs of the various archive repositories and libraries without which the raw materials of history could not be accessed; principally in this case those at the National Archives, the British Library, the National Records of Scotland, the National Library of Scotland and the Special Collections of Edinburgh University Library. On a more personal note, members of the family have kindly given hospitality when I was in my all too fleeting visits to Scotland to view relevant material and to walk the battlefields. My son went with me to Dunkeld; at least by the trip's end he was able to say how far the Soldier's Leap was and to recite the chorus of 'Bonnie Dundee'. Last, but not least, Ralzan Rattray spent a day with me, driving me and walking me around the key points of the Killiecrankie battlefield, as well as sharing his knowledge of the battle and providing some of the illustrative matter for the book. Professor Frank Tallett and Dr Piotr Stolarski were kind enough to read the draft and make useful comments.

The Series Editor would like to thank Mr Stephen Ede Borrett for his assistance on the colours and flags carried in the campaign and Mr Alan Turton for his work on the pen and ink sketches.

This book is dedicated to Ralzan Rattray.

Introduction

The Jacobite campaigns (also known as rebellions or risings, according to preference) are one of the staples of Scottish, and to a lesser extent, British, English and European history. The term Jacobite was born in 1689. It meant a supporter of James II (1633–1701), and later his legitimate son, James Francis Stuart (1688–1766) and eldest grandson, Charles Edward Stuart (1720–1788) taken from the Latin for James, Jacobus, and was used for decades thereafter. Yet their historical coverage has been very diverse, given that the attempts by the Stuarts and their supporters to regain the thrones lost in 1688 were to persist until 1759. The lion's share of historical interest, whether in books, literature, song and film, has been on the attempt made in 1745, concentrating on Charles Edward Stuart (often known as Bonnie Prince Charlie), the climatic Battle of Culloden and the campaign as a whole. Earlier attempts to restore the Stuarts tend to receive short shrift. That being said, the present century has seen five books published on the Fifteen (more than in the whole of the twentieth century). Understandably, the 1708 and 1719 attempts which were as much invasion attempts by France and Spain as domestic insurrections, and led respectively to a great 'what if' and a skirmish in the Highlands, have gained even less coverage (one book apiece in the current century).

However, another relatively neglected field is that of the first attempt made in Scotland to restore James II to his throne. Indeed, it can be argued that there has only ever been one full-length history of this campaign. Hopkins' ground breaking book[1] is a study of Highland history from the Restoration to Glencoe and its aftermath, dealing with political matters as well as marches and battles in a very well researched and detailed manner. It is not primarily a military history, and though it does not ignore the fighting, focuses rather more on the political intrigues of late seventeenth-century Scotland than on the battles and the men who fought in them.

This book covers the military campaign in Scotland from 1689–1691, often known as the first Jacobite rebellion or rising, but the term campaign is probably better. Often this has been relegated to a bit part in wider studies.[2]

1 Paul Hopkins, *Glencoe and the End of the Highland War* (Edinburgh: John Donald, 1989).

2 Charles Petrie, *The Jacobite Movement* (London; Eyre and Spottiswoode, 1932); Bruce Lenman, *The Jacobite Risings in Britain, 1689–1746* (London: Methuen, 1980); Lenman, *The Jacobite*

The Scottish aspects of the campaign have also been subsumed in larger works, such as a recent book about the conflict within the three kingdoms.[3] This concentrates on Ireland, perhaps naturally, for this is where the bulk of the fighting occurred.

The myriad books about battles in Scotland and Britain invariably cover the battles here, albeit in minimal detail. As stated, Bonnie Prince Charlie and Culloden are the foci of the majority of works on the 1745 campaign, for 1689–1691, it is the Jacobites' first leader, 'Bonnie Dundee' (about whom there have been more biographies than any other figure in the Jacobite period other than the Bonnie Prince).[4] Given the predominance of these, the impression has sometimes been given that the campaign died with Dundee at Killiecrankie on 27 July 1689. Even a recent work which claims, as its subtitle to be a study of the campaign, ends with his death.[5]

Most, if not all, of these books, though they give an account of the campaign and the battle, seem to show a limited understanding of military realities. To date, the best account of that battle is that by Reid,[6] which as always with this author, who is a former soldier, shows a great grasp of tactical reality; however there is limited recourse to any manuscript sources. In any case, it is a booklet than a full-length study, as his later works on the Fifteen and Forty Five were. The even smaller pamphlet, produced by the National Trust for Scotland in 1978 is slender indeed, and passes off dubious material about the battle as if it was fact. A more recent version is larger and better, though focusses on the wildlife of the district, too, as does the visitor centre.[7]

Glencoe, which forms a bloody coda to the campaign, is also well known due to copious writings. Apart from the aforementioned extensive study by Hopkins there are a number of popular histories, mostly fired by a great sense of justifiable indignation.[8] These books cover the campaign prior to the massacre. A now unobtainable book, published in 2002, covers both.[9] Killiecrankie and Glencoe also have visitor centres devoted to them (as has Culloden) and are also the subject of poems and novels, though as yet no film or TV treatment. Since 2015 there have been re-enactment groups and others at Killiecrankie in late July to inform and entertain the public about the battle on its anniversary, and it has been the subject of a TV archaeology

Clans of the Great Glen, 1650–1784 (London: Methuen, 1984); Michael Barthorp, *The Jacobite Rebellions, 1689–1745* (London: Osprey Publishing, 1982); Daniel Szechi, *The Jacobites: Britain and Europe, 1688–1788* (Manchester: Manchester University Press, 1994).

3 John Barratt, *Battles for the Three Kingdoms, 1689–92* (Stroud: Sutton Publishing, 2006).

4 Charles Stanford Terry, *John Graham of Claverhouse, Viscount Dundee* (London: Archibald Constable and Co., 1905); Alastair and Henrietta Tayler, *John Claverhouse* (London: Duckworth, 1938); Magnus Linkwater and Christian Hesketh, *John Graham of Claverhouse, Bonnie Dundee: For King and Conscience* (Edinburgh: Cannongate, 1989); Andrew Scott, *Bonnie Dundee* (Edinburgh: John Donald, 2000).

5 Christina Fforde, *A Summer in Lochaber* (Colonsay: House of Lochaber, 2002).

6 Anon, *The Killiecrankie Story* (National Trust for Scotland, 1978); Lyndsey Bowditch, Benjamin Notley, Euan O'She and Louise Medine, *Killiecrankie* (National Trust for Scotland, 2015).

7 Stuart Reid, *Killiecrankie* (Leigh on Sea: Partizan Press, 1989).

8 John Buchan, *The Massacre of Glencoe* (London: Peter Davies, 1934); John Prebble, *Glencoe: The Story of the Massacre* (London: Penguin, 1967): John Sadler, *Glencoe: The Infamous Massacre* (Stroud: Amberley, 2008).

9 Niall Barr, *Killing Times: Killiecrankie and Glencoe* (Stroud: Tempus, 2002).

programme as well as two recent excavations, all of which have served to raise its profile.

Yet there is more to the subject than Dundee, Killiecrankie and Glencoe, as Hopkins' book illustrates, as important as all these are. Another battle in the campaign has never had a non-fiction book dedicated to it, though there has been a recent novel. The reason for this may be that this was not a Jacobite victory, nor an atrocity story (though was vicious enough), and so has not captured the popular imagination. Or it may be that it lacks the English versus Scottish dimension that featured in the later attempts to restore the Stuarts.

We need to examine the era as a whole. The 1689-1691 campaign would not have come about had there not been a revolution in Britain in the year before its onset. This event is often known by the name given by those who in retrospect celebrated it, namely the Glorious Revolution. Less well known, but arguably more important in the long term than the Civil Wars of 1642–1651, it certainly has been not ignored by historians in recent times, though the majority focus on it as being an episode of primarily English history. Tim Harris overturned this view in 2006 by examining the Scottish and Irish as well as the English dimension.[10]

This book is solely concerned with the military campaigns in Scotland from 1689-1691 and in the battles in particular. It focuses on the officers and men who served on both sides, examining how they operated and how they fought, as has been the case with Professor Childs in his accounts of the fighting in Ireland and in the Low Countries in the 1690s, as well as his books studying the army of the later Stuarts from 1660–1702 in the unfashionable era betwixt the giants of Cromwell and Marlborough.[11]

To an extent, therefore, this is old fashioned/popular military history, but it is, it is hoped, also informed by an awareness of the concerns of the so-called 'New Military History' and underpinned by thorough research into primary sources both printed and manuscript, as well as an examination on the ground of the major encounters. It begins by examining the political and religious struggles in seventeenth-century Scotland, especially from the Restoration of 1660 to the Revolution of 1688, in order to show the political and religious fault lines and personalities in Scotland without which there could have been no armed conflict. Chapter two takes the reader through the initial campaign from March to July 1689, marked by skirmishes and manoeuvre. The next chapters examine the opposing forces from general to private, together with equipment and tactics. Chapter five details the battle of Killiecrankie, with chapters six and seven having the battles of Dunkeld and Cromdale as their highlights, but also dealing with the wider campaign of which they were part. The final chapter covers the drift towards a settlement

10 Tim Harris, *Revolution: The Great Crisis of the British Monarchy, 1685–1720* (London: Allen Books, 2006).

11 John Childs, *The Nine Years War and the British Army, 1688–1697* (Manchester: Manchester University Press, 1991); Childs, *James II, the Army and the Glorious Revolution* (Manchester: Manchester University Press, 1980), Childs, *The Williamite War in Ireland, 1688–1691* (London: Hambledon Continuum, 2007).

Lieutenant-General Hugh Mackay, c 1640–1692 by William Barnard. (National Galleries of Scotland)

in 1691 and the treaties which ended the conflict, at least temporarily, as well as a brief account of the massacre of Glencoe.

This is primarily a military history, examining the officers and men who fought at the three major military encounters in Scotland in 1689–1690, as well as blow by blow accounts of these battles, using primary sources, both manuscript, published and archaeological, to do so. It is one which deals with military history in its wider context. It employs archival as well as printed primary sources, from both England and Scotland from the National Archives, National Library of Scotland and the National Records of Scotland. These include a plethora of published letters and memoirs by some of the participants, governmental bodies, civilians and rank and file. Contemporary newspapers, military treatises and poems as well as manuscripts from numerous Scottish and English repositories are also used. It will provide a fuller picture of the military campaign and will serve to dispel myths which still adhere to it.

1

Seventeenth Century Scotland, 1660–1688

The Jacobite campaign of 1689–1691 in Scotland was apparently caused by the dynastic struggle between two branches of the Stuart royal family, headed by James VII and II (1633–1701) and his son-in-law, William I and III (1650–1702) over who should rule Britain. Yet it had deeper roots, which stretched backwards into Scotland's history in the previous century and a half. Religious and political dissension had built up over time and periodically erupted into violence which challenged and even overthrew monarchs.

It should be noted that religion was no small matter with minimal impact on political life in the seventeenth century. This was an age of near universal Christian belief. The European world, stemming from the Protestant reformation of the sixteenth century, was divided into Catholic and Protestant. These latter were often of a form which was hierarchical, with bishops and akin to Catholicism, though acknowledging the country's monarch, not the Pope, as its head. But there were other forms of Protestantism which were administratively looser and did not recognise a secular ruler as their Head but God alone. Where one denomination in a country was a minority its communicants were often legally discriminated against.

Each denomination of Christianity viewed the others with suspicion, not only because of their religious differences, but because of their secular implications. Catholics were often seen by Protestants as being responsible for arbitrary and despotic rule; in the late seventeenth century France was held up as an example of such; Protestants being severely repressed there, especially after the revocation of the Edict of Nantes in 1685 (though Protestant Sweden and Prussia were autocratic, too, the latter favoured religious toleration). Apart from during the Commonwealth of the 1640s–1650s, Protestant nonconformists in Britain were fined for non-worship in the established churches; Catholic worship was also illegal in theory from the sixteenth to the eighteenth centuries. Fines and even imprisonment were imposed on those not attending Anglican worship. Religious dissidents were also barred from the universities, the professions, civil and military, and government. This was not just bigotry but because it was feared that members of minority denominations who could not acknowledge the legitimacy of the state church (and thus the monarch who was its head since Henry VIII) and so could not be loyal to it, because membership depended on making oaths of allegiance to the established church and state. Sometimes this could be a self-fulfilling prophecy. De facto toleration could occur and religious minorities were often only in real danger at times of crisis, either real or imagined, such as during the fallout from the so-called Popish Plot of 1678–9, when a number of Catholic priests in England were executed.

Having said all this, Protestant and Catholic states could act together against a common enemy who would necessarily be a co-religionist. Protestant Sweden was allied to Catholic France against Catholic Spain and Austria in the Thirty Years' War (1618–1648). The Pope backed the Protestant invasion of Britain in 1688 against the incumbent Catholic monarch, due to his being the ally of the Pope's enemy, the Catholic Louis XIV (1638–1715) of France. *Raison d'etat* trumped confessional solidarity. Protestant England allied with Catholic France against Catholic Spain in the 1650s, and two decades later Protestant England and Catholic France fought Protestant Holland.

By the seventeenth century adherence to the Catholic Church in Britain had diminished to the extent that only about 2 percent of the population were Catholic (this was in England and Scotland; in Ireland the majority were Catholic despite settlement by Protestants from the former two). A Presbyterian form of Protestantism was established in Scotland in the later sixteenth century, unlike the case in England where some of the trappings of Catholicism remained as the Church of England. Under threat by Charles I (1600–1649) in 1638 of the danger of an imposed Prayer Book, the Scots broke out in rebellion, leading to the Bishops' Wars which led to the nationwide Civil Wars of the 1640s. In Scotland, the Presbyterians backed the Parliamentary cause, whilst the Marquess of Montrose (1612–1650), with Highland and Irish support, initially defeated them in a series of battles in 1644–5, but was overcome in the latter year. Although Scotland then backed Charles I and, following his execution, his son, Charles II (1630–1685), they were beaten by Cromwell's army at Preston, Dunbar and Worcester (1648–1651). There was an enforced Union and a military garrison in the country in the 1650s. The Presbyterian Church flourished, however, as episcopacy was abolished along with the House of Lords and the monarchy.

The restoration of the monarchy in the form of the charismatic and politically astute Charles II in 1660 led to much that had been established in the past two decades being swept aside in Scotland as well as in England. For Scotland, the key restorative steps were the re-establishment of episcopacy and the confirmation that the monarch was Head of the Church in Scotland (which Presbyterians saw as being obliged to equate the King with Jesus). Lay patronage of clerical benefices was restored, giving power back to the landowners, which resulted in many of them adhering to episcopacy until at least the middle of the next century and thus supporting the Jacobite cause. All this reinforced Charles II's power. The Presbyterians could be fined for attending their own places of worship, as was also the case in England. A third of the clergy in Scotland in 1661 (a far greater proportion than in England) were ejected from their livings as they were unable to conform to these new ecclesiastical strictures. In 1670 an Act was passed which could lead to active Presbyterians being executed for attending field conventicles where they worshipped with their own ministers. Landowners could be punished if their tenants attended these assemblies. Many then attended their meetings bearing arms.[1]

Writings of the Presbyterians, possibly intended for posterity, describe their sufferings at this time. Gabriel Semple wrote, of the years following the Restoration:

> The souldiers drove the ministers out of Galloway and Nithsdale where the meetings were most frequent, so many of them came privately to Edinburgh and lurked there and preached more privately, at which time souldiers did sadly distress the country where the meetings had been held, these that went not to church by fining, imprisoning, driving of all their cattle, which did much exasperate the people'.[2]

In 1666, there were references to Presbyterians being 'killed, many tortured, many gibbeted and their heads and hands poled'.[3]

Persecution was stepped up in the following decades. Regular troops and Highland clansmen were quartered on districts where Presbyterians dwelt and worshipped, chiefly in the south-west of Scotland. Field conventicles were held by worshippers 'with great contempt of the regular clergy'. Where meeting houses did exist, the Scottish Privy Council (the royal appointed executive government agency in Scotland) would send orders for the regular troops in that district to demolish them, as Captain John Graham of Claverhouse (1648–1689) noted in January 1679: on finding one he wrote 'the walls wer throwen down, and timber burnt'. They would extract fines, arrest worshippers, steal, torture (the latter perfectly legitimate in Scotland) and even kill Presbyterians. Graham referred to searches by his troopers for ministers and prisoners being taken away under military guard. Soldiers took 'free quarter' from civilians. Troops would also commit crimes apart from those sanctioned by their officers, Graham referring to 'ane accompt of a disorder committed by some of our men in the cuntrey'. The government saw their enemies as seditious; there had been Presbyterian rebellions in 1666 and 1679 and the brutal murder of Archbishop Sharp in 1679. An extreme branch of the Presbyterians, the Cameronians, declared war against Charles II but this group was not representative of all Presbyterians.[4]

In 1678, there were similar complaints by Presbyterians, 'the western shires were by an act of councell given up to be harassed and plundered by these savages for no other cause but because some few in these western places had at some times go to publicke worshippe of God in these meetings of people called conventikles'. Apart from the depredations of the regular

1 Tim Harris, *Revolution: The Great Crisis of the British Monarchy, 1685–1720* (London: Allen Books, 2006), pp.21–22.

2 David George Mullan (ed.), 'Protestant Piety in Early Modern Scotland: Letters, Lives and Covenants, 1650–1712', Scottish Historical Society, Series 5, Vol. 17 (2008), p.157.

3 *Ibid.*, p.170.

4 *Ibid.*; *Dundee Letters: Letters of John Graham of Claverhouse, Viscount Dundee* (Edinburgh: Bannantyne Club, 1826), pp.2, 4-5, 10, 22.

troops, there were also the Highland Host which arrived in the country around Glasgow and Stirling to harass the Presbyterians there: 'Highlanders in swarms through the country their to ly, plunder and pillage, and avail orders for more havock'. The Highlanders quartered themselves on private householders; twenty being in one house and 1,400 in another 900, for example.[5]

The Presbyterians were not unresisting. On 21 April 1679, Graham wrote, 'I fynd Mr Welch is accustoming both ends of the country to face the Kings forces, and certainly intends to brak out in ane open rebellion'.[6] Later that month, Graham refers to arresting a man who 'does not deny bot he is listed as on who is to defend thes feild conventikls in arms'. Graham's soldiers were certainly eager for a fight, 'a great desyr to be at those rogues', as was he. This might be because they were, perhaps unsurprisingly, resisted by those they oppressed. On 29 May, Graham wrote of a shoemaker firing on his men near Falkirk, before he was apprehended. Apparently 'He is otherwayes a great rogue, and frequents field conventikles, and they say, taks upon him to exercise'.[7]

It was even possible for the Covenanters to take on the King's men in open battle and worst them, as occurred in the skirmish at Drumclog, to the south of Glasgow, on 30 May 1679. When Graham's troop of horse came in sight of a Covenanter meeting, 'we found them drawen up in battell upon a most advantageous ground'. They could only be reached by passing through ponds. They 'consisted of four battalions of foot, and all well armed with fusils and pitchforks, and three squadrons of horse'. Battle commenced, with both sides sending out skirmishing parties. When those of the Covenanters fell back, they sent forward a battalion of their infantry, against which 60 dragoons were pushed forward and made them run. Then there was a general engagement, with Graham's men standing on the defensive, his men firing a volley when the enemy were within 10 paces. This did not beat off the attack, which developed into a melee. Two of Graham's officers were hit and his horse was wounded by a pitchfork. Graham was carried off by his horse and this demoralised his men who 'fell into disorder'. They were pursued by the Covenanters' horsemen. Eight or 10 of the troopers were killed and others wounded, though Graham saved the troops' standards. The reverse encouraged other country people to show hostility to the troops and Graham wrote, 'This may be counted the beginning of the rebellion in my opinion'.[8]

Following the fighting at Drumclog, the Cameronians took heart and the government sent stronger forces to join the Scottish militia to crush what was now deemed a rebellion. Battle occurred on 3 June at Bothwell Bridge, just to the east of Glasgow. This time the forces involved on both sides were rather more formidable. The King's forces were led by his eldest son, the 30-year-old James Scott (1649–1685), Duke of Monmouth, who was Captain General. The Covenanters, allegedly 7,000 strong, had barricaded Bothwell Bridge.

5 Mullan (ed.), 'Protestant Piety', pp.171–173.
6 *Dundee Letters*, pp.18–19.
7 *Ibid.*, pp.23, 25, 27.
8 *Ibid.*, pp.29–30.

Monmouth asked them if they would like to negotiate to avoid bloodshed, but the only terms he could grant would be that they must first surrender and then plead for mercy. This they would not accept and so hostilities began. Cannon fired on the Covenanters and then the bridge was attacked. The defenders fell back, allowing the King's men to cross the bridge and form up for an attack. There was further artillery fire as a prelude to the assault. The Covenanters' cavalry seems to have been the first to flee, 'leaving their flying foot to the mercy of our arms, who pursued them with all diligence and zeal, and have killed some hundreds of them and taken many hundreds prisoner'. According to the account of John Maitland, Duke of Lauderdale (1616–1682), Monmouth's casualties were minimal.[9]

Lauderdale then wrote, 'We send the flying packet with great joy, that your Grace may give His Majesty the good and happy news of a total and absolute victory obtained this day over the rebels by His Majesty's Forces'.[10] A few of the 1,100-1,200 prisoners were hanged, 'dyeing very obstinately; some justifying the rebellion' whilst others were transported to the Americas.[11]

Military action against the Covenanters continued after their defeat at Bothwell Bridge. Graham wrote in February 1682, 'The first thing I mynd to doe is to fll to work with all that have been in the rebellion, or accessory their too by giving men, money or armes; … and after, field conventikles, for what remains of the laws against fanaticks'. He was convinced that only a permanent military presence would be effective otherwise many would 'fall back to their old ways; so that it is in vain to think of any settlement here, without a constant force pleased in garrison; and this is the opinion of all honest men here, and their desir'. However, some Scots clearly welcomed the military presence in suppressing the Presbyterians.[12]

Yet it would be wrong to see the soldiery as being wholly fixed on a military solution. Graham also wrote, 'I will threaten much, but forebear sever execution for a whyll, for fear people should grou desperate and increase too much for the number of our enimys'. Again, he made paradoxical comments; 'to put laws severly against great and small in exicution, which is very just; but what effects does that produce, but mor to exasperate and alienat the hearts of the whole body of the people, for it renders them desperate when it gains on'. It was not intended that there was any 'desein to ruin any of his subjects … nor I to enrich myself', rather than to reclaim 'any who would resolve to conform and leive regularly'.[13]

Yet violence was to be applied where it was deemed to be necessary. As to a particularly militant Covenanter, McClurg-Smith of Menegeff, Graham wrote in March 1682, 'I am resolved to hang him for it is necessary I make some example of severity less rebellion be thought cheap here'. When one

9 Andrew Browning (ed.), *English Historical Documents, VIII*, (London: Eyre and Spottiswoode, 1953), p.625.

10 *Ibid.*

11 Narcissus Luttrell, *A Brief Relation of State Affairs, 1678–1714*, I (Oxford: Oxford University Press, 1857), pp.20, 31.

12 Andrew Murray Scott (ed.), 'Letters of John Graham of Claverhouse', *SHS Miscellany 11*, 5th series, Vol. 3. (1990), pp.170, 174.

13 *Ibid.*, pp.170, 174.

John Brown was found, with ammunition on his property, and who would not swear he would not oppose the King nor take the oaths required, 'I caused shoot him dead'. He complained that there were insufficient troops to do the work. Resistance was not at an end, for that June he noted that there were 'severall parties of Whigues in armes to number of 6 or 700'. In 1684 he referred to 'that plague of presbitry' and there was a skirmish that year with 200 Covenanters, who fired at his troops, wounding some, before fleeing. Graham wrote of 'this unseasonable trouble these dogs give me'. The subsequent search for the Covenanters failed and was followed by another skirmish.[14]

However, support in Scotland for the Stuart monarchy certainly existed, especially among the bulk of the country's rulers; active rebels were very much the minority. The Presbyterians were quite possibility a majority of the Scottish population, but they were unable, and in most cases, unwilling, to overthrow the existing order in Church and State. The latter were firmly in the hands of the King's brother, James, Duke of York, from 1679–1682, working in Charles II's name, of course. James worked with his natural allies, the Episcopal Church and the secular establishment, against the radical threat.[15] Some saw the Presbyterians as dangerous politically as well as being denominationally unsound. John Evelyn (1620–1706), an English Anglican Royalist, wrote in his diary on the occasion of the Presbyterian revolt of 1679, 'a Rebellion in Scotland of the Phanatics there; so as there was a sad prospect of publique affaires'.[16]

Certainly when James arrived in Scotland in 1679, he was 'nobly entertained' when he was met by the nobility, members of the privy council, and the gentry on the borders. The city magistrates received him 'with all the splendour and joy imaginable'. He received a similar reception in Glasgow in 1682. In 1680 and in 1681 Charles' birthday was celebrated in Edinburgh with 'great joy and solemnity'. On the latter occasion, bells rang, guns fired, there were trumpets and bonfires. In that same year the Scottish Parliament observed that there was no doubt that the throne would pass to the King's brother on his death (there had been much debate in England whether this should happen), but they also asserted the necessity for maintaining the anti-Catholic laws; an uneasy combination given that James, as heir, was Catholic. Other loyalist statements included asserting the royal prerogative and outlawing field conventicles. When Lord Belhaven objected he was briefly gaoled after his 'words put the house in a heat'.[17]

Acts of defiance continued, however. On Christmas day of 1680 students in Edinburgh burnt an effigy of the pope. Covenanters would burn Acts of Parliament in public in 1682. There were rumours of plots to kill the King and his brother. Whilst these were latter were illusory, in the summer of 1684 they did kill two soldiers.[18]

---

14 *Ibid.*, pp.179, 182, 230, 217, 220, 223.
15 Harris, *Revolution*, pp.33–34.
16 John Evelyn, *Diary* (London: Everyman, 2006), p.595.
17 Luttrell, *Brief Relation*, I, pp.26–27, 46, 117, 122, 138, 124.
18 *Ibid.*, pp.61–62, 162, 316, 322.

In February 1685, when Charles II died, he was succeeded by his younger brother, James. As Duke of York he was not unknown to the Scots, due to his presence there earlier in the decade. As in England, his accession was greeted in Scotland with apparent congratulations from his subjects. Colin Lindsay, the third Earl of Balcarres (1652–1721) wrote, 'Never King succeeded to a throne more with the love and esteem of his subjects than your Majesty'.[19] The Corporation of Aberdeen, on 18 February, recorded James' accession with the following comment, 'whom God preserve and bless with a long glorious happie life and a prosperous reigne'. That day there were all possible manifestations of loyalty; loyal healths were drunk, volleys of gunfire were heard, bells were rung, there was music and bonfires were lit. Along the populace there were 'great acclamations of joy from the whole citizens and others ... crying with uplifted hands, God save King James the seventh'[20] The capital was loyal, too, 'Letters from Edinburgh speak of the great joy and satisfaction in that kingdom upon the proclaiming of His Majesty's there'. Loyal addresses were sent from both Edinburgh and Glasgow.[21]

This should not have been surprising because Charles had replaced those disloyal to him in positions of power in the corporations, in Parliament, the Privy Council and in the Church, with those who were his supporters. Loyal addresses were sent and in the streets there were bonfires and free drinks for the people. Parliament supported him and was willing to grant James the revenues he needed to govern. The clergy preached loyalist sermons. James promised he would uphold the laws and defend his subjects' religion. Evelyn wrote thus in his diary that the new monarch attested that:

> ... he had ben misrepresented as affecting arbitrary power, they should find the contrary ... that he would endeavour to maintaine the Government both in Church & state as by Law establish'd, its Principles Being so firme for Monarchy, & the members of it shewing themselves so good & Loyal subjects, & that he would never depart from the just rights & prerogative of the Crown, so would he never Invade any man's propriety: but as he had often adventured his life in defence of the Nation, so he would still proceed, & preserve it in all its lawful rites & libertyes.[22]

Initially it seemed a workable arrangement. There were relatively few signs of open discontent, though a minister in Dumfriesshire was brutally assaulted for his loyalty to the new king.[23] However, a few years previously one of his brother's ministers, had raised the following doubts about James:

> This good prince has all the weaknesses of his father without his strength. He loves, as he saith, to be served in his own way, and he is as very a papist as the

19 Earl of Balcarres, *Memoirs touching the Revolution in Scotland* (Edinburgh: Bannatyne Club, 1841), p.2.

20 *Extracts from the Council Registers of the Burgh of Aberdeen, 1643–1747* (Edinburgh, 1832), p.305.

21 Luttrell, *Brief Relation*, I, pp.330, 338, 339.

22 Evelyn, *Diary*, p.709.

23 Harris, *Revolution*, pp.46–65.

> pope himself, which will be his ruin ... if he had the empire of the whole world he would venture the los if it, for his ambition is to shine in a red letter after his death.[24]

There was immediate and dangerous opposition, however, from exiled discontents who had been involved in conspiracy in Charles' latter years. In Holland Charles II's eldest illegitimate son, Monmouth, victor at Bothwell Bridge, and Archibald Campbell (1629–1685), the ninth Earl of Argyll, planned to arrive in England and Scotland simultaneously to bring down the new king. Argyll's father had been executed by the Stuarts in 1661 and he had initially loyally served them until he was accused of treason in 1681, sentenced to death but escaped abroad. His standard bore the words, 'No Popery, no prelacy, no erastianism'. Both expeditions failed and their leaders were beheaded. The reasons for such were due to a failure to co-ordinate their efforts against James II, tactical errors, military failings and a lack of expected support.[25]

Argyll had arrived in his old ancestral lands in March 1685. He came with three ships containing 300 men and arms and equipment for thousands more. Apparently, 'They all knew how odious the King's person, as well as his religion, was in Scotland'. He hoped to rally his former tenants, then march to Edinburgh via Glasgow. According to Sir Ewan Cameron of Lochiel (1629–1719), 'The newes of Argile's landing ... made such a noise, that people of all ranks and degrees were in the utmost confusion and consternation'. After having a peak of 2,500 men, desertions reduced it to 1,500, 'all High landers except a few Dutch officers and Scotch fugitives'. Most Presbyterian and the radical Covenanters did not join him because he did not support their cause. The army in Scotland and the militia were summoned to act against Argyll. They were led by John Murray (1631–1703), the first Marquis of Atholl.[26]

There was a stand off in June with Argyll camped near Loch Fyne near Inveraray. There was concern he might attempt a surprise attack on his enemies at night time, but Atholl, who was at Inverary, sat back and did little. Eventually after a brief skirmish, Argyll retreated to Glenderrowen and later to Portnadernag. His support falling apart, the rebellion ended and Argyll was captured near Glasgow. He was executed at Edinburgh on 1 July without any need for a trial as he had been already found guilty of treason in 1681. Some of his followers were also killed; others were transported. In England, Monmouth's rebels were crushed in battle at Sedgemoor, Somerset, on 5–6 July. James was as secure as ever, and more so, because he had not only smashed his enemies (though some supporters fled) but he had an excuse to increase his military strength by raising additional regiments in both England and Scotland in peacetime; supported in this by loyal Parliaments in both countries.[27]

---

24 John Kenyon, *The Stuarts* (London: Fontana, 1970), p.144.

25 Harris, *Revolution*, pp.73–5; Luttrell, *Brief Relation*, I, p.350.

26 J. MacKnight (ed.), *Memoirs of Lochiel* (Glasgow: Maitland Club, 1842), pp.210–1; Browning, *English Historical Documents*, p.627.

27 Harris, *Revolution*, pp.76–80, 88; Cameron, *Memoirs*, pp.212–216.

Atholl family coat of arms. (Author, 2017)

James II had triumphed because his enemies had minority support. The majority stood with him or at least did not side with his opponents; as had been the case under his brother. Yet most would not support him without question. Confident in his successes against his enemies, the King then took his next steps as part of his policy to forward the position of his fellow Catholics and this was to lead to his downfall. Catholics were a minority, making up about 2 percent of the population in Scotland. Unlike their English equivalents they had not suffered much legal discrimination in worship had even been able to hold government offices until 1681, following the anti-popery scare known as the Popish Plot. In the sixteenth and seventeenth centuries Parliament had passed anti-Catholic legislation and James was determined to dismantle this in order to restore Catholicism as a major part of British religious life. James decided to launch his policies in Scotland before attempting them in England.[28]

He did this by promoting Catholics to positions of power within the state. In Edinburgh in 1686, his lord chancellor, James Drummond (1648–1716), the fourth Earl of Perth, had a Catholic chapel established. This was resisted by 'the common people' who raised a 'tumult or stir'. Popular opposition was insufficient but if allied to elite opposition, the prognosis for James was poor. He tried to force the Scottish Parliament in the same year to pass laws to ease the lot of the Catholics, but in this Parliament was no so obliging and most of its members did not support him. Parliament was thus suspended.[29]

Then in 1687 the King, using his royal prerogative to bypass Parliament, passed an edict of Toleration to all denominations (including all Protestant nonconformists), to promote the lot of Catholics by enabling them to worship without restrictions. All this did very little to help Catholics, but antagonised his supporters in the Episcopal Church by attacking their monopoly on religious authority that he had, in his coronation oath, sworn to defend. This provoked both the establishment, whom had supported him previously, and led to popular anti-Catholicism. Balcarres wrote, 'The fears and jealousies both parties had of the Roman Catholics did not a little heighten these discontents'.[30] In Edinburgh where mass was celebrated openly in 1686, there had been riots in the streets, which had to be suppressed by troops. The

28 Harris, *Revolution*, p.145.
29 Luttrell, *Brief Relation*, pp.372, 376, 381.
30 Balcarres, *Memoirs*, p.4.

governor of the castle was turfed out and replaced by the Catholic George Gordon (c.1649–1716), first Duke of Gordon.[31]

This was quite apart from the actions of the Presbyterians who were also his long-established opponents. Despite their weakened condition, following years of persecution, in his late brother's reign, James' declaration of Toleration allowed them to worship and, inadvertently, to organise in the open. Exiled and imprisoned ministers, no friends of King James, returned and congregations were re-established. This did not immediately challenge the King but it did mean that they were in a position to take action should the opportunity arise.[32] They 'do not like the indulgence there, and many may refuse the benefit of it, because they will not take the oath', though some Quakers and Presbyterian ministers sent him addresses of thanks. Covenanters remained at war with the regime and in July 1688 killed six soldiers whilst rescuing some of their own.[33]

By 1688, in both England and Scotland, James had thrown away an almost impregnable position that he had enjoyed since the summer of 1685. He retained some supporters, but he had lost many others who were appalled by his religious and political moves which ran contrary to theirs. It was now not only the Covenanters who were in opposition but many in the political elite as well as some of the common people: the situation in England was similar. In the autumn of that year, James faced the external threat of a Dutch invasion by his son-in-law, the Protestant Prince William of Orange (1650–1702), ruler of Holland, who was married to his eldest daughter, Mary (1662–1694). This had been prompted by the birth to James' Queen, of a legitimate son, James Francis Stuart, on 10 June 1688 and the invitation to William by seven leading Englishmen. William, who had the ear of some prominent Scots about him, wanted to utilise British resources against the expansionist aims of France under Louis XIV. The birth of the heir meant that there could be a long line of Catholic kings and that James' policies would not die with him, for he was already middle aged and older than his brother had been when he had died. Celebrations of the royal birth were muted in Scotland; some were put on (the royal boroughs sent an address congratulating him on the birth of his son, as did the archbishops and bishops) but many stayed away and troops had to be on hand to prevent them being disrupted.[34] In Aberdeen, though, on 27 June, there were 'thanksgiving and rejoiceing for the happie birth of the Prince'.[35] Yet some of the King's natural supporters, the Episcopalian clergy, did not pray for the new Prince of Wales. Presbyterian ministers were 'making insinuations to their people of the danger from Popery and arbitrary power'.[36]

To deal with this impending invasion, James had his Scottish army, described by Balcarres thus, '3,000 effective men, vigorous, well disciplined

31 Harris, *Revolution*, pp.151–3.

32 *Ibid.*, p.176.

33 Luttrell, *Brief Relation*, I, p.398, 407, 411, 445.

34 Harris, *Revolution*, pp.367–8; Luttrell, *Brief Relation*, pp.454, 474.

35 *Extracts ... Aberdeen*, p.309.

36 Balcarres, *Memoirs*, p.5.

and clothed, to a man, hearty in your cause', marched south to England leaving his northerly kingdom unusually vulnerable.[37] The army was composed of three regiments of infantry, two of cavalry and a further cavalry troop.[38] When Graham, now a colonel of cavalry, received these orders on 10 October, he wrote that he would obey 'with all convenient dilligence'.[39] Others in Scotland rallied to James' side. The Privy Council and the bishops assured him of their support and their abhorrence towards the invasion. So did the Scottish burghs. Glasgow Council raised the militia. The Privy Council also instructed Sir Ewan Cameron and Sir John Drummond of Machanie to summon militia to Kirkmichael and eventually they had 1,200 men with them in October. Cameron wrote 'They effectually kept that country in obedience'.[40] There was a loyal address from the Privy Council, including the signatures of Balcarres, Perth, Graham, the Duke of Atholl and the archbishops, addressed to James II, asserting that they were 'ready to expose our Lives and Fortunes in Defence of your sacred Person'.[41]

There was also support for William, too. In Dumfriesshire, nobility and gentry avoided serving in the militia. Presbyterians looked forward to his arrival. They gathered together and many moved to Edinburgh, unmolested by the militia. Meanwhile, William and his multinational army of Dutch, Danes, Englishmen, Scots and Germans arrived in south-west England on 5 November and slowly marched towards London, gathering support on the way. James marched his forces towards them and they gathered near Salisbury. A number of high level defections, but only a small number of rank and file, went over to William. A notable defector was John Churchill (1650–1722), once a key supporter of the King. Despite James' bravery in warfare in previous decades, he felt he had to give way and his forces, superior in numbers, retreated without a fight. By the end of December James had fled the country, having been granted exile in France, his forces disbanded and William's army was in London. William made contact with his supporters in Scotland.[42]

The removal of the Scottish army also meant that popular hostility against Catholicism and James could be manifest. Before, Balcarres noted, the 'disaffected' had 'lived quietly', but now 'all the disaffected in the nation thought they had met with their just time … a whole nation exposed'.[43] Government in Scotland was beginning to break down. The Earl of Perth and the Privy Council were in conflict with the leading Scottish Catholics, 'who all advised to give way to necessity, and since they had no power to maintain the government, it would look better the quit voluntarily'.[44]

In Edinburgh, students and the populace ('the rabble met in great numbers') engaged in demonstrations and violence against Catholic chapels

37 *Ibid.*, p.12.
38 *London Gazette*, 2411, 17–20 Dec. 1688.
39 Scott, 'Letters', p.233.
40 Cameron, *Memoirs*, p.231; Harris, *Revolution*, p.370.
41 *London Gazette*, 2388, 4–8 Oct. 1689.
42 Harris, *Revolution*, pp.370–1.
43 Balcarres, *Memoirs*, p.11.
44 *Ibid.*, p.15.

and property. Some soldiers tried to restore order and killed some of the rioters but took some fatalities themselves. Such actions also took place elsewhere. Similar violence occurred in London and in other towns and cities in England, too.[45] As a contemporary newspaper noted, 'The Protestants are up in arms in several parts of this kingdom, declaring with the Prince of Orange, for the Protestant religion and a free Parliament. The rabble of this city [Edinburgh] have demolished most of the Romish chapels and have pulled down several Popish houses'.[46] The Earl of Perth, James' foremost representative in Scotland, fled. Firstly he went to Lochaber, under Cameron's protection, then planned to take a ship to Ireland where he believed his royal master was. Taking ship at Kircaldy, on the Fife coast, he was captured and imprisoned in Stirling Castle.[47]

There was only one note of open defiance against William in Scotland: 'The Duke of Gordon is returned into the castle [of Edinburgh] and is resolved to hold the same against any opposition'.[48] Yet a deputation from the city council was allowed into the castle and Gordon assured them, 'he did not intend, nor should there be any the least damage done to the city by the castle'.[49]

There was also other popular action throughout Scotland, beginning at the end of the year and continuing into the summer of 1689. This was taken by Presbyterians against the Episcopalian clergy. They were known as 'rabblings' in which the latter were forcibly elected from their churches and their manses, to be replaced by Presbyterian ministers. This happened in perhaps between 200 and 300 parishes and can be seen as an attempt to overturn the Protestant religious settlement of 1660, not just attacking Catholic chapels (which were illegal).[50] James II wrote to the Pope in February deploring such behaviour, 'Nor is that madness confined to England, with equal fury and no less destruction it has invaded Scotland, where every sort of cruelty is practised on men of the Catholic name by the partisans of Orange'.[51]

By the end of the year, Scotland was divided. Some supported James. Cameron, for example, was extremely dispirited, 'Thus disappointed, he returned to Lochaber, where he continued all that winter, mediating how he could best serve the King'.[52] Others were more open in their resistance; Gordon refused to surrender Edinburgh Castle. Viscount Dundee (as Graham was now known) was also open in his continued loyalty to James. This was a minority, however. There were Episcopalians who wished to maintain their church but were ambivalent about their support for James and might co-operate with William. Others were as yet undecided, being guided by self interest. Finally there were the Presbyterians who desired a radical

45 Harris, *Revolution*, pp.372–5.
46 *Universal Intelligencer*, 4, 18–22 Dec. 1688.
47 Cameron, *Memoirs*, pp.231–2.
48 *Universal Intelligencer*, 4, 18–22 Dec. 1688.
49 *English Courant*, 7, 28 Dec. 1688–2 Jan. 1689.
50 Harris, *Revolution*, pp.376–378.
51 *Calendar of the Stuart Papers belonging to His Majesty the King Preserved at Windsor Castle*, I (London: HMSO, 1902), p.36.
52 Cameron, *Memoirs*, p.232.

overhaul of the Scottish religious settlement and supported William.[53] Some former supporters had changed tack, the burgh of Aberdeen now passed a loyal address to William on 8 January and on 29 May was to order official celebrations when he accepted the Crown.[54] A declaration was passed in Scotland in favour of the Prince of Orange and the Protestant religion.[55] William's declaration was read out on the first day of 1689 in Edinburgh to jubilation in public and apparently 'Glasgow had don it last week & most of the touns'.[56]

Meanwhile in London, on 7 January 1689, William assembled all the Scottish nobility and gentry there to decide what should happen in his northern kingdom. William, third Duke of Hamilton (1634–1694), was elected as their spokesman. They agreed that William should be given temporary authority there but that a Convention of Estates meet at the Scottish capital on 14 March 1689 to settle the country's future government.[57] Meanwhile in England, after some deliberation, William and his wife Mary were offered the throne of England by the Convention assembled in February and they accepted; he became William III.

Amongst those influential Scots whom William spoke to were the foresaid Balcarres and Dundee. Neither agreed to support him. Late in February they were accompanied by 24 cavalrymen, presumably of his own regiment, and rode to Scotland. In the meantime, William had guaranteed Dundee's protection provided he lived peaceably and he had agreed 'unless he was forced to it, he would live quietly'.[58] When Dundee and Balcarres returned to Edinburgh, the latter believed it was in a state 'of great tranquillity and generally well affected'. They met Gordon and persuaded him to hold the castle for James. The latter, however, did not make preparations for a siege and did not arrange for a supply of provisions to be laid up there.[59]

There were, however, concerns about law and order in Scotland among William's supporters, who had no armed forces to support them, and a letter of 19 January spoke of Major General Hugh Mackay (1640–1692), who had arrived in England in the previous year with William's invasion force, and a loyal supporter of William, suggesting that a troop of Guards be sent, 'I cannot see how it should be otherwise for we must have som guards … that troop should suffice'.[60] There were fears that clans loyal to James might march southwards, 'the Highlanders [being] ready to rise upon a word given' and by the end of February there were reports of discontents in Edinburgh, including disbanded army officers. For William's supporters, there was some immediate relief for men from the West Country had arrived to defend the

53 Harris, *Revolution*, pp.380–6.
54 *Extracts … Aberdeen*, p.311.
55 Luttrell, *Brief Relation*, p.492.
56 National Library of Scotland, MS7026, f.98.
57 Harris, *Revolution*, pp.379–80.
58 Gilbert Burnet, *History of My Own Time*, IV (Oxford: Clarendon, 1823), p.39; Balcarres, *Memoirs*, p.xix.
59 *Ibid.*, pp.23–24.
60 NLS, MS7026, f.106.

Convention.[61] As the Convention was preparing to meet, tension in the capital was apparent: 'They were pleased to call them rable, about 2000 men came out of the west & growing dayly & Earl Dundee has another sort of rable 30 or 40 troupers … who walk up and down with him'.[62]

William was concerned, with no army in Scotland, that the country might fall into the hands of his opponents. After all the small Scottish army brought southwards in November 1688 had been mostly ordered overseas (leading Dumbarton's regiment to mutiny). On 4 February 1689 Mackay referred to William ordering the regiment of Scottish dragoons, now led by Sir Thomas Livingstone, northwards. However Lord Dunmore, their former colonel, was instructed to pay their arrears. This caused delays and so they did not march until at least two more months had passed.[63]

Therefore Mackay received the following instructions from William III on 7 March 1689:

> You are to command our forces that are to be in Scotland, and you shall take the advice and assistance of the Lord Melvill, to whom Wee have given instructions to that effect.
>
> You shall strengthen the regiments sent from hence to Scotland to number of marching foot in each company; and if you find necessity, you shall levey more regiments; and if the occasions that may occur admit not of a delay, you shall give commissions to officers that are to levey or command them.
>
> If the Castle of Edinburgh be not rendered according to our former orders, you shall treat for the rendering of it; and if you finde need, you shall give assurance of indemnity to the Duke of Gordon, Leut Collonell Windrome [in command of the garrison at Edinburgh castle], and – to whom Wee have already sent passes and protections; and you shall give such other gratifications to such as you see convenient, that the Castle may be put in the hands of confident persons, both commanders and souldiers. You shall doe the like for the Castle of Dumbarton.[64]

Mackay was in London, but was unwell, 'not being recovered of a great sickness whereby he had been attacked shortly after his landing in England'. However, convinced that the cause was right, he hastened to obey. He, three regiments of the Scots-Dutch Brigade, namely Mackay's, Balfour's and Ramsay's (about 1,100 infantry in all) together with arms and ammunition for the new regiments to be raised there, took ship to Scotland as this was the quickest way of getting there. They boarded barges on the Thames on 13 March to take them to the transport ships. Once they had departed, the journey took between eight and 10 days.[65] These regiments arrived on 27 March (a day after Mackay) and were initially quartered in Leith, Dalkeith and Musselburgh. They had each been over 600 strong in November 1688 and

---

61 *Ibid.*, ff.143, 147.

62 *Ibid.*, 158.

63 *Ibid.*, MS 3740, 80.

64 Hugh Mackay, *Memoirs of the War carried on in Scotland and Ireland, 1689–1691* (Edinburgh: Bannatyne Club, 1833), p.221.

65 *Ibid.*, pp.3–4.

on 27 March Mackay was allowed by the Convention to send out recruiting parties to increase their strength; it is not known how successful these were. The city was ordered to provide Mackay with horses and carriages.[66]

He was also provided with sums of money from the English Treasury. Firstly, on 12 March, it was ordered that £7,500 be given for the specific use of the Dutch troops. A further £10,000 was sent on 15 March to him for his use in Scotland. On 19 March an additional £4,000 was provided. To put this into context, £971 3s 8d paid for a single regiment of infantry, Hastings', to cover costs from 14 December 1688 to 20 January 1689. The cost of a whole infantry regiment for a year was about £7,500–7,600.[67]

Elections for the Convention in Edinburgh were held and the men chosen were 188 in number; clergy, nobility and gentry. Some, such as the bishops and Dundee, supported James but far more were against him. The Presbyterian interest was strong among them, and became more so as some of James' supporters and some of the Episcopalians withdrew from the gathering in Edinburgh. They first met on 14 March. Although there was some discussion about a possible union with England, nothing came of this. The real question was who should be king and how should Scotland be governed in Church and state. On 16 March, James had not helped his own position by typically sending a hectoring and threatening letter to the Convention; in contrast, William was conciliatory and mild.[68]

James' supporters in Scotland, including those who left the Convention at Edinburgh, discussed holding an alternate Convention at Stirling. In order to hold this meeting they needed physical security. They had hoped that Atholl, who had led the forces against Argyll in 1685, might be able to have provided it, but he was irresolute and remained in England, refusing to commit himself. Even in Edinburgh some did not feel safe. Men from the West of Scotland had been summoned by the supporters of William 'never was seen so contemptible a rabble'. Dundee apparently feared for his life, claiming 'he knew six or seven of the western rebels who had undertaken to assassinate him'. Despite identifying his would be killers, they were not arrested and so he was eager to leave the city. Balcarres tried to argue against it because it could give alarm to their fellows and bring an end to the plan for the Convention at Stirling.[69] In the meantime the Edinburgh convention requested more immediate support. Lord Leven obliged them by raising 800 men into a regiment of infantry in two hours on 18 March for the defence of the capital.[70]

The English Parliament decided that James had abdicated the throne, but the Scottish Convention did not agree to this polite fiction. Instead, Sir John Dalrymple (1648–1707) suggested that the Crown had been forfeited by James by his acting illegally. A majority agreed with him and they declared

66 Evan Whyte Melville Balfour-Maitland, 'Estate Proceedings, An Account of the Proceedings of the Estates of Scotland, 1689–1690', *SHS*, series IV (1954), vol. I, p.19; NLS, MS 7026, 170.

67 *Calendar of Treasury Books*, IX, Part 1, 1689–1692 (London: HMSO, 19), pp.6, 9, 377, 128, 911.

68 Harris, *Revolution*, pp.387–90.

69 Balcarres, *Memoirs*, pp.29–31.

70 Balfour-Maitland, 'Estates', I, p.8.

that the throne was vacant. Hamilton suggested it be offered to William and this course of action was sanctioned by those present. Messengers were despatched southwards to pass on the news and to request that their grievances be settled in due course.[71]

Dundee decided he could not risk staying in Edinburgh. On 18 March, he planned to meet other Jacobites there, but did not do so and instead went to the castle. He met Gordon near the postern gate 'and had long discourse with him in French' according to one account. Gordon was told there about the intention to raise the Jacobite standard at Stirling and then the castle would be relieved. Dundee was seen by his enemies meeting Gordon and the Convention. Dundee then rode out of Edinburgh with about 60 horsemen. The Duke of Hamilton ordered Major Hugh Buntine and cavalry to ride after Dundee, but without success.[72]

The meeting of the Convention, on 19 March, 'being informed that the Viscount of Dundee and the Lord Livingstoun, with several others, are in armes, at or near the toun of Linlothgow, without any warrand from the Estates' had a herald 'to charge the saids Viscount Dundee and Lord Livingstoun to appear befor the Meeting of Estates, within twenty four hours after the charges, undir the pain of treason'.[73] There were fears that 'the clans of the Highlands were gathering together' and a proclamation was issued to raise the militia. Meanwhile, Gordon had been requested to leave Edinburgh Castle as he was a Catholic and so incapable of legally holding any military or civil office. He refused and so the castle was blockaded.[74]

Meanwhile, James II had reluctantly returned to the only one of his kingdoms which was not largely hostile towards him, Ireland, and had established his court in Dublin. The bulk of the population as well as the standing army there, stood by him, principally on religious grounds, given that the majority, unlike the rest of Britain, were Catholic. French aid was forthcoming, and soon the Protestant minority in Ireland were looking increasingly beleaguered in their Ulster strongholds. The fight to retake the British Isles from him whom some deemed a usurper had begun, with an apparently strong base in Ireland and support from the Continent. Dundee had initially desired to join James there, requesting that the Estates grant him a pass to go to Ireland. They refused. Had they seen their way to doing so, then the violence he was about to precipitate might have been confined to Ireland and there might have been no warfare in Scotland at that time.[75] This was not to be the case, as we shall see.

71 Browning, *English Historical Documents*, p.634.

72 Balcarres, *Memoirs*, pp.30–31; NLS, MS7026, f.163.

73 Dundee, *Letters*, p.32n.

74 Balfour-Maitland, 'Estates', I, pp.1–3.

75 *Ibid.*, p.11.

2

The Campaign begins, 1689

In the interim, George Hamilton of Binny, in conjunction with the Duke of Hamilton, summoned 400 armed citizens of Glasgow to surround the Parliament House in Edinburgh. The Earl of Leven had formed a regiment of infantry and the Earl of Argyll brought his Highlanders to the capital.[1] Despite this, the Convention was still concerned about Dundee. Livingstone had complied and was discharged from his posts. Lieutenant General James Douglas, commander of the Scottish Army from March to December 1688, had also contacted Dundee and asked him to come over to the new king's cause, but to no avail.[2]

Having been sent the letter from the Convention, the ball was now firmly in Dundee's court. He initially responded to it by writing one of his own. Dundee sent a letter from his home at Dudhope, near the city of Dundee on, 27 March, to Hamilton to explain his current position:

> May it please your Grace,
> The coming of an herauld and trumpeter to summon a man to lay down arms, that is living in peace at home, seems to me a very extraordinary thing, and, I suppose, will do so to all that hears of it. While I attended the Convention at Edinburgh, I complained often of many people's being in arms without authority, which was notoriously known to be true, even the wild hill men; and, no summons to lay down arms under the pain of treason being given them, I thought it unsafe for me to remain longer among them. And because some few of my friends did me the favour to convey me out of the reach of these murderers, and that my Lord Levingstone and several other officers took occasion to come away at the same time, thus must be called being in arms. We did not exceed the number allowed by the Meeting of Estates: my Lord Levingstone and I might have had each of us ten; and four or five officers that were in company might have had a certain number allowed them; which being, it will be found we exceeded not. I am sure it is far short of the number my Lord Lorne was seen to march with. And, tho I had got away with some more than ordinary, who can blame me, when designs of murdering me was made appear? Besides it is known to every body, that,

1 Balfour-Maitland, 'Estates', I, p.2.
2 Mackay, *Memoirs*, p.221; Balcarres, *Memoirs*, p.32–3.

> before we came within sixteen miles of this, my Lord Levingstone went off to his brother, my Lord Strathmoir's house; and most of the officers, and several of the company, went to the respective homes or relations: and, if any of them did me the favour to come along with me, must that be called being in arms? Sure, when your Grace represents this to the Meeting of the States, they will discharge such a groundless pursuit, and think my appearance before them unnecessary. Besides, tho' it were necessary for me to go and attend the Meeting, I cannot come with freedom and safety, because I am informed there are men of war, and foreign troops in the passage; and, till I know what they are, and what are their orders, the Meeting cannot blame me for not coming. Then, my Lord, seeing the summons has proceeded on a groundless story, I hope the Meeting of States will think it unreasonable, I should leave my wife in the condition she is in. If there be any body that, notwithstanding of all that is said, think I ought to appear, I beg the favour of a delay till my wife is brought to bed; and, in the meantime, I will either give security or paroll not to disturb the peace. Seeing this pursuit is so groundless, and so reasonable things offered, and the Meeting composed of prudent men and men of honour, and your Grace presiding in it, I have no reason to fear farther trouble.
>
> I am,
> May it please your Grace,
> Your most humble servant,
> Dundie
>
> I beg your Grace will cause read this to the Meeting, because it is all the defence I have made. I sent another to your Grace from Dumbliein, with the reasons of my leaving Edinburgh: I know not if it be come to your hands'.[3]

The Convention's response to this was to declare Dundee to be a traitor and this was proclaimed in public at the city's market cross on 30 March.[4]

Dundee's actions were to lead to civil war in Scotland. Had he accommodated the Convention's wishes, it seems likely that there would have been no armed conflict in Scotland. Yet he was not the man to back down. He was doubtless motivated by loyalty to James, a man he had known personally for a decade and whom he had served as a soldier.

There were certainly hopes entertained in Ireland for support to be sent from there to the Jacobites in Scotland. James' lord lieutenant, the Earl of Tyrconnell, wrote on 15 March, 'I hope before the end of July to have the honour to embrace you in Scotland'. James told Balcarres that his wish was to despatch 5,000 soldiers including 250 cavalry there, 'being resolved to come ourself as soon as it is possible for us to do it with safety … we have thought to send 5,000 men … we desire to know your opinion of this number'.[5] The former de facto monarch had had protestations of support from Scotland,

3 Dundee, *Letters*, pp.32–34.

4 Rev. Alexander Murdoch (ed.), 'The Grameid: an heroic poem on the Campaign of 1689', *SHS* I, Vol. 3 (1888), p.46n.

5 *Report on the Manuscripts of the Duke of Buccleuch and Queensberry preserved at Montague House, Whitehall* (London: HMSO, 1903), II, pp. 36, 38.

referring to 'from whence he had received a sincere acknowledgement of duty and affection from many persons of distinction there' but though he could not go there in person at once, trusted that his cause 'would not be so entirely abandoned in that country'.[6] An incursion from Ireland was also feared by Mackay, writing on 16 April, 'I venture that King James may adventur over to the highlands with some men for there lays all his hops and Dundee is gon to the hils'.[7] Yet James, lacking French ships to convoy his troops over to Scotland, was unable to assist; France's priorities were, as ever during the Jacobite campaigns up to 1746, Continental not British.

Dundee's actions clearly rattled the government. Meanwhile they had two pressing intertwined issues which were close at hand; finance and security. On 18 March the Estates of the Scottish Parliament raised the question that there must be money to pay the troops; ten regiments of infantry made up of 600 men each, 12 troops of horse of 50 men in each and a regiment of dragoons of 300 men, which were deemed necessary to defend the new succession; a far greater number than had been in the pre-1689 Scottish army. Initially Edinburgh merchants made up the shortfall with loans. On 26 March the city militia were summoned and provided with 20 day's provisions.[8]

The regular troops for the new army were slowly being raised. Commissions to enlist men were given to noblemen loyal to the new status quo. Leven's was the first. On 19 April commissions were given to James, Earl of Angus, who raised 1,000 men (soon increased to 1,200, divided into 20 companies); whilst John, Earl of Glencairn, John, Lord Blantyre and John, Lord Bargany all raised about 600 men each. They were initially armed at their colonel's expense, but were paid by the government. Archibald, Earl of Argyll, Alexander, Viscount Kenmure, Ludovic Grant and Charles, Earl of Mar all raised regiments, too, each of 600 men divided into 10 companies. Each colonel had the authority to grant commissions for the officers under him. By 22 April 10 troops of horse had been raised, each numbering about 50 men. By the end of April the men were being armed; Bargany receiving 200 muskets and 150 pikes; Glencairn's being given both types of weapons, too, though Bargany's did not receive bandoliers for their musket balls until early May. Mar's had seven out of 10 companies raised by 13 May. Meanwhile, Mackay had been given a warrant to beat the drum to raise men for infantry and cavalry units.[9] Leven's men, who were from Argyll, Glasgow and the Western Isles, were ordered to come to Edinburgh, arriving by 26 March. They were then sent to Fife on 2 April.[10]

The nearest enemy was Gordon's garrison in Edinburgh Castle. There had been musketry fire from there in late March, but it had only wounded some of those in the city. Continued low-level fire from the castle in April led to the Estates discussing whether an attempt should be made to storm it.[11] Mackay

6 J.S. Clarke, *Life of James the Second*, II (London, 1816) p.323.

7 NLS, MS 7026, 184.

8 Mackay, *Memoirs*, p.5; Balfour-Maitland, 'Estates', I, pp.6, 10, 17.

9 Balfour-Maitland, 'Estates, I', pp.8, 19, 44, 47, 49, 50, 55, 59–60, 70, 91.

10 *Ibid.*, pp.18, 25.

11 *Ibid.*, pp.15, 29.

had a trench constructed about that part of the castle facing the country to hinder any communication of intelligence and provisions from outside the city. He placed sentries in the city to prevent anyone from there assisting the garrison, but realised that there was insufficient strength to assault it, given his lack of artillery and bombs and the intrinsic strength of the castle, which was to withstand Jacobite attempts to take it in 1715 and 1745.[12]

There was also concern for the security of Stirling Castle, 'the first post of the kingdom', not far to the north of Edinburgh, held by Mar, whose loyalties were uncertain, despite being given a commission to raise a regiment. Mackay sent a company of 50 infantry headed by a captain there in order to form the garrison. Given that the garrison's senior officers were but lieutenants, Mackay's captain would be the highest ranking and could therefore take command without causing Mar any offence.[13]

In case the Scottish forces were insufficient, others from the English army were ordered to be stationed throughout the north of England:[14]

Unit	Location
Langton's Horse	Carlisle
Beaumont's Foot	Carlisle
Hewitt's Horse	Penrith
Royal Regiment of Dragoons	Newcastle
Villiers' Horse	Northumberland
Royal Regiment of Horse	Berwick
Cavendish's Horse	Newcastle
Livingstone's Dragoons	Berwick
Colchester's Horse	Alnwick
Beveridge's Foot	Kendal
Berkeley's Dragoons	Berwick
Levenson's Dragoons	Kendal

On 14 May, three regiments and one regiment of dragoons were requested for Scotland.[15] One of these may have been Berkeley's, ordered to march north on 15 May. Sir John Lanier's was to march north on 20 May. Mackay asked Lanier to go to Edinburgh, which he did. He particularly desired more cavalry.[16]

Troops summoned to northern England and even Scotland, from the English army came from throughout England. In January and February, Hastings' infantry regiment was marched from the Scilly Isles, Plymouth and Hackney to Leicester. By the beginning of April they were at Berwick.[17] On 8 March, Colchester's Horse were ordered from Kent to Alnwick and 20 days later, Berkeley's dragoons were ordered from Lichfield to Berwick. In early

12 Mackay, *Memoirs*, pp.6–7.
13 *Ibid.*, pp.5–6.
14 TNA, WO5/5, pp.67–251.
15 Balfour-Maitland, 'Estates', I, p.92.
16 NLS, MS 3740, 82, 84.
17 TNA, WO5/5, pp.44, 47, 68, 122.

April there were orders for six regiments of horse, three of dragoons and five of infantry to march to Berwick, Carlisle, Kendal, Penrith, Newcastle and Morpeth, all near to the Scottish border.[18]

On 22–23 April English cavalry were quartered in Edinburgh and the horses provided with fodder. Price's company of infantry was sent to Stirling to disperse any Jacobites there and then to provide a garrison for Drummond Castle. Yet as time went on, the quartering of horses in Scotland was found to be difficult, due to shortages of fodder, so Lanier's horse and dragoon regiments were sent back to Northumberland on 8 May.[19]

Meanwhile, towards the end of the second week of April, Dundee raised the standard of James II 'in a proud circle of youths' at Dudhope. He then went to the tower on Glenogilvy.[20] Livingstone's cavalry regiment was sent to Stirling to join Lauder's infantry (taken from Balfour's regiment) to prevent any Jacobite advance into the Lowlands. The former were also, following Dundee's reply to the Convention, and noting his intention to make war, to go to Angus to prevent him forming any body of supporters and if possible to seize him.[21] On 20 April Livingstone decided to take Dundee at the latter's country house of Glenogilvy, but though this was done without warning, on arrival he found that Dundee had left on the 19th; Dundee having heard that they were approaching him with hostile intent.[22]

Mackay was concerned now that Dundee was at liberty in northern Scotland. He later wrote of his fears, 'the consequence of letting Dundee, who wanted not his arguments, to persuade men to his measures, play his personage among the nobility and gentry of the north, and knowing that all the Duke of Gordon's interest, which is considerable in command of men, should joyn with him as one man', he took steps to try and secure the Highlands for his monarchs. First of all he concerted with loyalist Highland magnates. The Master of Forbes' eldest son was an enemy of Gordon, and went northwards to dissuade men from joining Dundee, to counter his arguments and to raise his own forces. Mackay also contacted Atholl who pledged his loyalty, despite also allegedly supporting James, to raise 400 men from his tenants to deter Dundee's men from marching through his lands. Finally he asked Mar, who was now deemed trustworthy, to raise men and to keep Dundee's force under observation on the braes of Mar. The laird of Grant was also asked to hinder Dundee's progress through Strathspey, especially by guarding the fords of the Spey.[23] These schemes met with very mixed results. Mar sickened and died. His tenants then joined Dundee. Grant was too slow in going northwards. Atholl's tenants took against him and followed the lead of his steward, Patrick Stewart of Ballechin, and declared for Dundee.[24]

Mackay did not think, though, there was any immediate danger to the capital. Arms had been distributed to the Presbyterians of the west country,

18 *Ibid*., pp.96, 117, 129.
19 Balfour-Maitland, 'Estates', I, pp.51, 74.
20 Murdoch, 'Grameid', pp.46, 49.
21 Mackay, *Memoirs*, p.6.
22 *Ibid*., pp.7–8; Murdoch, 'Grameid', p.49.
23 Mackay, *Memoirs*, pp.8–10.
24 *Ibid*., p.10.

who could presumably counter an incursion from Ireland, which the Convention in Edinburgh feared. Mackay saw Dundee as the principal hope for James and believed that if he marched against him he might 'in a short time frustrate the practices of Dundee in the north' and to deter any other Jacobites there. He therefore left Brigadier Barthold Balfour in Edinburgh to await Lanier and a reinforcement of English troops.[25]

By the end of April troops began to march northwards in earnest. Mackay's command left Edinburgh on 30 April. He hoped to apprehend Dundee and had every confidence of doing so. He had heard that Dundee had fled to Gordon's lands where 'he hopes to find assistance there as a sinking man lays hold on every twig'.[26] Mackay's command in Scotland consisted of his three 'Dutch' regiments of infantry, now about 1,200 men in all, Livingstone's regiment of dragoons and Colchester's of English horse, numbering about 180 each. The total force was 1,560 men, excluding the newly raised Scottish army.[27] Mackay's field force, though, was composed only of a minority of the troops in Scotland; 560 men consisting of the two regiments of cavalry aforesaid and 200 men from the Anglo-Dutch regiments, for the bulk were deemed necessary at Edinburgh. He had chosen those who were already trained and formed as combat was likely. After all, Dundee was thought to only have about 60 horsemen. Some thought fighting might not be necessary. William had intimated to Mackay that financial inducements 'among the Highlanders being thought the likeliest way to satisfy them' and the sum of £5,000–6,000 was suggested as being given to him, but it is uncertain that this sum was readily available and certainly the new king's 'hope in some time our affairs will be in so good a posture' was a trifle premature.[28]

The newly raised troops were also being thrown forward, clearly after only minimal training. They were given less ambitious tasks as befitted their lack of readiness for a fight. On 27 April, Angus' were in Argyllshire; 400 in Kintyre and the remainder in Lorn and thereabouts, where they were given permission to requisition boats if needed. They were given a barrel of gunpowder from Glasgow.[29] Angus' men were needed there because of the fears that the Jacobite army in Ireland might try to land men, perhaps 5,000 infantry and 200 cavalry or supplies there, as ships with 6,000 stand of arms had been seized in late April.[30] In this they had some success; on 10 May reporting that a boat and its occupants, including a servant of MacLean and one of the sheriff of Bute, had been taken at Greenock with suspicious correspondence from Ireland.[31]

Dundee needed to attract followers to his cause in the divided Scotland of 1689. The Jacobites hoped for the support of Scottish landowners who could bring significant numbers of men to the field of battle for potential or actual warfare. Dundee was not himself a significant military or political

25 *Ibid.*, p.11.
26 Balfour-Maitland, 'Estates', I, p.62.
27 Mackay, *Memoirs*, p.235.
28 *Manuscripts of the Duke of Buccleuch*, II, p.43.
29 Balfour-Maitland, 'Estates', I, pp.60, 77
30 *Ibid.*, pp.46–47.
31 *Ibid.*, p.77.

figure. So he turned to other means, by using a mixture of suggesting rewards for support, by emphasising the success of the cause in Ireland and aid from sympathisers in England and France. Some of the letters he wrote to potential supporters survive and they provide evidence of his attempts to boost the Jacobite cause.

Independently of Dundee, others in the Highlands had also turned their thoughts to a possible restoration. Such a one was Sir Ewan Cameron of Lochiel, chief of one of the largest clans. He had been sent a letter from James. It was very similar to that which was to be received by Dundee, asking him to be ready with his followers when called upon, with promises that they would be reimbursed and rewarded – or punished if they did not assist. Commissions to appoint officers would be sent. According to Cameron, after receiving this message, he 'made a visite to all the Chiefs that were near him, and wrote to those at a distance, and found them all heartily inclined to joyn him in a confederacy for restoring King James'.[32]

A general meeting was called upon for 13 May at Dalcomera, in Lochaber. In the meantime they wrote to James to assure him of their loyalty and their willingness to hazard all in his cause. They also asked James to send them 'a proper person to lead them', possibly James, Duke of Berwick and an illegitimate son of James II.[33] This suggests that Dundee, in Scotland, was not initially envisaged as their leader.

Yet despite their asking for a general to be sent, there was a man close at hand who would fit that role, namely Dundee, 'such was the high opinion generally intertained of his conduct and courage, that Cameron had private intimation sent him from all quarters, that so soon as his lordship could get a body of troops together, and that the season of the year was fit for action, they would risk their lives and fortunes under his command'. The initial success of the Jacobites in Ireland also acted as a spur to encourage their fellows in Scotland.[34]

Dundee was told that he should join his fellow Jacobites in Lochaber and that a detachment of various clans under MacDonald of Keppoch would escort him there. Before he did so, he made a tour of the northern Highlands to gauge potential support for the cause. He did not then call men to arms but told them to be ready when the call came, as it assuredly would. Returning home to his wife who was about to give birth, he heard alarming news.[35]

Meanwhile, the Convention in Edinburgh had been very active in drawing up a blueprint for Scotland's political and religious future. On 4 April they declared that the throne was now vacant and that it should be offered to William and Mary. A week later they drew up a Claim of Right, stating in unequivocal terms, that:

> James the Second, being a professed papist, did assume the regal power and acted as king without ever taking the oath required by law, whereby the king at his

32 Cameron, *Memoirs*, p.233–4.
33 *Ibid.*, p.234.
34 *Ibid.*, p.236.
35 *Ibid.*, p.237.

> accession to the government is obliged to swear to maintain the Protestant religion and rule according to the laudable laws; and did by the advice of wicked and evil councillors invade the fundamental constitution of this kingdom, and altered it from a legal, limited monarchy, to an arbitrary, despotic power … did increase that power to the subversion of the Protestant religion and to the violation of the laws and liberties of the kingdom.

There followed the Articles of Grievances, a list of how James had used his royal powers illegally to promote Catholics to positions of power contrary the laws passed by Parliament, to the detriment of established institutions and creating a large standing army in peacetime. William was lauded thus, 'Whereas His Royal highness, then Prince of Orange, now King of England, whom it hath pleased Almighty God to make the glorious instrument of delivering these kingdoms from popery and arbitrary power'. In future the monarch had to be a Protestant, laws against the establishment of Catholic schools, chapels and printing presses had to be made and upheld, laws were not to be suspended by the monarch nor was a standing army legal unless by Parliamentary consent. The Convention then did 'resolve that William and Mary … be declared King and queen of Scotland'.[36]

This was no unconditional offer of the Crown. There could be no reversion to Catholicism for the monarchy. William formally accepted on 11 May and began appointing men to the government. George, first Earl of Melville (1636–1707) was made Secretary of State (based in London and so with access to William) and Hamilton was commissioner to the Parliament. The Convention also decreed that episcopacy be abolished and a Presbyterian order be established. Clergy who did not swear allegiance to the new status quo or refused to pray for William and Mary lost their livings. William would have preferred not to have had this happen, but needed the Scottish Parliament's support so acquiesced. On 25 April 1690 royal supremacy over the Church in Scotland was abolished and Presbyterian ministers ejected since 1661 were restored. Lay patronage of the Church was abolished. Power lay with the General Assembly of the Church and with the parish elders and heritors. These were far reaching and radical changes, indicating a real shift in power away from the monarch and bishops and towards the Presbyterian clergy.[37] Yet the Episcopal Church did not want for supporters.

The populace in Edinburgh seemed to accept this, for when the new monarchs were proclaimed, 'the solemnity was very great, with expressions of joy, and the evening concluded with ringing of bells, bonfires, etc.'[38]

The revolutionary actions of the Convention, indeed, its very being, did not take place in an uncontested vacuum. Edinburgh Castle was still in the hands of a key Scottish supporter of James II, who had not given up hopes of reclaiming his thrones, though he was basing his return to power from Ireland, backed with French troops as well as Catholic Irishmen. James'

36 Browning, *Documents*, pp.635–8.
37 Harris, *Revolution*, pp.406–8.
38 Luttrell, *Brief Relation*, I, p.522.

Scottish supporters also began to stir and we will now return to their actions, which were certainly heeded by their opponents in the Convention.

In the last days of April, Dundee was riding about the Highlands with his small cavalry force. After leaving the Glenogilvy, they rode to Kirriemuir, passed the north Esk, climbed Cairn O'Mount, crossed the Dee, then went by Kincardine O'Neil and reached Keith on 21 April. He was joined at Castle Gordon on 22 April by James Seton (1644–1694), Earl of Dunfermline, and a small body of horsemen.[39] The party left to evade Mackay and rode northwards. On 1 May, Dundee and his 60 riders were at Elgin en route to Forroes and then to Inverness.[40]

Arriving at Inverness he met MacDonald of Keppoch there. This chief disobeyed his orders and was busy seizing and ransoming the city's magistrates. Dundee was dismayed by this, being 'extremely provocked' and 'expostulated the matter with him in very sharp terms'. This was because MacDonald's actions could be viewed as those of 'a common robber, and the enemy of mankind', though this was the Highland way. Dundee saw their role as James' representative so that they need to have 'the character of a patriot'. MacDonald made his excuses and slunk home, rather than conducting Dundee to Lochaber as he had been tasked with.[41]

Mackay was at Wheytloumes on 1 May and was marching towards the city of Dundee with, thought the Jacobites, 'considerable force'. Leaving a detachment there of two troops of Livingstone's Dragoons and their lieutenant colonel to 'keep the province of Angus in awe', he then went to Brechin, with the remaining 450 men, then to Fettercairn. He lost further men by the majority of the horses of Colchester's Regiment being unable to subsist in the hills, so the major, who was unwell, and 80 of his men were left at Brechin; Mackay taking only 40 of them with him. Waiting until he had information where Dundee was, Mackay learnt that he had marched to Strathbogie, the Duke of Gordon's country, and so resolved to follow him. The Master of Forbes met him with 500–600 men but they 'were so ill armed and appeared to little like the work' that they were dismissed with thanks.[42]

Mackay missed Dundee, who had left Strathbogie. Hearing that there was a large body of Jacobites across the Spey and fearful of the possible consequences for the government's prestige, of a retreat or a rout, he pressed on, hoping for the best, towards Elgin, but saw no action. Mackay summoned the 80 cavalrymen left at Brechin and called for loyalist Highlanders. He finally arrived at Inverness. He then had the city defended by palisades in the streets and by 300 armed men, mostly inhabitants. Strathnaver and Grant were ordered by Mackay to levy the men for the regiments that they had been commissioned colonels of. Believing he needed reinforcements in order to have the Highlands more settled, he wrote to Brigadier Balfour at Edinburgh, requesting he sent Colonel Ramsay with 600 men picked from the Dutch regiments, to march via Atholl and Badenoch, in which latter county he

39 Murdoch, 'Grameid', pp.49–54.

40 James Grant (ed.), 'Seafield Correspondence', *SHS*, 2, 3 (1912), p.49.

41 Cameron, *Memoirs*, p.237.

42 Mackay, *Memoirs*, pp.11–13.

would meet them. Misunderstandings and the fear of a French invasion led to the despatch of these men being delayed as they crossed from Leith to Burntisland. Meanwhile, Mackay contacted Glengarry and Cameron with monetary proposals in return for them switching allegiances, but in neither case did they respond positively.[43]

It was a disappointed Dundee who returned to the Lowlands via Badenoch. But it was then that he received his commission to act as commander of the Jacobite troops in Scotland.

> James R,
> Right trusty and well-beloved cosen and councellor, we greet you well. Whereas we have been informed by Sir Archbold Kennedy of your faithful and loyall deportment in this conjucture, we would not delay any time to send you our royall and most hearty thanks, and to let you know that, by the blessing of Almighty God, wee are come safe to this kingdome, notwithstanding the malicious designs of our enemies, and that our affairs are in such a condition, by the present posture of this country, and the assistance wee have brought with us, and that which wee have yet coming after us, that wee are not only in a condition to defend this kingdome, but to send you such supplyes as you may judge fit for our service. Wee have, therefore, resolved to send our commission of Lieutenant General to you, to command all such forces as can be raised there, and to command likeways such as wee shall send from this to your assistance, being resolved to come ourself, as soon as it is possible for us to doe it with safety, and that all the things of our army here (which wee intend to have very numberous) shall be put in order. Wee have thought of sending five thousand men, whereof one hundred horse, and one hundred and fifty dragoons, believing that a greater number of horse and dragoons will be inconvenient to ship over to you, and that you may get some there. Wee desire to know your opinion of this number, and what you propose to us for their subsisting in the country, and that you would let us know where you think fit wee should land them, with what else you may think convenient for our service.
>
> Wee have sent letters to the chiefs of the clans, and to the most of the nobility wee had reason to judge faithful to our interest: and by the forces we send over, commissions shall be sent blancke, to be filled up at your sight. The officers of our standing army wee will require to attend you by proclamation, and such as are with us wee shall immediately prepare for the journey, as soon as we heare from you. And, as soon as our forces, or any considerable body, can be brought together, wee think fit that the Nobility and Gentry should call the Bishops and Burroughs, and by our authority call a Convention of States to declare for us, and put the kingdom in a posture of defence. Wee need not tell you the necessity you lye under to defend yourselves. The Presbeterians are not good masters in any government, much less with you, where their particular quarrels are revenged in these publick confusions. But, assure yourselves, we will stand by you; and, if it shall please God to give success to our just cause, wee will let the ancient Cavalier party know that they are the only true basis the monarchy can rest upon

43 *Ibid.*, pp.13–19.

> in Scotland; and wee have found such effects of our mercy in times past, as will make us now raise our friends, upon the ruine of our enemys. What may be fit for you to know more, the bearer will informe you; only wee think fit to add that, as it was never our intention to maintain the national Protestant religion, so now wee will confirm it to our subjects, and their property, and libertie, which, let them fancy to themselves what they will, can never be assured to them by any other means. As for yourself, you may be assured, as your services to us all along have been eminent, soe when it pleases God to putt it in our power, the reward shall be the same. In the meantime, expecting your answer to the particulars, and what else you think fit for our service, wee bid you heartily farewell.
>
> Given at our Court in Dublin Castle, the 29th of March 1689, and in the fifth year of our reign.
>
> By His Majesties' command.
>
> Melfort[44]

There were other commissions to several Highland chiefs, which Dundee instantly despatched. The MacPhersons were enthusiastic, but claimed they needed to wait for the call of their superior, the Duke of Gordon, before acting.[45]

For the Jacobites, there were promises of support from the clans, but more aid was thought to be needed. Dundee had been proactive, too. In late April he had written to Sir Lachlan Mackintosh, seeking his help. In May he wrote to Cluny MacPherson, aware that Mackay had also tried to enlist his aid. Moral blackmail was applied and Dundee wrote 'I knou your constant loyalty, your honor and your conscience'.[46]

Dundee had avoided Mackay's larger force and by 9 May was at Kilcummin, to the south of Mackay who was now at Inverness. Meanwhile, Dundee, knowing that some of the clans had invited him to their country, was impatient to meet them and issued a letter arranging this rendezvous for 18 May at Lochaber. In the second week of May, Dundee had some small successes over his enemies with his 120 horsemen. The first was to take the public money held by tax collectors in Dunkeld, arriving on 10 May. Riding southward, he seized the lairds of Pollock and Blair, some of their militia men, 40 horses and arms at Perth, as well as taking the public money. This had been a bloodless coup at two in the morning of Saturday 11 May. Apparently he told the prisoners, 'You take prisoners for the prince of Orange, and we take prisoners for King James and there's an end to it'.[47]

He collected money from Angus and then so disconcerted Lord Rollo at Dundee that he and his troops left the city. Yet Dundee did not attempt to take it, which he arrived outside on 13 May, not wanting to lose any time and believing he lacked the strength to do so, though one report stated he made an attempt and was repulsed. The town had been barricaded and there were two troops of Livingstone's cavalry there, though none attacked

---

44 Dundee, *Letters*, pp.35–37.

45 Scott, 'Letters', p.238.

46 *Ibid.*, pp.235–237.

47 Murdoch, 'Grameid', pp.59–60; *Acts of the Parliament of Scotland, IX,* p.54.

the smaller Jacobite force outside the little city, the lieutenant colonel being 'either a traitor or a coward' according to Mackay. Eventually, having received assurances of support, he rode the long and difficult route to Glen Roy. On arrival he was 'received by Lochiell with all imaginable honour and respect'.[48]

Throughout May the Scottish government's forces were being posted throughout towns and cities to deter any further raids such as these, which Dundee had carried out at Dunkeld and Perth. On 13 May, seven companies of Mar's regiment were sent to Coupar. A week later, Angus' men, still not completely armed (on this date there was an order for them to be equipped with another 400 muskets and 400 pikes) were ordered to march to Falkirk, Kilsyth, St. Ninian's and an unidentified location called 'Lenbor'. Once there, their lieutenant colonel, William Cleland, put patrols at various fords at Cardross, Newbridge and Fraser. Balfour's regiment was sent to Glasgow and Kenmure's to Dumfries; Mar's remaining companies and Leven's were to garrison Fife. The Estates thought that the Scottish forces were insufficient so on 14 May asked Lanier to summon Berkeley's Horse and Hastings' Foot, both stationed at Berwick, to march northwards, along with another two infantry battalions as soon as possible.[49]

First blood was spilt in the second week of May. Captain William Young of Bargany's reported a skirmish there in a letter of 20 May. He claimed that his men had killed 'many' Highlanders, others fleeing in boats or to the mountains. This is what has been described as the skirmish at Loup in Kintyre, when on 16 May, Young and several companies of Bargany's infantry fought some of Sir Alexander MacLean's men. Total casualties were in single figures but the MacLeans ran and so this potentially decisive route from Ireland was closed to the Jacobites.[50]

Once more troops had been raised they were ordered on 27–31 May to march to garrison other towns. Glencairn's to Inverary, Kenmure's to Stirling, Strathnver's to Kinross, Mar's to Dundee, Blantyre's to Dumbarton and Killiclick and Angus' to Dunkeld and Doune. Of the cavalry, Belhaven's went to Foulis and Gorthie, Eglington's to Drummond Castle, Annandale's to Calderwester. This was to deny these towns to the Jacobites, though it also reduced the possible size of a field army.[51]

Meanwhile, James was told of his supporters' progress, and they requested 'his Majesty to come over in person to Scotland, where he generally had the hearts of the people'. They also craved military support, too, claiming that 'his Irish troops, who were worth little in their own country, united with his French auxillarys and Highlanders, would perform wonders, and compose a very formidable army, that would soon make him master of his enemys'. They reminded him how the alliance of Irish and Highlanders under Montrose in

48 Cameron, *Memoirs*, p.239; Balfour-Maitland, 'Estates', I, p.89; Mackay, *Memoirs*, p.20.

49 Balfour-Maitland, 'Estates', I, pp.95, 101, 92.

50 *Ibid.*, pp.95, 100; Hopkins, 'Loup Hill. 16 May 1689. The First Battle of Dundee's Highland War', *Kintyre Antiquarian and Natural History Society*, web edition, 18 and 19 June 1998.

51 *Register of the Privy Council of Scotland*, 3rd series, vol. 13, 1686–1689 (Edinburgh, 1932), pp.382–383, 398.

1644 had secured numerous victories. If James could not come, could he at least send the Duke of Berwick.[52]

Not all of the clans supported the Jacobite cause. Mackay attempted to reduce the number of his enemies by non-military means as well as by fighting. The laird of Grant was a zealous supporter of William and even went to the expense of raising his own regiment. Mackintosh declared his clan to be neutral and others in the north of Scotland followed his example. However, attempts to suborn Cameron with both cash and honours were unsuccessful.[53]

Support was anticipated and whilst it was taking its time to arrive, some of the correspondence between Mackay and Ramsay was intercepted by the Jacobites. It revealed that Ramsay was to march through Atholl by an order given on 28 May by Balfour and then meet Mackay at Inverness. Dundee planned to attack Ramsay, who, he believed, had either 700 or 1,200 soldiers. Yet Ramsay, marching from Edinburgh to Perth (arriving there on 22 May) with only 600 infantry on his way to Inverness, reached Blair and halted. He was a day's march from his rendezvous with Mackay. It was there that he was confronted with about 1,000 Athollmen opposed to him, who also magnified the numbers of Dundee's men who lay between him and Mackay. Ramsay did not know the country in order to find an alternative route. He decided to retire to Perth. But he had to act quickly and to speed his march, gunpowder was blown up. Marching through both day and night was required. Although he returned to Perth 'in great confusion', several men deserted; some stragglers were reported as being killed (this may have led to several Jacobite prisoners being hanged in early June). Ramsay had already written to Mackay to let him know of his situation. Dundee, too, knew of Ramsay's movements.[54]

Mackay wrote that he was very disappointed about this lack of union. He wrote that if it had been achieved, 'I could easily have beat or chassed the rebels, without the least hazard' but by failing to meet it 'hath extreamley altered the face of affairs'.[55]

Some of the clans gathered at Lochaber on 18 May, as planned, some being summoned by the fiery cross. Rousing speeches were made by Dundee and Allen Macdonell of Glengarry inveigling against William III and his supporters and praising the loyalty of the clansmen towards James as their rightful lord. According to Cameron, Dundee had 1,800 men, half of whom were Camerons, but another source has him with about 1,500 men (200–300 Glengarrys, 200 Clanranalds, Stewarts of Appin and MacDonalds of Glencoe being another 200 men, 600 Camerons and 200 of Keppoch's). John Phillip (c.1656–c.1713) of Almerieclose, near Arbroath, a graduate from St. Andrews University and an ardent supporter of Dundee, claimed there were

52 Cameron, *Memoirs*, pp.239–240.

53 *Ibid.*, p.240.

54 *Ibid.*, pp.240–1; Dundee, *Letters*, pp.57–8, Mackay, *Memoirs*, pp.21–22; Balfour-Maitland, 'Estates', I, pp. 115, 125.

55 Mackay, *Memoirs*, p.232.

at least 3,400 men; in addition to those clans represented above there were Sir Donald MacDonald's, MacLean's, and several smaller clans.[56]

Mackay, on hearing news that Ramsay was in retreat, left Inverness with 240 cavalry, the 200 Dutch infantry and 200 Highlanders on 26 May, taking only two days' provisions with him. There was a hope that he might be able to join Ramsay and 'secure that junction at all hazards'. He ordered Strathnaver to bring 200 armed men to Inverness, 'which he judged of great importance for the service'. He was unaware that Dundee had the relatively considerable force that he now possessed, for he wanted to prevent him from entering Gordon's country to raise additional men.[57]

There was some small Jacobite success at this time. On the same day that Mackay left Inverness, the better informed Dundee was active, and was aware that Ramsay's force had retreated to Perth. The castle of Ruthven in Badenoch was garrisoned by Captain John Forbes of Grant's regiment of infantry. His men were presumably ill armed and equipped, for Mackay wrote that Grant's men were 'without cloaths, arms or discipline'.[58] MacDonald of Keppoch was sent with a detachment there and summoned the garrison to surrender. Dundee's men had surprised the garrison and were aware that they had a very low stock of provisions. Mackay was critical, writing, 'for such as had the charge to furnish him [with provisions] neglected it too long, and he being a young souldier did not think of the nixt best remedy, viz., to take it from the inhabitants, when the security of the post did absolutely require it'. The garrison were offered the choice of giving up the fort or being destroyed in the assault. On refusing to surrender, Keppoch surrounded it, had his men fire at the garrison and to fix ladders as if to prepare to attack it. Forbes then declared that he would cede the fort if no relief arrived within three days. The Jacobites did not force the issue and with no help arriving, Forbes surrendered the castle, but on terms. He and his men, with their baggage, were permitted to leave unmolested. The fort was then burnt.[59]

Mackay had camped with his 200 Dutch infantry, Livingstone's Dragoons, Colchester's Horse and 100 Highlanders; around 500 men in all, near the Spey at Chilly Alvie. He was a half mile distant from Dundee. It was 'in a position difficult to attack' with a wooden bridge at its front, a stream to the right, a wood to the left and the Spey behind. Feeling that he needed more men, he ordered Berkeley's Dragoons and Leslie's infantry from Forfar and Coupar to march towards him. Yet supplies were a problem, the men being 'reduced to great wants of provisions and forage' despite Mackay's attempts to have them supplied by the Grants. Dundee, now numerically the stronger of the two, advanced towards him, 'The earth was trembling under the heavy tramp of his cavalry'. Yet hearing a report of forces to his rear, Dundee sent his brother with some infantry to investigate while despatching forward

56 Murdoch, 'Grameid', pp.96–143; Cameron, *Memoirs*, p.240.

57 Mackay, *Memoirs*, pp.21–22.

58 *Ibid.*, p.40.

59 Cameron, *Memoirs*, p.241; Mackay, *Memoirs*, p.31; Murdoch, 'Grameid', pp.173–175.

towards Mackay one Captain Andrew Bruce (who had served with him at Bothwell Bridge) with a dozen cavalry.[60]

Bruce found Mackay 'holding his safe post within his cap' and addressed both Mackay in withering terms and also taunted the men of Livingstone's Dragoons who were thought to be sympathetic to the Jacobite cause. Mackay had his troops open fire but Bruce withdrew and reported to Dundee, who brought his entire force towards Mackay. Keppoch and his men, now they had dealt with Ruthven Fort, joined them. Outnumbered as he rightly believed himself to be, Mackay withdrew; the Jacobites claiming 'with precipitate flight left his camp secretly at night'.[61]

Mackay had to retreat in part because of the supply situation but also because of the disparity of troop numbers. The two regiments requested had not arrived, but the two troops of Livingstone's dragoons from Dundee had. Captain Forbes from Ruthven and two men from Livingstone's told him that a number of officers from this regiment were in league with the Jacobites. Mackay had them arrested and sent to Bala Castle 'to be kept in civil imprisonment and well entertained'. He had the choice of three routes; to return to Inverness, to travel to Glenlivet, both of which he thought Dundee might anticipate and so counter, or to march along the Spey and he chose the latter option after holding a council of his officers.[62]

The ensuing pursuit lasted four days. It took them through Abernethy and Cromdale. Phillip wrote, of Dundee, 'He shakes the earth with the clang of the trumpet and affrights the stars with the fire flailing muskets'. The retreat for Mackay was fraught with supply difficulties and they stopped at Balvany to bake bread for the men. At Glenlivet, the pursuers caught sight of their prey, or rather a detachment of cavalry that Mackay and his nephew had posted to watch for their pursuers. The Jacobite army prepared for battle by drawing their weapons, forming into ranks and cast off their shoes. Marching up Glenlivet and down Strathdon, Dundee hoped to cut Mackay off and the army sang 'The King shall enjoy his own again' and 'speeds headlong after the flying army'. Night favoured Mackay's retreat, but Dundee proceeded against him. He believed that he could have attacked his enemy, but Mackay would not oblige him and marched his forces through the night. Captain Frazer was ordered by Dundee to take a troop of cavalry and some infantry to attack Mackay's rear and provoke a confrontation. Yet Mackay managed to march his troops faster and the pursuit was called off.[63]

Ben Rinnes was reached. Dundee had 'compelled him to retreat with routed troops' who eventually halted at Edinglassie, home to loyalist Sir George Gordon, sheriff of Banff.[64] On the morning of this flight, Mackay heard the welcome news that Berkeley's and Leslie's regiments would meet

60 Murdoch, 'Grameid', pp.176–177; Mackay, *Memoirs*, pp.25–27, 29.

61 Murdoch, 'Grameid', pp.177–181.

62 Mackay, *Memoirs*, pp.27–28.

63 Murdoch, 'Grameid', pp.182–186; Mackay, *Memoirs*, p.32.

64 Murdoch, 'Grameid', pp.186–190.

him later that day, which was 'news to his great satisfaction; they arrived with him at Suy Hill at noon and at six in the evening respectively.[65]

After these exhausting forced marches, the Jacobites rested at Edinglassie, plundering the laird's house there. Fortunately they were well supplied with provisions which had been left by Mackay's forces during their flight. Their sojourn here did not last long. Two deserters from Livingstone's dragoons told them that Mackay had been reinforced at Clatt by Berkeley's Dragoons and Leslie's regiment of English infantry, making in all nearly 1,000 men (this occurred on 11 June), so was emboldened to confront Dundee, whom he believed was in a state of disorder, so marched for Edinglassie, reaching it two days later, on 6 June. Dundee and his officers had already learnt of Mackay's reinforcements and imminent advance, as they were seated at dinner on the previous day. After flattering his colleagues by noting that the enemy had been 'repulsed by your eminent valour', he decided that they should retreat to the hills, 'not being able to encounter such a great number of horse and foot in the Champian country with such a handfull' and was unanimously supported by those present. This was not particularly because they would be outnumbered, but because of Mackay's superiority in cavalry, 'which the Highlanders att that time feared above all things'.[66]

At this point, Dundee was had been told by one of the messengers, who served in Livingstone's Dragoons, that the officers (these included cornets Ramsay, Murray, Lewis and Hay and Lieutenant David Gary) and men of the regiment were secretly supportive of James. Dundee encouraged this and stated his intention to attack Mackay at daybreak. It was not to be. When the two men returned to their unit, Captain Forbes, formerly commander at Ruthven, met them, learnt of their intentions and told Mackay about it. The two were arrested, as was Lieutenant Colonel William Douglas of Kilsyth, and the regiment was never able to aid James.[67]

Meanwhile, Keppoch and his men took the opportunity to pillage Macintosh country, resulting in the gain of much booty, including sheep and cattle. He burnt Dunachton Castle. When Dundee heard of this, he became angry and in front of the force's officers, claimed that he 'would much rather choise to serve as a common souldier among disciplined troops, than to command such men as he'. Keppoch's private gain was nothing as to the damage that such ravages would do to the army's reputation. Keppoch felt humiliated at such a rebuke. He apologised, promised to never behave in such a manner ever again. He would be sure to obey orders.[68]

Dundee had his stragglers recalled in order to retreat. The reasons for this, though, were not revealed to the men for fear that they might lead to a collapse in morale, which was 'then much elated'. The army was assembled and the men were told that they needed to march to join other Jacobite clans.

65 Mackay, *Memoirs*, pp.34–35.

66 *Ibid*., pp.243–4; T. Thomson (ed.), *Acts of the Parliament of Scotland*, Edinburgh, 1814–1875) [Henceforth *APS*]; Balfour-Maitland, 'Estates', I, pp.130–1; National Records of Scotland, CH12/12/1717.

67 Cameron, *Memoirs*, pp.241–2; *RPCS*, 3rd series, 15, 1690 (Edinburgh, 1967), p.46.

68 *Ibid*., p.243; Murdoch, 'Grameid', p.180.

Some, ignorant of the real reason for moving off, did not follow, but remained to pillage the countryside. Of these, some, perhaps 18–20, were caught by the followers of the laird of Grant and Gordon of Edinglassie, both of whom supported William, and were hanged for their crimes of plundering.[69] Apart from this, the retreat to Badenoch was 'without any disorder tho the enemy being perustule of him'.[70]

Meanwhile the bulk of the army stayed with Dundee and marched in good order, with a strong rearguard, marching by Auchindoune Castle and then Cromdale. Mackay's forces were too slow moving to catch up with them; he sent Sir Thomas Livingstone, with 200 dragoons, including his own regiment to pursue them. There was, however, a skirmish in early June which showed that Highlanders could defeat cavalry. Sir John MacLean's command numbered either 200, 300 or 500 men and as they were marching along the banks of the Spey in Badenoch, to join Dundee, took a wrong turn and were endangered by the newly arrived Berkeley's Dragoons, possibly 300 strong, under Lieutenant Colonel Francis Hawley, believing they had met friends. It was evening and Dundee, though unaware of the risks they were running, knew of their whereabouts and was concerned that they might lose their way. He sent men from MacDonalds of Glencoe's clan to guide them.[71]

The MacLeans were soon disabused of their notions when the dragoons gave them 'a dreadful discharge from their fire vomiting weapons'. They returned it, and 'sent a shower of bullets fired from his guns'. The MacLeans threw off their plaids and drew up on a hill called Knockbrecht, the speckled hill. It was impossible that the dragoons could follow them up the hill on horseback. They dismounted to fight, as dragoons were capable of doing. The MacLeans 'fell doun upon them with sword in hand, cut severall of them to pieces before they could recover their sadles, killed the commanding officer, who was shot dead, made many prisoners, and seized more of their horses'. Another version stated, 'with javelin and iron spear, and dart and pointed stake, and from high rock he drives the proud enemy headlong with great stones'. This may have been an exaggeration. Another version of events notes that apparently five or six dragoons were killed, as was a captain, and others were wounded. Balcarres wrote that 14 dragoons and one captain were slain. There was also a pursuit. When the Macleans arrived in Dundee's camp on the following morning, they did so in triumph, bringing their captures for all there to see, having stripped the bodies of their fallen foes. There had previously been alarm within the Jacobite camp, on hearing gunfire in the night, which had echoed in the hills, and a party of men had been preparing to investigate. Indeed, Dundee thought that this encounter might have been but a prelude to a more general engagement.[72]

69 Cameron, *Memoirs*, 244; NLS, MS 3738, f26r.

70 NRS, CH12/12/1717.

71 Cameron, *Memoirs*, p.244; Mackay, *Memoirs*, p.221.

72 Cameron, *Memoirs*, pp.244–7; *London Gazette* 2463, 17–20 June 1689; Murdoch, 'Grameid', pp.211–217; NLS, MS 3738, f26r.

However, according to Mackay, the skirmish was a Jacobite defeat. He wrote that Livingstone's dragoons were also involved and attacked MacLean's forces, killing 80–100 men and would have done greater damage had the force been concentrated instead of being split into two. The adjutant, on discovering the Jacobites, had not been able to depart with the information to his colonel without the Jacobites' knowledge of his activity.[73]

The Jacobite army continued its march to Lochaber. They were joined by Sir Alexander MacLean, with 200 Argyllshire men, mostly of MacDonald of Largo and Gallusky's men. At Keppoch they halted for two days. Lack of provisions (the cows were too lean and the market towns were held by the government) led to Dundee dismissing his men, except for his few cavalry and the newly arrived 200, on the understanding that the others reconvene in a day's notice when needed. More men came to Dundee, at this time, however. These were Sir Donald MacDonald and about 700 men and the Clanranalds; another 600 under their youthful captain and his tutor.[74] Alexander MacDonald and Colonel Hector MacNeill met them.[75] Mackay wrote on 13 June, 'I found that for the most part they were separate, everyone returning home to his own country and Dundee as was said to be in the braes of Lochaber sick of a flew, but whose people can equally com together againe for their equipage is prepared'.[76] On 14 June Dundee was in Glen Roy.

Mackay thought that he was unable to pursue Dundee. On 19 June he put this down to the 'inaccessibleness of the ground where I found the enemy posted for hors, which was my greatest strength and for the conveyance of subsistence to retire down the river of Spey'.[77] He told Hamilton on 4 July that 'it is a mater to ruin a troope and at last have no security by it to follow them in their hills because when they are pressed being in body they can separate themselves and escape as in their hills and forests and if we should separate to hunt them out they knowing the paths and mountaine ways better than wee can gather againe and beat our separate partys'.[78] However, in 1746 it was proved possible for regular troops to successfully pursue the Jacobites in their own rugged terrain.

The lack of support for the Williamite cause was another cause for concern, 'a disposition of the country in general excepting a few families to favour our enemys, if they could get their passage to the low country'. Mackay had made overtures to the Frasers and Mackenzies, but without success and feared the former might overwhelm Argyllshire if they joined Dundee.[79]

What was needed was, as had been accomplished in Cromwell's day and what had been mooted after its demolition, a permanent garrison 'at Inverlochy which may very speedily be executed if the lords of the council give present orders', though this would be no small undertaking. Mackay reasoned that to build a fort there would need supplies of biscuit, cheese

73 Mackay, *Memoirs*, pp.38–39.
74 Cameron, *Memoirs*, 247–8.
75 NRS, CH12/12/1717.
76 NRS, GD406/1/3605.
77 NRS, GD406/1/3606.
78 NRS, GD1/406/3607.
79 NRS, GD406/1/3606.

and butter from Glasgow for 4,000 men for six weeks, two frigates to convoy these as well as horses and 1,500 pioneers from Ross, Inverary, Murray and Nairnshire with spades, pickaxes and shovels, as well as wrights to cut and prepare the palisades for the fortress.[80] Meanwhile, Argyll had to remain at Perth with his troops in case Dundee tried to return to the town.[81]

Ramsay, having informed the Privy Council as to what had happened to him, was given additional forces; 200 men from Leven's regiment and 100 from Hastings' and together with the 600 Anglo-Dutch already allocated to him, marched northwards again, to Inverness via Atholl and Badenoch. Mackay was unaware of this, otherwise he alleged he could have used them to attack Dundee.[82]

Eventually Ramsay and Mackay met. Mackay had ordered him northwards again, through Atholl, Dunkeld and to Inverness. Once Mackay had Ramsay's forces, he allocated the troops as follows: Berkeley's were sent to Strathbogie, the Dutch to Elgin, and at Inverness were posted Leven's, Hastings', Livingstone's Dragoons and 200 Highlanders. The troops at Inverness were led by Livingstone.[83]

Meanwhile, Dundee had issues of his own to resolve. At a council of war, Dundee proposed using the time that they had, before the others rejoined them, in training the men in the habits of regular armies. Many agreed with this, especially the Lowland officers and the young chiefs present, perhaps impressed by his two decades of military experience. Cameron was strongly opposed, however. He argued 'That to pretend to alter any thing in their old custome of fighting, whereof they are exceedingly tenacious, would intirely ruin them, and make them no better than new-raised troops'. But, fighting under their own chiefs and with Dundee as their leader, 'they were equall to as many of the best disciplined veteran troopes in the kingdome'. He referred to the victories of the Highlanders under Montrose (though presumably not Montrose's ultimate defeat) and the skirmishes during the present campaign. He elaborated on the Highland method of war in detail (as will be explained in the next chapter). Cameron's 'oppinion determined the councill' and Dundee was impressed, remarking 'he was certain of victory from men of soe much naturall courage and ferocity'.[84]

Dundee now awaited the return of those who had temporarily left the army. There was some dissension and distractions to contend with, however. Bad blood existed between the Grants and the Camerons on account of some of the latter straggling having been hanged by the Grants for pillaging. The Camerons had their revenge by stealing Grants' cattle and killing some of the men, but this embroiled them in a quarrel with the MacDonalds of Glengarry as one of the clan had been slain in the raid in late June. The latter had been connived at by Dundee and the provisions they took were certainly very useful for the army. Glengarry took his grievances up with Dundee and

80 *Ibid.*, 3607.

81 *Ibid.*

82 Mackay, *Memoirs*, p.39.

83 *Ibid.*, p.40.

84 Cameron, *Memoirs*, pp.251–2.

demanded the Camerons be punished. Dundee argued that the Camerons were not regularly paid nor disciplined and were not under military law. The provocation they were under had been great. Glengarry was extremely unhappy and angry with such a judgement, but lacking most of his clan with him, could do little.[85]

Support was less than hoped for, but Dundee had high hopes of additional magnates coming out for him. On 27 June he informed the Earl of Melfort, James' secretary of state, that the Earls of Panmure, Southesk, Strathmore and Kinnaird were all 'right and at home', so presumably capable of joining him. Others were in Edinburgh but 'under caution'. According to Dundee, 'All these will break out, and many more, when the King lands, or any from him. Most of the gentry on this side of the Forth, and many on the other, will do so too'. Dunfermline and David Halyburton of Pictur were with him, as was Lord Dunkeld 'and many other gentlemen who deserve well, for they suffer great hardships'.[86]

Some, though, had absented themselves. Sir George Mackenzie of Rosehaugh, 'a very honest man, firm beyond belief' and Atholl, 'who did not know what to do' had gone to England. Others were under house arrest; such as Earls Hume, Errol, Aberdeen and John Campbell, of Breadalbane (1634–1717). The bishops' behaviour was unclear, Dundee described them as 'the kirk invisible', though the lesser clergy 'generally stand right'.[87]

Worse, some Scottish magnates were hostile to the Jacobite cause, as we would expect. The Duke of Queensberry supported William and his brother was promoted. The Viscount of Tarbat was 'a great villain'. The second Marquis of Douglas was 'now a great knave, as well as beast'. Dr Gilbert Burnet (1643–1715), a leading Scottish clergyman and supporter of William, had apparently led others into William's camp.[88]

Dundee also anticipated troops from Ireland, writing to Melfort thus, 'I beg you will send us ammunition, and three or four thousand arms of different sorts, some horse, some foot'. Ideally he wanted 5,000–6,000 men and about 600–800 horses, 'but rather more; for had I had horse … I would not have feared them'. He suggested that the troops could land in Inverlochy, it being far from the enemy, then march to Murray via Inverness or to Angus by Atholl or to Perth by Glencoe. Or they could arrive at Kintyre, where Dundee could meet them. He had tried to convince his enemy that the Irish would land in the west, not the north, to decoy them to the place where they would not arrive.[89]

One reason why he expected support from James' main army in Ireland was because he heard news that Londonderry, a beleaguered Protestant stronghold in Ulster, was about to fall to the Jacobites, 'Mr Hay, who came hither yesterday from Ireland, gives account that, above three weeks ago, he was at the siege, and then hors flesh was sold for sixpence a pound, and for

85 *Ibid.*, pp.253–5.
86 Dundee, *Letters*, pp.50–51.
87 *Ibid.*, pp.48–49.
88 *Ibid.*, pp.49–50.
89 *Ibid.*, pp.51–53.

cannon bullets they were shooting lumps of brick wrapped in peuter plates. It is now certainly rendert'. Relief attempts had been beaten back.[90]

Dundee emphasised the immediacy of reinforcements to convince waverers to flock to the Jacobite banner. Writing to Cluny MacPherson on 19 May, he had told him, 'I have nou received letters from Yrland by which I am sure nothing but want of fair wynd can hinder the landing of a considerable force in this country from there, and that the King will be with us very soon'. Little did Dundee know that Mackay had been writing to Cluny too; on 19 May trusting that he would not 'joyn with a companie of Papists'.[91]

The lack of immediate mass Irish support may have been because James' forces there had other fish to fry, namely the reduction of the Protestant strongholds in Ulster as well as facing William's forces under the Duke of Schomberg now pouring into the country. But it may also because ships of the Royal Navy had been sent to cruise the waters between Scotland and Ireland. In May Commander Potter and 180 men were in HMS *Warwick* there. A month later this complement had risen to eight ships and by 1 August there were nine ships in all, including HMS *Dartmouth* under Captain John Leake. By 1 October there were 16 ships including the *Fanfan* under Edward Pottinger whilst HMS *Dartmouth* was then under John Every's command. Part of their role would have been to safeguard troops and supplies to William's forces in Ireland as well as preventing Jacobites crossing the sea to aid Dundee.[92]

On 19 July Dundee wrote to the Earl of Murray, son of Atholl (who was himself safely absent in Bath). He flattered his correspondent, 'knowing as I doe from your Lordships owne mouth your principles, and considering your educatione and the loyaltie of your people', he was convinced that he would come out into the open for James. Potential reward was also dangled below the Earl, 'by declaring openly for the liberty of your country, and the lawfull right of your undoubted sovereign, you may acquire to yourself and family great honours and rewairds, and the everlasting blessing of Almighty God, which is above all'.[93]

Murray was also told that James had made a declaration 'that he will secure the Protestant religion as by law established' and return the religious status quo in Scotland to what it had been after the Restoration of 1660. Dissenters would be guaranteed 'liberty of conscience' and this would satisfy all his subjects in matters of faith. There would be an indemnity to all who had not supported the King or even had opposed him except for those who came over with William in 1688 or had voted for William as King in 1689.[94] Dundee also made personal pledges on religion, telling Cluny MacPherson, 'I am as much concerned in the Protestant religion as any man and will doe my indeavors to see it secured'.[95]

---

90 Dundee, *Letters*, p.39.

91 Scott, 'Letters', p.237; 'Gleanings from the Cluny Charter Chest', *Transactions of the Gaelic Society of Inverness*, XX (1894–1896), p.229).

92 TNA, ADM8/2.

93 Dundee, *Letters*, pp.72–4.

94 *Ibid.*, pp.74–76.

95 Scott, 'Letters', p.237.

Murray, appeared determined to support the Jacobites and raised his tenants, to the number of 1,200 men. They could defend their country until Dundee was able to join them. However, Murray was not wholeheartedly for the Jacobite cause and his baillie, Patrick Stewart of Ballechin, suspected his real intentions. He occupied Blair Castle, one of the seats of the Atholl family, and when Murray demanded entry into his own home, it was refused him. Murray then wrote to Mackay to tell him of this and to urge him to march towards the castle.[96]

Meanwhile Lanier had arrived in Edinburgh from England, by 25 May. He wrote on that day that 'The castle is blockt up, we not having Forces nor Guns to attack it in force: the governor has been very favourable hitherto in not firing his guns on the Town, which I believe he will doe when he sees that he is vigorously attackt'.[97] He had sent Berkeley's Horse and two battalions of English infantry northwards, one of which was presumably Hastings', and noted that his own regiment was only 20 miles from Edinburgh. He did not relish the prospect of a drawn-out campaign due to supply difficulties: 'I hope the Forces will not be long in this Country they not knowing what belongs of Forage, neither is there any hay or straw to be had and little or no grass the spring being late here'.[98]

He soon left Edinburgh and by 29 May had arrived in Perth. This was in order to 'assemble what forces I can that if he be present to march', fearing that Dundee was between Perth and Mackay. He was concerned about the state of the troops, 'many of them can get noe arms and I never saw any country so unprovided for necessaries of war … it is not to be imagined how the horse and dragoons that come from England are fallen away and it will require time and as good quarters to make them good again'. As for the horses, only fodder for goats existed. Yet he remained confident, 'I think we shall put an end to this in a little while'.[99]

He had entered into negotiations with Gordon. The latter was given an ultimatum, but Gordon broke off talks and some small shot was fired from the castle. Hamilton informed Lanier that he did not want the castle bombarded for fear that the city's property would be damaged in retaliation. Lanier insisted that his two 18-pounder cannon be allowed to open fire and that he would inform the King if Hamilton continued to refused to allow it. Gordon gave in, due to a lack of supplies, and Lanier proceeded to prepare the guns.[100] Gordon surrendered Edinburgh Castle on 13 June and Lanier put a garrison of 200 men into it.[101] A minor, but embarrassing irritant had been removed. Lanier believed that now the castle had fallen, there was no longer any need for English troops to remain in Scotland and that they should march back to the borders. He wrote to William Blaythwayt, the secretary of state for war, on 23 June, 'I tarry here only to have instructions which I shall

96 *Ibid.*, 255–6.
97 NLS, MS 3740, 86.
98 *Ibid.*
99 *Ibid.*, 88.
100 *Report on the Manuscripts of F.W. Leyborne- Popham, Esq. of Littlecote, Co. Wilts* (London: HMSO, 1899), pp.268–269.
101 Luttrell, *Brief Relation*, I, p.547.

expect from you only, and the sooner we move from hence will be the better for our horses'. He added 'the Regiments are very weak by the great loss of horses'.[102]

Dundee knew of the loyalties of the Athollmen and on 10 July ordered them to meet him at Blair in arms. To encourage them, he promised them he had 4,000 men and would tell James of their actions. There was also a threat, letting them know that any who refused the call would be deemed traitors.[103] He wrote again, on 18 July to Cluny, ''tis high time for you to draw to armes, which I desire you to do with all your men and followers'. Four days later he wrote again, referring to Irish support having arrived and that French help was soon anticipated (he also told him of the alleged fall of Londonderry) and that 'All mankind almost nou begs our assistance'. Dundee was clearly desperate to have the MacPhersons, suggesting an air of begging, as he wrote again on the 20th, the 22nd and the 26th, writing appeals such as, 'It is nou no nor time to look on when all your neighbours ar ingadged, I assur you it will pove your ruin if you doe, so you will doe well to drawe to armes or be looked on as rebelles' and finally on the 26th, 'if you have a regard to preserve yourself and to serve the King be in arms timorou' at Blair Castle. Apart from Cluny's men, Dundee also desired provisions for 1,500.[104] Likewise on 10 July he implored that the Robertsons of Strachloch and Bleaktoune to 'rise in arms and come to Blair of Atholl'. He had, he said, 4,000 men from the Highlands and more were expected to arrive from Ireland. Not to rise would be deemed the act of a traitor.[105]

Threats were employed. There was also an allegation that 'They threaten to kill all who refuse to join them' and in 1690 William MacIntosh of Aberador claimed that the MacDonalds 'threaten all the petitioner's tenants with death who would not joyn with them'.[106]

The MacDonalds did respond to Dundee and were marching to join him by 18 July when they left Loch Eil, marching northwards. They stopped by Loch Lochy on 22–25 July, awaiting the Glengarrys. On that latter day they marched by Glen Roy, Glenturret, the Pass of Drummond, Druimuachder and arrived in Atholl on the next day. There, on the banks of Alt Chulian they were told by a horseman of Mackay's march from Dunkeld to Killiecrankie. Apparently the men were 'eager for the foray'.[107]

Melville wrote to Mackay on 4 June to state that he had been instructed by William to tell him to return to the Lowlands to secure Edinburgh and Glasgow 'for the safety if the country rather than goe in pursuit of Dunde through the Highlands which would render the horse unserviceable through want of forrage travelling in bad wayes'.[108] Hamilton told Mackay on 8 June that the English cavalry in Scotland should be sent there, but he left the details to Mackay's discretion. He also thought that the newly raised Scots

102 NLS, MS 3740, 90.
103 Scott, 'Letters', p.249.
104 *Ibid.*, pp.256, 260, 263.
105 *The Manuscripts of the Duke of Athole and the Earl of Home* (London: HMSO, 1891), pp.38–39.
106 *HMC Athole*, p.41; Thomson, *Acts*, IX, p.207.
107 A.H. Miller (ed.), 'Eye Witness Account of Killiecrankie', *Scottish History Review*, III (1905), p.66.
108 Mackay, *Memoirs*, p.40.

forces should also be sent to the west.[109] There were also fears of an incursion from Ireland, though Mackay wrote that the Duke of Portland assured him that there was 'no thing to feare from that parte' or he would have marched southwards immediately.[110] By 13 June he had despatched Colchester's cavalry southwards, in order to assuage the politicians' fears.[111]

On 20 June, Mackay decided to march more of his forces, principally 500 men from the Dutch regiments, southward. He reasoned that he could not pursue his enemy into difficult terrain and he would be unable to subsist his forces there. Furthermore, he was unwell. His illness of earlier in the year had returned and so he was unable to ride a horse, a key ingredient for an active commander in the field. He told Hamilton, 'I will nevertheless leave this country as well provided as I can'.[112] In order to keep a grip on the north he left Livingstone with his own cavalry regiment, Leslie's regiment, 200 men from Leven's regiment and 100 from Hastings'. In all, about 1,000 men. Berkeley's cavalry garrisoned Aberdeen. There were to be 72 soldiers at Abergeldie and 100 each at Braan and Cultaylend from Reay's and Balngowen's units.[113]

Mackay mused over the successes and difficulties of the previous two months. Positively, he believed that 'had I not been here to oppose the rebels these two tyms, they descended since my north cumming, that the most parte benorth Tay had been by this time in open rebellion'. Yet he bemoaned his lack of troops and the difficulties they had faced in regard to the lack of supplies, both of which would need to be bettered in future for him to succeed.[114] Once he was reasonably sure that he had left the north garrisoned, he marched south with all the Anglo-Dutch troops he had with him, about 800, and Berkeley's Dragoons.

To date, neither side could claim success. Dundee was still at large and had the potential to gather a reasonably sized force, by Scottish standards, in the west and north-west of the Highlands. He had bested his enemy at Ruthven and perhaps at Knockbrecht, too. Yet he had not gained control of any major source of supply, had not broken into the Lowlands, let alone England, as occurred to his successors in 1715 and 1745. He was unable to keep together any force of size together due to the lack of supplies. Nor had he received any significant help from Ireland; though had he, the difficulties of feeding them would have been significant. Edinburgh castle had been lost to the Jacobite cause and the potential 'fifth column' of Livingstone's dragoons was no more. Yet they remained as a potent force for James, and Mackay had been unable to destroy them, due to a lack of numbers, lack of supplies, difficulties in terrain and the lack of a forward base in the north-west. There had been no battle as at no simultaneous point did both sides desire one – the skirmish at Knockbrecht had been an accidental clash.

109 William Fraser, *Melvilles Earls of Melville and the Leslies Earls of Leven*, (Edinburgh, 1890), III, p.127.

110 Mackay, *Memoirs*, pp.226–7.

111 NRS, GD406/1/3065.

112 Mackay, *Memoirs*, p.226.

113 *Ibid.*

114 Mackay, *Memoirs*, pp.41, 237.

On 12 July, Mackay was back in Edinburgh and was disconsolate at the thought that his plan for placing a garrison at Inverlochy could not be put into operation that year 'because the rains begin soon in the Highlands'. He believed that 'to subdue the rebels, to which there must needs a Fort be built'. There was also a lack of materials needed for construction. Mackay proposed the scheme to the council for the men, horses and meal necessary for the expedition. The government were slow in formulating a response and eventually offered too few men, too late. It also tied Mackay to Edinburgh for two weeks, whilst Dundee secured Atholl and Badenoch.[115]

Mackay was still in Edinburgh on 20 July, dealing with the question of the dubious loyalty of those in Livingstone's Regiment. However, two days later, he was preparing to leave to confront Dundee, by marching to Stirling and then to Perth. He was confident of the result, 'it seems they will have a last pull for it, for in their own mynds I doe believe that this small succour will more discouradge sort of them, more then it will raise their hops'.[116]

Provisions and baggage horses had been prepared on 19 July for Mackay's march north, planned for three day's hence.[117] The Privy Council ordered county magistrates to assist in this. Meanwhile a price was put on Dundee's head, of 18,000 Scots marks. Troops were gathering for him to use: on 14 July Bargany's, Blantyre's and Kenmure's were to gather at Stirling. Six troops of cavalry were also hastening there. Not all were content; there had been a mutiny over lack of pay among Bargany's and a sergeant, a drummer and a few others had been arrested.[118]

Mackay took six regiments of foot 'making at most 3000 men' and four troops of both horse and dragoons. He intended to meet Argyll with the forces at his command. Of his own forces, Hastings' and Leven's were depleted in numbers as detachments had been made from them at Inverness. What determined him to march was a letter from Lord Murray telling him that his father's castle had been taken for the Jacobites by the steward there. Murray told him he had no hopes of persuading his father's tenants of switching their allegiance to William. He would therefore go to Atholl and gather the tenants and retake the castle. Mackay replied that all he wanted was that Murray try to keep the men from joining the Jacobites.[119]

Although Mackay was eager to march towards Atholl to prevent Dundee from marching to Lochaber, delays in the government's provision of meal and horses to transport it, meant eight or 10 days passed before Mackay could follow Murray into Perthshire. Eventually Mackay 'prest with all earnestness his dispatch to secure at least the country of Athole with others adjacent, from casting themselves headlong in the adverse party'. As part of this he intended to retake Blair Castle and so took four petards with him to destroy

115 *Ibid.*, pp.227, 230.

116 Mackay, *Memoirs*, pp.44–45.

117 *Ibid.*, p.245.

118 Balfour-Maitland, 'Estates, I', pp.173–174.

119 *RPCS*, 13, pp.481, 510.

its gates, and then leave a strong garrison there.[120] He even threatened to hang Ballechin from the castle walls if he denied him entry.[121]

Two days later after leaving Edinburgh, he was at Stirling. He seemed less sure of the government's position, 'it is not an easie commission that the King hath given mee to keep a kingdom peaceable'. This was because of division between the government's supporters. Two officers who were also MPs threatened to resign their commissions rather than leave the House. Mackay suggested that men should stay in their political roles in Edinburgh whilst their troops accompanied him to battle as he thought that resignations might lead their men to being 'greatly disgusted'. He also felt himself 'to be straitned for provisions in this expedition'. It was here that he ordered the majority of the cavalry to march to Perth to rendezvous with him there.[122]

Mackay told Hamilton, 'coming here to Stirling I find what wherewith be great deficiencie in the fournishing of the hors for the transport of meal. I am affrayed of the inevitable evill which will follow if the forces should want subsistance'. There were provisions arriving for two weeks, but he needed them for four weeks, and that they were at Perth. He reiterated the need for a garrison at Inverlochy. Without such a supply he would have to retire from the theatre of operations without any opportunity to engage the enemy.[123]

It was when he was at Stirling that a letter from Murray arrived, telling him that Dundee was in Badenoch and was marching to Atholl. If Mackay did not arrive there first, he could not promise him that the 1,500 Atholl men would not join Dundee. Because of this, and the fear that men from the Isles, Badenoch, Monteith and Marr might join Dundee, Mackay realised he could not halt his command's march at Perth to await the cavalry he had ordered to rendezvous with him there. Anything that looked like faint heartedness in his forces might encourage other Jacobites to rise for James II. Possession of the castle at Blair would stem Jacobite recruits from Atholl.[124]

Mackay was also confident in his own forces. This was despite the fact that 'all of them [were] almost new raised levies'. He thought that the Jacobites had 'shewed nothing that looked like briskness' in the opening stages of the campaign (though he had retreated from them on one occasion). So because of his confidence and the need to secure the castle, Mackay eschewed the additional four troops of dragoons and two of horse that he would otherwise have had in his little army.[125]

Dundee learnt of his enemy's advance towards Blair Atholl and began to summon his forces there on 21 July. If the castle fell, it could cut his communications between northern and western Scotland. Blair Castle was also seen as a strategic site in March 1746 as it was then fought over again. He was impressed by the loyalty of the Athollmen and marched the men he had at his immediate command all, 1,800, towards Blair. Orders were given

---

120 Mackay, *Memoirs*, pp.46–47.
121 *HMC Athole*, p.41.
122 Mackay, *Memoirs*, pp.47–48.
123 *Ibid.*, pp.48, 246.
124 NRS, GD406/1/3608, 3609.
125 Mackay, *Memoirs*, pp.48–49.

for the rest of his army to follow him. There were only 240 Camerons with him, so John, the eldest son, was sent with messengers into Morvine, Swynart, Ardnamurchan and elsewhere to bring up the rest of the clansmen.[126] MacNeill had his men march all that night and next day until they arrived there the third day; they being at Blair Atholl on the evening of 25 July.[127]

Dundee marched to Atholl with all speed. En route he was joined by Major General Cannon and Colonel Purcell from Ireland with 300 men, a far cry from the numbers requested and promised and the Highlanders were 'miserably dissapoynted'. Several Scottish and English officers came from Ireland, too, such as Captain Robert Charters and Lieutenant Colonel Douglas. However, they received the news that the ships sent from Ireland with provisions had been taken there in the Isle of Mull, apparently because Cannon had stayed there too long and news of his whereabouts became known to the enemy. Dundee was not outwardly dismayed and his men, though half starved, had faith in him and were in good spirits as a serious military confrontation loomed before them.[128]

Mackay was certainly eager for battle but was unsure as late as 26 July whether Dundee would oblige him, writing then to the Lord of Weemys, 'I doe not believe that Dundee is so neare, though I wish he were, let his forces be what they will'.[129] This sense of confidence and lack of knowledge about Dundee's whereabouts was shared by Lanier at Edinburgh, who wrote on 23 July, 'I suppose soe considerable a force going against them will rout them out'.[130]

Meanwhile, Mackay marched from Perth to Dunkeld, where he told Hamilton, that he must take the castle 'for is impossible an army can passe without som prejudice particularly to the corns where grass is wanting … I shall doe all the diligence I can towards the reduction of Blair Castle and the settling a garrison in it to serve us as a magazine', though it would need to be made stronger by the employment of pioneers.[131] At midnight on 26 July he had a letter from Murray. This told him that he had lost the race. Dundee was in Atholl and Murray had left Blair and travelled through the pass of Killiecrankie, southbound. Murray told Mackay that he had left men to secure the near side of the pass for Mackay's benefit.[132]

The first major clash of arms was now imminent as the armies were to fight over the possession of Blair Castle. Battles over the possession of a fortress were not uncommon as they represented a tangible gain. It is now time to pause from the narrative to discuss the forces opposed to one another, considering their officers, men, tactics and equipment. Ironically on the day of the battle, Melville had written this to Hamilton, 'I am very glad you thinke the hazard is not so great now from Viscount Dundee'.[133]

---

126 *Ibid.*, p.49.
127 Cameron, *Memoirs*, p.256.
128 NRS, CH12/12/1717.
129 *Ibid.*, p.257; Thomson, *APS*.
130 NLS, MS 3740, 94.
131 NRS, GD406/1/3069.
132 Mackay, *Memoirs*, p.49.
133 Fraser, *Melvilles*, II, p.138.

3

The Jacobite Army

A great deal of work has been carried out on the Jacobite Army of 1745; to a lesser extent on those of the campaigns 30 years previously. There is, though, only a little written about the Jacobite army of 1689. There are some references in a more general survey of Jacobite forces in 1689–1746 and when examining uniform details.[1] John Barratt has a chapter in his book about the Irish and Highland armies operating in the British Isles in 1689–1691, but it is quite general in effect and says little that is specific.[2] Stuart Reid also spends a few pages discussing the Jacobite army, too. He notes that contrary to popular opinion, the Highlanders were not a warrior people but were mostly made up of peasant conscripts armed with Lochaber axes, dirks and half-pikes; only the front line elite had swords, targes and guns, and whose only hope in battle was to charge as a fire fight was impracticable.[3]

The purpose of this chapter is to examine the officers and men of the Jacobite forces operating in Scotland from 1689–1691. This is to assess their fighting capabilities; their strengths and weaknesses in order to ascertain what threat they posed to the new status quo in Church and State. We will begin with the senior officers to the junior, then to the rank and file, their equipment, tactics, organisation and motivations.

Unlike the high command of the later Jacobite campaigns (such as the Earl of Mar, the Duke of Perth, Lord George Murray and Thomas Forster, as well as James and Charles Stuart), that of 1689–91 was made up of experienced and professional soldiers. There has been several biographies of the campaign's most famous leader, Dundee, but virtually nothing on his successors, Cannon and Buchan, though they had rather lengthier periods of command than did he. Biographers are strongly supportive of him, emphasising his loyalty to his monarch, his leadership abilities, his bravery and military talents and do their best to counter nineteenth-century allegations that he was 'Bluidy Clavers', being harsh and vicious in campaigning against the Covenanters in the later 1670s and 1680s. As with James Wolfe in 1759 at Quebec and

1 Barthorp, *Jacobite Risings*, pp.16–22, 31.

2 Barratt, *Battles for the Three Kingdoms*, pp.30–35.

3 Reid, *Killiecrankie*, pp.44–48.

Lord Nelson in 1805 at Trafalgar, Dundee had the dubious fortune to die victorious in battle and this has helped grant him posthumous hero/martyr status. The Catholic poet John Dryden's translation of a contemporary verse by Dr John Pitcairn that Dundee was the 'last and best of Scots', which is admittedly partisan, has been upheld by subsequent biographers. Even an enemy, Dr Burnet, referred to him as 'an able officer and a man of good parts, and of some very valuable virtues'.[4]

Viscount Dundee was born John Graham of Claverhouse in about 1648. Although his career was that of a professional soldier, unlike most of his ilk, whether Jacobite or not, he had attended university. He was a student at St. Salvator's College, St. Andrews University, as did, over a decade later, one of the Jacobites' most doughtiest foes, William Cleland, as we shall see in the following chapter. Next he was an excise commissioner, in 1669, but in 1672 became a volunteer in Lockhart's Regiment, then in the service of Louis XIV in the French war against the Dutch. Service alongside foreign armies was commonplace for Britons in the seventeenth century, especially the Scots, who desired a military career. He finished the war, however, as a captain of the Dutch Guards fighting against the French.[5]

In 1678 he was serving on Scottish soil as a captain of an independent troop of horse. This was principally in action to enforce the law against the illegal conventicles, as noted in chapter one. His military reputation was marked by his reverse at Drumclog in 1679. From the point of view of the Presbyterians, his name became accursed because of his actions in dealing with them in these years, but his soubriquet of 'Bluidy Clavers' was to exaggerate the severity inflicted by himself and on his orders. The government approved of his measures and he became colonel in 1682, a brigadier general in 1685 and was made a viscount in 1688. His military experience was, however, limited and he had never held an independent military command at a senior level. Politically, Dundee was a loyal supporter of James II, as Duke of York as well as King, and knew him socially. However, unlike some of James' supporters, he was an Episcopalian rather than a Catholic, though believed in his royal master's adherence to religious toleration for all. A contemporary source stated of Dundee, 'who had for ever before his eyes ideas of glory, the duty of a soldier and the example of the great Montrose', who was related to Dundee.[6]

John Graham of Claverhouse.

Dundee was able to inspire his men by his actions, as described by a contemporary:

4 Tayler, *John Graham*, p.215; Burnet, *History*, III, p.345.
5 ODNB, Vol. 23, pp.214–21.
6 John Dalrymple, *Memoirs of Great Britain and Ireland*, II, (Dublin: David Hey, 1773) p.300.

> If anything good was brought to him to eat, he sent it to a faint or sick soldier. If a soldier was weary, he offered to carry his arms. He kept those who were under him from sinking from under their fatigue, not so much by exhortation as by preventing them attending to their sufferings … he walked on foot with his men, now by the side of one clan, and anon by that of another. He amused them with jokes, he flattered them with his knowledge of their genealogies, he animated them by a result of the deeds of their ancestors and of the verses of their bards.[7]

In the nineteenth century, with the onset of romantic Jacobitism which turned Charles Edward Stuart into Bonnie Prince Charlie, Dundee became Bonnie Dundee, a term first coined, perhaps inevitably, by the novelist Sir Walter Scott, and a song was written from Scott's poem:

Bonnie Dundee

Lords of Convention, 'twas Claverhouse spoke
"Ere the King's Crown go down There are heads to be broke
Then each cavalier who loves honour and me
Let him follow the bonnets of Bonnie Dundee

Chorus:
'Come fill up my cap, Come fill up my can,
Come saddle my horses, And call out my men;
Unhook the West Port, And let us go home
For its up with the bonnets of Bonnie Dundee

Dundee he is mounted, he rides up the street,
The bells they ring backward, The drums they are beat;
But the Provost (douce man) said "just e'en let it be,
For the town is weel rid o' that de'il Viscount Dundee".
Chorus

There are hills beyond Pentland, and lands beyond Forth,
If there's lords in the south, there are chiefs in the north
There are brave Duine wassels 3000 times 3 will cry hey for the bonnets of Bonnie Dundee
Then awa' to the hills, to the lea, to the rocks
Ere I own a usurper I' sprouck wi' the fox.
And tremble false Whigs in the midst of my bonnets and me.
Chorus[8]

Against this welter of sympathy for Dundee, there is a sole modern jarring note. A critical voice comes from Bruce Lenman, referring to Dundee as 'a simple if ambitious soldier' and possessing 'heroic simplicity', and damningly, 'a career hitherto more marked by the qualities of a conscientious political

7 Quoted from Fforde, *Summer in Lochaber*, pp.39, 136.
8 *Musical Bouquet*, nd.

policeman than by those of a master of tactics'. He later describes Dundee as 'primarily a very unimaginative soldier for whom the arrival of an order from a superior terminated all speculative thought, if indeed he ever indulged in such'.[9] A recent biographer of Dundee has been critical of this stance, citing his boldness in declaring war single handed against William.[10]

Alexander Cannon was the second of the Jacobite generals of the campaign. As with Dundee he had his first taste of soldiering on the Continent with the Scots Brigade. In 1685 he became colonel of Pembroke's newly formed English infantry regiment as James II expanded his army in the wake of the Monmouth Rebellion. He then became colonel of the Queen's Regiment of Horse, a role he held until 1688. He briefly served in Ireland, where he was promoted to major general, such was the want of professional soldiers to lead the expanded Irish army, before arriving in Scotland in early July 1689. He had little experience of battle, none of leading irregular troops and had never previously enjoyed independent command and was described by a contemporary thus, 'tho a good and experienced officer, not being conversant with the ways and humours of the Highlanders and unacquainted with their method of making war'.[11]

The third of the campaign's Jacobite generals was Thomas Buchan (c.1641–1724). As with Dundee and Cannon, he was a professional soldier, from Aberdeenshire and a Catholic convert. As with the two just mentioned he had initially served with a Scottish regiment in French service against the Dutch. As befitted a man of his age, he had began soldiering in 1668 and by 1671 was a captain in the Royal Scots, serving in the War of Devolution (1667–1668) and in the War of the Dutch (1672–1678). Likewise, he ended the latter war in the Scots Brigade in the service of Holland. By 1680 he was a lieutenant colonel in, ironically, Mackay's battalion, but in 1682 was serving in Mar's regiment. Two years later he was back in Scotland and as with Dundee, was involved in internal policing against the Presbyterians, though was far from being over-zealous. By 1688 he was a brigadier and went to Ireland to be with James in 1689, though was defeated in the minor battle of Windmill Hill on 4 June 1689, prior to departing for Scotland.[12]

There were some other Jacobite officers who had military experience. One such was Sir George Barclay (c.1636–1710). He had soldiered abroad and in Scotland up to 1685. He then had been appointed as a major in the newly established regiment of Edward Hales' Foot. As a Catholic he was a natural supporter of a Catholic monarch who was eager to appoint co-religionists as officers in his expanding army. He was also knighted by the King, was briefly with him in Ireland before crossing the sea to Scotland and was an officer with the MacDonalds at Killiecrankie.[13] Other experienced soldiers joined the Jacobites, too. Lieutenant Colonel Douglas from Ireland

9 Lenman, *Jacobite Risings*, pp.30–31, 41.
10 Murray, *Bonnie Dundee*, p.235.
11 Dalton, *Army Lists*, II, pp.11, 54; Clarke, *James II*, II, p,352.
12 *ODNB*, 8, pp.458–459.
13 *Ibid.*, 3, p. 765.

had once been a major of dragoons.[14] Gavin Hamilton had been a captain in the Queen's Regiment before joining Dundee.[15] Dunfermline had served in the Dutch wars and was later to lead Dundee's cavalry.[16] A number of officers arrived from Ireland: 14 officers of field rank, nine captains, seven lieutenants, four cornets and two quartermasters.[17] Other Jacobite officers had served in the Anglo-Dutch Brigade on the Continent and had left it to return to Britain at James II's command in early 1688.[18] Known Jacobites with military experience are noted in the appendix. Given that James II had possessed regular forces prior to 1689 it is not surprising that some of those officers continued to serve him following his deposition.

Not all had been or were professional soldiers. Most of the officers were so because they were clan chiefs or their sons and senior tacksmen (a chief's principal tenants). These included Sir Ewan Cameron and his son John (though as a form of insurance, another son held a commission in a Scottish government regiment). Then there was Alastair Dubh Macdonell of Glengarry, described as being 'brave, loyal and wonderfully sagacious', Sir Donald MacDonald as 'conducting all his actions by the strictest notions of religion and morality … possessed of a very opulent fortune … he lived in great affluence' and Alastair MacDonald of Glencoe as being 'strong, active and of the biggest size; much loved by his neighbours and blameless in his conduct. He was a person of great integrity, honour, good nature and courage, and his loyalty to King James was such that he continued in arms from Dundee's first appearing in the Highlands till the fatal treaty'.[19] Episcopalian clergymen were also present in the ranks. Robert Arbuthnot, born in 1669, was a minister's son and joined Dundee.[20] Some clergy were also part of the army. One was Robert Stewart, Episcopalian minister of Balquhidder.[21] There were also a number of NCOs from the standing army in the Jacobite ranks, such as Caddel and Chesnat, the latter from Stirlingshire, who had been sergeants in Colonel Collier's regiment.[22]

The clan leaders were a mixed lot. At one end were hoary veterans such as Sir Ewan, who had fought against Cromwell and for his own ends in the 1650s, before being knighted by James in 1682. His clan had been involved in many raids in recent decades. Another in this mould was Glencoe. At the other end of the scale were young men, still in their teens. Alexander Robertson of Struan, aged 19 in 1689 (as was Sir John MacLean), later claimed his family had been brought up in 'the strictest principles of non Resistance and passive obedience' since the Bruce's times and that on his father's deathbed in the previous year he had sworn to follow the principles of his uncle in loyalty to the successors of Charles I and II. Once he had received a commission from

14 Thomson, *APS*, Appendix IX, p.56.
15 *RPCS*, 14, 1689, (Edinburgh, 1933), p.42.
16 Murdoch, 'Grameid', p.53n.
17 NRS, GD406/1/3535.
18 Mackay, *Memoirs*, p.59.
19 Murdoch, 'Grameid', pp.124n, 125n; Cameron, *Memoirs*, p.321.
20 *ODNB*, 2, p.325.
21 Thomson, *APS*, Appendix IX, p.59.
22 Balfour-Maitland, 'Estates', I, p.200.

James, 'Strowan remembering his father's instructions upon his deathbed, and being ambitious to serve the Crown, it was no wonder of such an age, he was fond of such a commission.'[23]

There are various descriptions of what the Jacobite offices wore and how they were armed. Dundee has been described as being 'with his armour on'. The elderly chief of the MacDonalds of Glencoe wore a buff coat, as did Sir John Drummond of Machanie. Some officers rode into battle and almost all carried a sword and pistols. Glencoe had 'a brass blunderbuss'. Sir Donald MacDonald wore a red coat. Keppoch had a steel targe.[24] Other officers wore mail coats, leather cuirasses and helmets, though the mail coat seems unlikely.[25]

The Jacobite army did not see themselves as rebels, but as legally constituted forces. Indeed, James II wrote to his potential supporters to stress this, as a letter dated from him to Glengarry of 27 March 1689 makes clear:

> Trusty and well beloved wee greet you well whereas the wickedness of our enemies has reduced our affaires to the necessity of requiring the assistance of our good subjects, these are to will and require you with all your friends and followers to be ready upon call to come to our assistance at such time and place as you shall be appointed, and we doe hereby assure you that all expences you may be at shall be fully reimbursed by us and that wee will stand to our former declarations in favour of the Protestant Religion, the liberty and Property of our subjects all which we wilfully secure to them and that we will reward abundantly such as have faithfully...we expect your ready obedience and therefore will send you our commission with power to you to name your other officers in the time for what you shall doe in obedience to these our Royal Commands and for raising, arming and training of men for securing and opposing our Enemy with your utmost force these shall be to you and others a sufficient warrant.[26]

The commissions, when they came, included the wording 'appointing you to be colonel of a regiment of Foot in our ancient kingdom of Scotland hereby giving power to name and appoint you lieutenant colonel, major, captains, lieutenants and ensigns ... exercise as well officers and soldiers'.[27]

Although it has been suggested in a military history of the risings that 'Such armies were really no more than a tribal horde, though perhaps more so in 1689',[28] the above letters show that James envisaged the Jacobite army as being organised along conventional military lines. Dundee, Cannon and Buchan, the Jacobite generals, were all regular army officers. Certainly, the list of Jacobite prisoners taken at Cromdale in 1690 show their ranks included captains, lieutenants and ensigns and so presumably this was widespread by then. When, and to what extent, the army was so organised is

23 NLS, ADV 13.1.8.
24 Thomson, *APS*, Appendix IX, pp.58–59.
25 Murdoch, 'Grameid', pp.122, 132.
26 Royal Archives, Cumberland Papers, 1/17.
27 *Ibid*., 18.
28 Barthorp, *Jacobite Risings*, p.19.

Weapons used at Killiecrankie. (Author, 2017)

another question, for it is possible that in 1689 such organisation was wholly lacking and the men fought by clan.

The Jacobite armies have been heavily romanticised since the nineteenth century. More recently they have been brought down to size. Stuart Reid has written that Dundee's army was formed of 'raw recruits and miserably armed'.[29]

The Jacobite army was an army of Highland Scottish irregulars, with a few Irish troops. It resembled more the forces led by Montrose in 1644–1645 rather than those Jacobite armies fielded in 1715, 1719 or 1745. These latter included Lowlanders, English and units of the Spanish and French armies. Viscount Montrose and Alasdair MacColla, had, in 1644–1645, an army of Scottish Highlanders and Irishmen. The former included the Camerons and the MacDonalds and were as much motivated by hatred to the Clan Campbell as any loyalty to Charles I. They had been initially successful, but their weakness was their propensity to plunder and to desert after battles.[30]

Whereas their enemies were conventionally armed with musket or pike and occasionally bayonet, the Jacobites' Highland infantry carried a multitude of weapons. These included double-headed Lochaber axes, long javelins and spears (perhaps half-pikes), clubs and bows and arrows, as well as the more conventional swords and guns. The pike, used by Scottish armies from Bannockburn to Flodden, had been discarded. After the battle of Killiecrankie, it is probable that many more of the Jacobite infantry also carried muskets that had recently been their enemies', but how well trained they were with these is another matter. Dundee's cavalry were 'All mounted and in bright armour', presumably meaning breastplates and perhaps back plates and helmets, too. They carried pistols and swords.[31]

The Rev. Thomas Morer, a chaplain in Mackay's army, described the Highland method of warfare thus:

29 Reid, *Killiecrankie*, p.16.

30 Trevor Royle, *Civil War: The War of the Three Kingdoms* (London: Littlebrown, 2005), pp.339–349.

31 Murdoch, 'Grameid', pp.119, 147.

> You shall seldom see them, though only taking air, without a sword and dirk, which is a short dagger … now they carry muskets and other firearms. And when they are on the defensive part they depend much on the targes and targets, which are shields of that form the Latins call by the name of clypeus, round and equidistant from the centre, and are made of the toughest wood they can get, lined within and covered without with skins, fenced with brass nails, and made so serviceable that no ordinary bullet, much less a sword, can penetrate to injure them or their masters, who have such an artificial way of twisting themselves within the compass of these shields that it is almost a vain attempt for their enemy to seek to annoy them. And indeed they fight with too much odds when they come so near us because they not only had the protection of their buckles but are withal very expert at their swords, which consist of the best blades now in being, and was therefore much sought after by our officers and soldiers, who were very well furnished with hem before we left the Highlands. Once or twice a year great numbers of them get together and make a descent into the Lowlands, where they plunder the inhabitants and so return back and disperse themselves. And this they are apt to do in the profoundest peace, it being not only natural to them to delight in rapine, but they do it on a kind of principle and in conformity to the prejudice they continually have to the Lowlanders, whom they generally take for so many enemies.[32]

Yet this image of the Highlanders, which can be found in the writings of others requires some qualification. Firstly, it has been written by an outsider, looking in, so runs the risk of being impressionistic. Certainly, some Highlanders did use swords and targets in battle and some carried muskets. Yet more recent research has put paid to some elements of the popular image of the Highlanders in this period as being an intrinsically military people. Inter-clan violence was in sharp decline throughout the seventeenth century and the last clan battle was in 1688. Bloodshed rarely occurred unless it was sponsored by the Crown, in order to bolster its authority as in the case of the campaigns of Montrose of 1644–1645 and afterwards. A survey of one clan in 1705 noted that only 12 percent carried weapons on a routine basis.[33]

Cameron of Lochiel described the Highland method of war to Dundee in 1689. After noting that the Ancient warriors commonly used broadswords and targes, he then stated:

> The Highlanders are the onely body of men that retain the old method, excepting in so far as they have of late taken the gun instead of the bow to introduce them into action: That so soohe as they are led against the enemy, they come to within a few paces of them, and having discharged their pieces in their very breasts they throw them down, and draw their swords: That the attack is so furious, that they commonly peirce their ranks, putt them into disorder, and determine the fate of the day in a few moments.[34]

32 Browning, *English Historical Documents*, VIII, p.663.
33 *Oxford Companion to Scottish History* (Oxford: Oxford University Press, 2007), p.96.
34 Cameron, *Memoirs*, p.251.

Iain MacAileian, a bard, gave an alternative description of the Highland attack:

> When charging down, when charging down,
> When charging down, undaunted,
> The men in plaid, the men in plaid
> Who would rush down the hillside
> Pressing on keenly, pressing on keenly,
> Stopping for nothing, in order
> After the gun, the sword ready
> Without any more motion[35]

To an extent the adoption of this method of warfare could not be avoided. It was necessity as well as Cameron's advocacy that led Dundee, a hitherto conventional soldier, to adopt it. The latter wrote on 27 June 1689 thus, 'When we first came out, I had but fifty pounds of powder; more I could not get; all the great towns and sea-ports were in rebellion [i.e. for the government], and had seized the powder, and would sell none. But I had one advantage, the Highlanders will not fire above once, and then take to the broadsword'.[36] Similarly, in Ireland, James' Irish forces lacked arms and ammunition, a difficulty posed for all armies lacking access to arsenals and magazines.[37]

Formal methods of warfare based on the primacy of musketry would not have been practicable because of the length of time required for drill and practice. They also need experienced NCOs to train the men. And they required a sufficient quantity of muskets, ball, powder and pikes. All these were lacking in the Jacobite army in May and June 1689.

The other point to grasp, argued Cameron, was the way in which the Highlanders had to be led in battle to be successful. The men needed to have confidence in their leaders and so 'even the most dareing and desperate attempt will not intimidate them if they have courage enough to lead them on. Under their chiefs they are equal to any; but acting as regular troops under officers they knew not, they were no better than any others'. Under formal discipline, the men would 'become meer formal machines, acted by the impulse of fear'. The lack of arms and ammunition, men and time to train them as well as disinclination all worked against Dundee's initial instincts.[38]

Mackay wrote about the various advantages that the Highlanders possessed. The first was that:

> The Highlanders of Scotland do by their way of living, and nature of their habitations, surpass the rest of the inhabitants of Scotland in valour and other qualities for the war, and that no new levies before they have been formed for a while, and served in a campaign, are comparable to them in their bills, especially

35 Quoted in Fforde, *Summer in Lochaber*, p.125.
36 Dundee, *Letters*, p.47.
37 Childs, *Williamite War*, p.41.
38 Cameron, *Memoirs*, pp.251–2.

> where they can boldly attempt without hazard of any considerable loss tho' worsted, because of their nimbleness and speed of feet.[39]

He added that the Highlanders 'if pressed, were able to march in one day as much as the regular troops could do in two'.[40] On the eve of the battle of Killiecrankie, he compared the Jacobite troops to those newly raised Scots forces: 'I esteem the Highlanders as good as these troops, their number great and better officer'd', but he also held them in contempt, writing in the same letter of 'these barbarians'.[41]

Some training does seem to have happened, according to Phillip, who wrote of the Highlanders:

> Practising for battle, he reviews his troops, and turns out his foaming squadrons on the plain. He develops his compact columns, and wheels them again into formation…he teaches the toilsome task of Mars, and how to meet the fire of the enemy and the heavy charge of swift cavalry, and how to charge by horse and foot.[42]

The clan system was partly defined by kinship; with the theory that all the clan had a common descent. It was also partly based on geography. Then there were the bonds of rent. The clan chief had a number of principal tenants known as tacksmen. They held land from the chief of long leases, perhaps for 90 years or for several lifetimes. Yet by the end of the seventeenth century, these leases were quite short term, being for 19 years or less. This had the result of reducing the power of the tacksmen for they could no longer assert their authority over their sub-tenants.[43]

Some clans marched along with flags and to the sound of music, as did their opponents. The Stewarts of Appin marched 'with a drum and several pipes'. They also had a flag.[44] John Philip refers to Dundee's units being encouraged by bagpipes and trumpet.[45] Philip, who carried the royal standard of the Scottish lion, described Dundee as 'a new phoenix rises from the ashes of Montrose' and in 1691 wrote a long heroic verse about the campaign up to the end of June 1689, regrettably ceasing prior to Killiecrankie.[46]

They were certainly a formidable sight, as Philip attested. Glencoe's men were 'all of gigantic mould, all mighty in strength'. Generally, they were deemed 'the target bearing giants of the hills'. Glengarry's men 'each of whom a tartan garb covers … in triple stripe' and Clanranalds had 'garments interwoven with thin red stripes and red buskin'. Appins wore 'fur bonnets'. In general it was a 'plaided army with floating banners'.[47]

---

39 Mackay, *Memoirs*, p.114.
40 *Ibid.*, p.115.
41 NRS, GD406/1/3609.
42 Quoted from Fforde, *Summer in Lochaber*, p.122.
43 *Oxford Companion to Scottish History*, pp.95–96.
44 Thomson, *APS*, Appendix, IX, p.57.
45 Murdoch, 'Grameid', pp. 104, 120.
46 *Ibid.*, p.40.
47 *Ibid.*, pp.123, 143, 205.

According to the Jacobite poet Iain Lom MacDonald, at least as regards his clan, the men had a semblance of military discipline. Sergeants gave commands. Sentries were kept at night. There were carts to transport supplies and the men carried knapsacks.[48]

Some men were recruited by their minister. Dundee noted, 'The poor ministers are solely oppressed over all. They generally stand right'.[49] Robert Stewart, immediately after Killiecrankie, enlisted 60 men from his own parish of Balquhidder.[50] There were references to priests in Banff encouraging support for the Jacobite cause in early 1690.[51]

Although the bulk of the army in Scotland in 1689–1690 was made up of Highland Scots, there were some Irishmen, too. The Irish troops were seen dismissively by some Scottish contemporaries; Ewan Cameron referred to them, in 1689, as being 'naked'. It is true that in transit from Ireland they lost 'a grate parte of theire provisions, cloaths, saddles, paper and commissions'. Yet he also wrote that, 'though raw, undisciplined, half starved and armless, were not inferior to the clans in courage … on all occasions … behaved with the same resolution; which shows of what service ane army of them might have been in any part of Brittain'.[52] Iain MacAilein noted, 'the sight of them was not lovely/theor get up was more like heads of beasts/than men of justice and reason'.[53] The basis of James II's Irish forces were the standing army of Ireland, which was one of the three armies (there was also an English and a Scottish one) of the British Crown in the years 1660–1707. This was rapidly expanded to 36,000 men in 1689 in order that James II could retake the entire island. The result, however, was a reduction in quality due to inadequate numbers of officers (most Protestant officers went over to William), arms and equipment and the lack of training. They were organised as regular troops with 13 companies for an infantry regiment. It is probable that the 300 strong contingent which was in Scotland in 1689 was a weak regiment and may well have lacked uniforms and have been under-equipped with muskets, powder, ball and pikes.[54]

Jacobite cavalry is usually described as being poor at best. Yet in 1689 it was deemed remarkably capable by Mackay. On one occasion he wrote about 'not daring to expose them [his cavalry] to the enemy's horse, which was composed of all gentlemen, reformed officers or such as had deserted'.[55] In 1682, Dundee had been appointed a colonel of the King's Regiment of Horse in Charles II's Scottish Army, composed of four troops, expanded to six in 1688. In October 1688, when the Scottish Army came to join that in England, Dundee led them, and some of his troopers stayed with him after the Revolution. Sir William Wallace, a captain, joined James in Ireland in 1689, but came to Scotland later that year and fought at Killiecrankie. David

48 Miller, 'Killiecrankie', p.65.
49 Dundee, *Letters*, pp.48–49.
50 Thomson, *APS*, Appendix, IX, p.59.
51 *RPCS*, 14, p.98.
52 Cameron, *Memoirs*, p.297; NRS, GD406/1/3535.
53 Quoted in Fforde, *Summer in Lochaber*, p.120.
54 Barratt, *Battles for the Three Kingdoms*, pp.30–33.
55 Mackay, *Memoirs*, pp.52–3.

Graham was the regiment's quartermaster and he also followed Dundee. Another five known Jacobites had served unfer Dundee as cavalry officers between 1678–1688 as noted in the appendix. Not all the officers did so: William, Earl of Annandale, a captain, joined William's cause. However, the kernel of trained regular soldiers in the Jacobite cavalry made them a force superior to the bulk of the Scottish government's cavalry who had only been raised in March 1689.[56] It is possible that the cavalry formed Dundee's bodyguard as he is said to have had 'a company of lusty men with him whom they called his guards'.[57] Until the battle of Dunkeld in August 1689, there was no Jacobite artillery; what there was there had presumably been taken from the battlefield of Killiecrankie, but was not to prove of much use, possibly due to lack of ball and powder, trained personnel or/and faulty tactical use.

Supply was haphazard. The majority of the Scots nobility and gentry were impoverished. Dundee had tapped the tax revenues of Dunkeld and Perth in May 1689, but there were few other 'legitimate' methods of securing funds with which to pay for munitions and wages. Irregular, or rather traditional, methods were used instead. Lord Forbes claimed that in 1689–1690, the Jacobites had taken £3,838 of goods from his estates, principally in the way of oxen, cows and sheep.[58]

The Jacobites were not all motivated by a love for James or a hatred of William. Viscount Tarbat claimed that it was due to Cameron's 'apprehension of the Earl of Argyll's appearant restauration and favour'. The previous earl had been exiled and then beheaded in 1685. His lands had been forfeited and Cameron now had some of these lands. The MacDonalds had many grievances with the Campbells, so all of these clans looked with askance about the return of Argyll to political prominence. Mackay concluded that despite protestations, 'on all sides, self interest lay at the bottom'.[59]

Plunder, too, was another motivation, especially for the rank and file and so may explain in part why they were willing to follow their masters. Given the poverty of Scotland and the Highlands in particular it is not surprising that pecuniary motives featured highly. Lanier wrote on 29 May, 'I believe it is more out of hopes of coming down into the Lowlands in hope of plunder than for any reason'.[60] John, Master of Sinclair, later wrote, 'The Highlandmen would rise out of hopes of plunder, and would doe as they had always done, which the historie of Montrose and since that, of my Lord Dundee, was enough to convince anie bodie of, which is, they would certainlie desert on three events'.[61] A petition to the Scottish Parliament noted, in 1690 that 'Colonel MacDonald in companie with the other rebels in armes did most barbarously and inhumanely ... burne, pillage and destroy the petitioners' dwelling houses ... carrying along with the haill portable goods...not leaving

56 Dalton, *Scottish Army*, pp.135, 142–143.
57 Thomson, *APS*, Appendix IX, p.58.
58 James Allardyce, *Historical Papers relating to the Jacobite Period, 1689–1746*, I, (Aberdeen: Spalding Club, 1895), pp.xiv–xvi.
59 Mackay, *Memoirs*, pp.18–19.
60 NLS, MS 3740, 88.
61 Walter Scott (ed.), *Memoirs of the Insurrection in Scotland of 1715* (Edinburgh: Abbotsford, 1858), p.26.

some of them so much as a pair of plaids for bedding'.[62] Yet as we note, such behaviour was not exclusive to the Jacobite army.

Religion, too, may have played its part. The clans were predominantly Episcopalian, though some such as that of Glencoe were Catholic. This would have made them natural opponents to any Presbyterian force, as had been proved by the Camerons' opposition to the Covenanters in Charles II's reign. Dundee was an Episcopalian and supported James II in part because of the latter's support for that Church.

The Jacobite army of 1689–1691 was professionally led by experienced regular officers and included a number of junior officers schooled in conventional warfare, too. However none had any experience of independent command at a senior level. The men they led were mostly irregulars under their own chiefs and their sons, and who were different to their enemies in both arms and tactics. The army's strength was limited in both numbers and material resources, nor did it have the financial backing a regular force possessed, nor much assistance from its nominal allies, in Ireland or France from both of which it had high hopes. Yet as an irregular force, well handled, the Highlanders and Irish could be deadly, as the Covenanters found to their cost in 1644–1645. This was no rabble to be easily disbursed as had occurred at the Pentland Hills in 1666 or at Bothwell Bridge in 1679.

62 Thomson, *APS*, IX, p.207.

4

William and Mary's Forces

Those forces opposed to the Jacobites in 1689–1690 have been relatively cursorily examined, and by the same authors who have looked at the Jacobite forces of the same period. Michael Barthorp was the first in a general examination of 'The Government Forces' from 1689–1746, suggesting the plug bayonets were in part responsible for the defeat at Killiecrankie.[1] Stuart Reid and John Barratt have also briefly explored the topic, in the books mentioned in the previous chapter; Reid's book on the Scottish army provides additional detail on the units themselves, one by one.[2] Charles Grant also discusses the British Army of the late seventeenth century, too, tactics, organisation, weapons, equipment and uniforms and again repeats the point about plug bayonets.[3] More generally, information about the British Army at this time has been provided by Professor Childs' works, though he was focusing on the army operating in England (to 1688), Ireland (1689–1691) and the Low Countries (1689–1697), but has much that is generally relevant about how armies existed on and off the battlefield.[4]

The purpose of this chapter is to examine the officers and men of the forces opposed to the Jacobites in Scotland, beginning, as with the previous chapter, with the high command before descending through the echelons. Equipment, tactics and organisation will be also examined. Fortunately these were more or less permanent standing forces with formal codes in terms of drill and pay and so far more is known about them compared to their Jacobite counterparts.

From the Restoration of 1660 to the union of 1707, Britain had one monarch but three military establishments. These originated from the Civil Wars of 1642–1651. Most of Cromwell's army had been paid off and disbanded after the restoration of the monarchy in 1660, but some had to be kept in pay, allied to some of the former Royalist army units. The English, Irish and Scottish armies were small and generally employed in internal

1 Barthorp, *Jacobite Risings*, pp.23–28, 31–32.

2 Reid, *The Last Scots Army, 1660–1714* (Leigh-on-Sea: Partizan Press, 2003).

3 Charles Stewart Grant, *From Pike to Shot, 1680–1720* (Wargames Research Group, 1986), pp.35–48.

4 Childs, *The British Army and The Nine Years War*, and *The Williamite Wars in Ireland*.

policing roles and to garrison castles, on formal occasions and to overawe political dissidents, though some had been employed more actively in Tangier, a colony in North Africa, held for Charles II during most of his reign before being discarded before its end.

These armies were viewed with a great deal of hostility in times of peace. In part this was because of their expense to those who paid taxes for their upkeep. But it was more the fact that they could be an aid to a ruler who wished to extend his authority without recourse to Parliament. This was no idle fear for it had happened overseas and in Britain under the Commonwealth of 1649–1660, during the closing years of Charles II's rule, 1681–1685 and throughout most of his brother's reign, 1685–1688. As noted, Presbyterians in Scotland had felt the heavy hand of the army in 1660–1688. Finally, the increases in the size of the armies following the defeat of the Monmouth Rebellion of 1685, and the introduction of Catholic officers (without Parliamentary approval) also gave rise to concerns that James II, considered by some to be authoritarian, might use it as a prop to bolster his rule and those policies deemed unpopular by his Protestant subjects.

Officers

In charge of the forces of the joint monarchy north of the border in 1689–1690 was Major General Hugh Mackay. Unusually for a general who lost a battle, historians have been kind towards him. Even Sir Charles Petrie, a leading Jacobite scholar in the early to mid-twentieth century, notes: 'MacKay, however, was no mean antagonist, and realizing that offence is the surest form of defence'.[5] According to Reid, Mackay was 'a competent rather than a brilliant general, but he was better than any of Dundee's successors'.[6] However, a recent biographer of Dundee wrote, 'Mackay was out of touch with the Highlands and the Highlanders; he understood little of their ways. He was a foreigner in his own land'.[7] Contemporaries had mixed opinions, however.

Dr Gilbert Burnet, a clergyman loyal to William III, wrote that he was:

> … a general officer that had served long in Holland with great reputation and who was the most pious man I ever knew in a military way… one of the best officers of the age, when he had nothing to do but obey and execute orders; for he was both diligent, obliging and brave, but he was not fitted for command.

Burnet believed that Mackay was too fearful of shedding blood unnecessarily and his piety made him mistrust his own sense.[8]

5 Petrie, *The Jacobite Movement*, p.84.

6 Reid, *Killiecrankie*, p.29.

7 Scott, *Bonnie Dundee*, pp.215–216.

8 Gilbert Burnet, *History of his own time* (London: Reeves and Turner, 1883), p.540.

Morer, an army chaplain who accompanied the army in 1689, had similar views:

> MacKay was a Highlander, tho' commander … certainly an honest gentleman, a zealous person and brave enough … where tho' his conduct was shamed [at Killiecrankie] his courage was not … a good soldier, with sufficient qualifications to be a colonel, but for a general officer, it seemed to be a preferment above his capacity. His ill conduct showed itself in divers ways.

Morer thought that Mackay's efforts at Killiecrankie and were poor and these will be noted in the subsequent chapter.[9]

After his death, Burnet composed an epitaph for him:

> He was a man of such strict principles that he would not have served in a war that he did not think lawful. He took great care of his soldiers' morals, and forced them to be both sober and just in their quarters. He spent all the time that he was master of in secret prayers, and in the reading of scriptures … when he had full leisure for his devotions he acted with a peculiar exaltation of courage. He had one every singular quality: in councils of war he delivered his opinion freely and maintained it with due zeal; but how positive soever he was in it, if the council of war overruled it, even though he was not convinced by it, yet to all others he justified it, and executed his part with the same zeal as if his own opinion had prevailed.[10]

An opinion of him from one of his principal enemies was magnanimous, however, 'he bears that of being a very generous enemy, a good officer, and very zealous in the service of his master'. There follows an account of his political and religious views and his fair-minded attitude towards Dundee and the Highlanders in general.[11]

Both Burnet and Morer identified Mackay's personal bravery, a great virtue in any soldier, of course, but both believed that he had been over-promoted and that he was unsuited to command an army, which, of course, he had no experience of, as was the case with his Jacobite enemies. He was also a devout Presbyterian. Yet he seems to have been a consensualist and unwilling to go against his junior officers. Whether this inability to impose his authority was a weakness is another question.

Other contemporaries were complimentary. The Prince de Vaudemont in a letter to William III in 1691 wrote that: 'Lanier [has] thought, Mackay skill and Colchester bravery'.[12] One Alexander Matheson of Ardross wrote that he had 'acquired the character of one of the first military commanders of his age, as well as that of an eminent Christian'.[13] Dutch general Ginkel

9 Morer, *A Short Account of Scotland*, pp.100–101.

10 Browning, English Historical Documents, p.930.

11 Cameron, *Memoirs*, pp.297–298.

12 David Chandler, *Marlborough as Military Commander* (London: Batsford, 1975) p.26.

13 NLS, MS 3742, f4r.

wrote that he was 'a man of great judgement and long experience'.[14] Unlike Dundee, Mackay has not attracted a modern biographer, but his career prior to 1689 can be briefly summarised. Mackay was a Highlander, of Scourie in Sutherland. He was a professional soldier and had almost three decades of soldiering behind him when he was entrusted by William to deal with his Scottish enemies in early 1689. In 1660 he had become an ensign in the Royal Scots in the monarch's new army. He was probably born in about 1640, though his birthdate is not known. There was no war in the British Isles and the regiment saw service under the French against the Dutch in the War of Devolution of 1667–1668. In 1669 he volunteered to fight the Turks alongside the Austrian forces. By 1672 he was a captain in the Royal Scots and initially the regiment fought with the French against the Dutch, in, the War of the Dutch, 1672–1678. However he resigned his commission and joined the Dutch. In 1674 he was put in charge of the 10 independent English companies in Dutch service. By 1677 he was a colonel and in 1685 a brigadier general. By now he was in charge of the Scots/English brigade of three infantry regiments in Dutch service. In 1688 he sailed with his men and his Dutch master, the Prince of Orange to topple James II.[15]

He also had a ruthless streak in him and was not afraid to put military needs above those of civilians if there were good military reasons for such activity.

Sir John Lanier was another senior officer on the government's side in Scotland in 1689. He was a veteran soldier of nearly two decades of experience, though, as with Mackay, he had never seen action in Scotland. As with Mackay, he had fought alongside the French in Flanders during Charles II's reign, then became lieutenant colonel in Monmouth's Regiment of Horse, part of the English army, in 1674–1678, before being knighted and becoming a brigadier. For the next few years he was governor of Jersey, improving the defences there. In 1688, now a major general, he defected to William during the invasion.[16]

Below the ranks of the generals were the regimental commanders. Some were professional soldiers, but even when not, they were not wholly inexperienced.

William Cleland (c.1661–1689), lieutenant colonel of Lord Angus' regiment, was not a professional soldier. As with Dundee he had attended St. Salvator's College in the University of St. Andrew's, though some years later, in 1676–1677 and in the following decade spent time in university in Holland. Yet he had seen combat at Drumclog and at Bothwell Bridge in 1679 as a Covenanter and had taken part in the Argyll rebellion in 1685, before coming over with William in 1688. He was appointed as lieutenant colonel to the regiment on 10 July 1689. He was also a poet and fired by religious zeal against the Jacobites.[17] Mackay wrote this of him: 'a sensible

14 Childs, *Williamite Wars*, p.334.

15 *ODNB*, 35, pp.510–511.

16 *Ibid.*, 32, pp.528–529.

17 *Ibid.*, 35, pp.16–17; *Calendar of State Papers Domestic of the Reign of William III Preserved at the Public Record Office, 1689–1690* (London: HMSO, 1913), p.184.

resolute man, though not much of a souldier'.[18] Some of the officers, whose background we know of, were members of the aristocracy or gentry, as was customary at this time. Patrick Grant, lieutenant colonel of his brother Grant's infantry regiment, was a nobleman. Two junior officers of the Royal Scots Dragoons were John Hay, son of the Marquis of Tullibardine and Sir William Douglas, son of the Duke of Roxburgh. Andrew Agnew, a lieutenant in that unit was the son of Sir Andrew Agnew of Wigtownshire. One of the cornets was a baronet's son. The lieutenant colonel of Kenmure's Foot was laird of Craigdarroch in Dumfrieshire. Sir Robert Hamilton was a captain in Leven's Foot. Captain Jacob Hildebrand was a baronet and Lieutenant Colonel George Ramsay (c.1652–1705) was an earl's son, as was Leven. John Ferguson of Craigdarroch, a lieutenant in Kenmure's regiment, was described as being 'descended of a good ancient family being in the flower of his age' and was married to the Lady Elizabeth. Not all officers were from landed society. John Blackadder (1664–1729), a lieutenant in Angus' Foot, was a Presbyterian preacher's son, as was Samuel Veitch (1668–1732).[19] Theodore Drury, an artillery officer who served in Mackay's regiment as a captain, was a French refugee, presumably a Huguenot expelled from France.[20]

Many of the officers had no military experience whatsoever. Of Livingstone's Dragoons, of the 10 officers serving in 1690 whom we know about, seven had their commissions dating from 1689 and the three cornets all from 1690.[21] An exception was Hamilton, who had seen service in the Dutch forces prior to becoming a captain in Leven's. His fellow captains had not.[22] Lieutenant Colonel George Ramsay, whose regiment fought at Killiecrankie, had served as a captain in an English regiment in the French service until 1674, then the Dutch and was a major in Wachope's regiment in 1685; lieutenant colonel in 1687. He had remained loyal to William during the recall of some of the Scots-Dutch Brigade in March 1688 and became a full colonel by the end of that year. Marlborough referred to him as 'a very brave man and a good soldier'.[23] Leven was an experienced officer, having served in the Prussian service as a colonel and then had raised a regiment of Scottish refugees in Germany and the Low Countries in 1688.[24]

Some regiments were better officered than others, Mackay referring to Leven's regiment having 'very good brisk gentlemen; the same advantage Hastings' had'.[25] Most were less than impressive, Mackay writing that he 'have a great want of experienced officers'.[26] This was especially the case with the officers of most of the newly raised units that the Scottish government had had created in March and April of 1689. He wrote that: 'the chief officers, being all noblemen of no service, chose the officers of their regiments

18 Mackay, *Memoirs*, p.71.
19 Dalton, *Army*, III, pp.30, 92, 87. 85; NRS, GD77/189.
20 *RPCS*, 14, p.421.
21 Dalton, *Army Lists*, III, p.30.
22 *Ibid.*, p.85
23 *ODNB*, 45 p.929.
24 *Ibid.*, 37, p.773.
25 Mackay, *Memoirs*, p.59.
26 *Ibid.*, p.278.

and troops, according as they had a kindness for their persons, or as they judged them popular'.[27] Yet Cleland was impressed with his captains and lieutenants, writing on 25 July 1689, 'The captains are universally brave men, the subalterns in one of the regiments are all good but on or two, and those I intend to turn out, and evrie too hot man, in a little tyme'.[28] Junior officers were not necessarily extremely young men: Lieutenant James Colt of Ramsay's was married and aged 31; John Nisbet of Kenmure's was 24 and a bachelor, as was the 28-year-old Lieutenant Hay.[29]

Men

Far less is known about the rank and file; only one seems to have written his memoirs, and in most cases not even their names are known. Those surviving muster rolls of the Scottish army at the National Records of Scotland only include Angus' regiment of all of the forces involved in the battles of the campaign, and they only list names and ranks; ages, previous occupations or parishes of origin are unrecorded. Pension records are the only other surviving records of individual members of the rank and file of what was to become the British Army after 1707, but they do not exist until 1715 and by that time most of the soldiers who fought in 1689–1690 had died or had already retired.

However, we do know a little about a handful of them; these may or may not be representative of the whole as they make up such a tiny proportion of such, and furthermore, as all were in receipt of pensions from 1719–1727 they were all inevitably very young in 1689. Even so, they must be examined because they are all that exist. Six men who served at Killiecrankie were all new recruits; one enlisted in 1686, one in 1688 and four in 1689. All had been born in 1660–1667 so had enlisted in their earlier twenties and were not much older at the time of battle. Another young recruit was Donald McBane, who had enlisted in Captain MacKenzie's company in 1687, aged 23. Yet another was Matthew Mathis of Angus' Foot, aged 20 in 1689. However Thomas O'Bryan of Hastings' was 35 years old in 1689, having served about five years in the army already.[30]

Some men had military experience. Hugh Ross had served several years as a soldier in Charles II's reign.[31] George Scot, in 1691, was described as 'ane distressed old souldier, adged about sixty nyne years … decrepit and infirme'. However, he had been employed on garrison duty at Edinburgh and Dumbarton Castles in recent years. This was often the lot of the older soldier, who was not employed in the field.[32]

27 *Ibid.*, p.7.
28 Fraser, *Melvilles and Leslies*, II, p.115.
29 Thomson, *APS*, Appendix, IX, pp.56, 59.
30 TNA, WO116/1.
31 *RPCS*, 15, p.151.
32 *Ibid.*, p.228.

Regrettably the pension records do not list previous occupation nor parish of origin, until the 1730s, and these men received their pensions between 1719–1727. McBane, who wrote his memoirs, had been an apprentice to a tobacco spinner in Inverness. His father was a local farmer/publican. He joined the army because he was unhappy with his employment, recording, 'My mistress began to lessen my Dish which I could not endure, I being a raw young Fellow would have eaten two days' meat in one day, so I went and listed myself a soldier'. How typical this was as a reason for enlistment cannot be known.[33] Some joined involuntarily, as in the case of Robert Mackenzie, born in Yorkshire in about 1669 and like McBane, a 20-year-old apprentice, though to a tailor, and who was pressed at Inverness by Captain Gordon into Strathnaver's regiment in 1689.[34]

Angus' regiment were rather different from most because of the devout nature of the men serving there. As the author of a book about one of their officers noted, 'Both officers and men were remarkable for the strictness and propriety of their moral conduct, and for the most exemplary attitude to the duties of religion. Their piety became proverbial.' Raised in May 1689 at Douglas, Lanarkshire by Lord Angus, they were 'chiefly of people residing in and about town'. They swore to be sober and to defend Protestantism against Catholicism.[35] These men were from Covenanting backgrounds and so, as Presbyterians, zealously opposed to James II and his supporters on religious grounds and on experiences and memories of past wrongs.

Each regiment was to have a surgeon and a mate, as from June 1689, but it would seem that this was not the case in reality, certainly not by the following month; with the exception of Angus', as will be noted in chapter six.[36]

Daily pay rates for the army in 1689 were as follows:[37]

Rank	Horse	Dragoons	Infantry
Colonel			12s
Lieutenant Colonel			7s
Major			5s
Captain	10s	8s	8s
Lieutenant	6s	5s	4s
Cornet	5s	n/a	n/a
Ensign	n/a	4s	3s
Surgeon and mate	n/a	n/a	5s
Quartermaster	4s	n/a	4s
Sergeant	n/a	2s 6d	1s 6d
Corporal	3s	1s 8d	1s
Drummer	2s 6d	1s 8d	1s 3d
Trooper/Private	1s 8d	1s 2d	6d

33 Donald McBane, *The Expert Sword-Man's Companion* (Glasgow: Fallen Book Company, 2015), pp.75–76.

34 TNA, WO116/1.

35 Andrew Crichton, *Life and Diary of Lt. Colonel John Blackadder* (Edinburgh: H.S. Baynes, 1825), pp.19, 21-22.

36 *RPCS*, 13, p.408.

37 Morer, A Short Account of Scotland, pp.151–155.

Life in the army during the Nine Years' War of 1688–1697 was not easy. Despite McBane's discontent with his food as a civilian, food in the army was, if anything, worse. A study has shown that soldiers had food totalling 1,700 calories and 40 grams of protein per day, well below that required; in the 1930s it was estimated that 3,800 calories and 160 grams of protein were needed per day by soldiers on active service. In theory in 1689 a soldier had 1½ pounds of bread and a slightly lesser amount of meat and cheese, with three pints of beer, per day. His food included rye bread, hard cheese, beer, meat and peas. Colonel Sir Robert Peyton observed in 1691, 'it being very hard for poor men that have no pay nor means of their own to live upon bread alone and do duty'. Marches of 12 miles per day were the best that could be expected. Of their pay, very little money was available for privates once deductions had been made for what food they received. On this he would be marching 10–12 miles a day, with a day of rest in every four.[38]

The supply of money to pay the army and for food to nourish the men and the horses was haphazard. The cash was always in arrears (at the onset of 1691 over a year's arrears were paid), occasionally provoking mutiny for its want. In 1691 an infantry captain related how he had had to pay his men from his own pocket for the entire previous year and wanted recompense. Supply was meant to be provided by the agents of 'local' government by order of the central state. However there are many references to troops commandeering accommodation and food from the towns they were staying in or passing through. Aberdeen and Banff later presented the Privy Council with detailed lists of what had been consumed unpaid for, by the army.[39]

Paying for these forces was a constant difficulty. Scotland was not a rich country (in 1660 it contributed £40,000 to the King's government, whereas England gave £1.2 million) During James II's reign the forces there eventually amounted to three regiments of infantry and three cavalry regiments, backed up by militia. In 1689 the cost of 10 fully manned regiments of infantry, 10 troops of Horse and one regiment of dragoons was, per month, £11,085, or if five regiments of infantry only were included, £7,105.[40] According to Viscount Tarbat, the cost of this army per year would be about £119,000. Yet Scotland's sources of income were limited. Eight months of the cess tax (levied on property), if all were paid, would amount to £48,000. Excise tax should yield £31,000 if all were paid, but £29,000 was a more realistic figure. Therefore income fell far short of expenditure on defence alone.[41] Tax revenues fell in 1689-1690 due to the difficulties in collection during the conflict.

Even when money was available it was not always forthcoming to the soldiers. Lord Blackwood was the commissioner for paying Angus' regiment, but because Cleland would not oblige him by making the lord's son the senior captain above others 'who had served abroad … being only a petite gentleman, no soger and last of all the captains in raising his company' was slow in making payments. Therefore Cleland had to pay the officers and men

38 Childs, *The Nine Years War*, pp.47–50.

39 *RPCS*, 16, 1691 (Edinburgh, 1970), pp.438–40, 50, 43–44, 199–200.

40 Mackay, *Memoirs*, p.297.

41 Fraser, *Melvilles and Leslies*, II, p.104.

out of his own pocket in 1689 'so that officers and sogers are considerably in my debt'.[42]

With little pay, men were not encouraged to marry. Yet several of the men in the Scots/English Dutch Brigade were married and some had children. Francis Opper had married Margaret Elshaph and they had five children.[43] Likewise, Richard Robertson of Kenmure's Foot had married and had five children, too.[44] James Dewar of Mackay's had married Janet Chalmers and they had had three children.[45] These may have accompanied the army on campaign in the way that camp followers often did.

Equipment and Tactics

Seventeenth-century field armies were composed of infantry, cavalry and artillery, as had been the case since the previous century and was to be so until the twentieth. At the end of the seventeenth century, armies in western Europe were in a state of transition between the pike and shot era and the horse and musket period. Pikes were being replaced by muskets with bayonets and matchlock muskets by flintlocks. The Danish Army was one of the first to make this switch, doing so in 1675–1679, whereas that of France did do not so fully until 1704.[46] The British armies made the changes in a more piecemeal fashion.

The most numerous of these arms were the infantry. In the case of the English these were divided into regiments and then 13 companies, each theoretically 50 privates strong (in reality the numbers per company varied; that of Angus' regiment in July 1689 varied from 47–62) plus officers: captain, lieutenant and ensign, five NCOs (two sergeants and three corporals) and two drummers. The senior officers: colonel, lieutenant colonel and major also commanded a company as well. However the Scots regiments raised in 1689 were initially ordered to be of 600 men divided into 10 companies, though Angus' was oddly enough envisaged as being 1,000 men of 20 companies. Each regiment was also supposed to have one surgeon, too.[47] A regiment took its name from its colonel, though was usually led into battle by its lieutenant colonel. The rank and file of the regiment were mostly armed with muskets, either matchlock or the newer flintlocks, but some (about one man in three) still carried pikes to ward off cavalry attacks and to engage enemy infantry in melee. Their successor was the musket and bayonet, introduced in France, and by 1704 it had completely replaced the pike.[48]

Matchlock muskets had been used throughout the seventeenth century, but unlike the first decades of the century they were now lighter and no longer needed a support to fire. They fired a lead ball of about one ounce at the

42 *Ibid.*, II, p.115.
43 *RPCS*, 15, pp.54–55.
44 *Ibid.*, p.123.
45 *Ibid.*, p.218.
46 Childs, *Williamite War*, p.194.
47 NRS, E100/13; Balfour-Maitland, 'Estates', I, p.44.
48 Grant, *From Pike to Shot*, pp.11, 43.

rate of one or two shots per minute. Men carried a bandolier of 12 wooden cartridges to carry powder charges, a bag of bullets and a powder horn. It took 44 movements to reload.[49] The powder used to propel the ball forward was ignited by the smouldering end of a two -foot-long cord, impregnated with saltpetre, known as the match cord. However in rainy or windy weather they were useless. As a contemporary military treatise observed, 'the Musket, which is often unfixt, requires always Powder, Bullet, and Match, and in windy or wet weather, often disappoints the service, especially if it be the match lock'. In melee, soldiers often used the butt end of the musket to club their enemies, but were also equipped with swords.[50]

Muskets had a maximum range of 250 yards but an effective one of a quarter of that. Throughout most of the seventeenth century a musketeer needed pikemen on hand to ward off cavalry. Officers were armed with swords and spontoons and their role was to direct the men not fight themselves, unless in self defence. Sergeants carried halberds. However, a new type of musket was being slowly introduced in the later seventeenth century. This was the flintlock musket: more reliable and faster to fire. In the British armies they were first employed in 1664, for seaborne troops, in 1683 for the Guards battalions and in 1685 for the Royal Fusiliers. It was not until 1691 that the entire infantry was issued with flintlocks and up to then regiments would be only armed with matchlock or flintlock only. Another innovation of this period was the bayonet in 1669: plug and socket (respectively one which disabled the musket from firing and the latter did not). This sharp blade made each musketeer into his own pikeman. These were not universally issued until 1691.[51]

Pikemen were armed with pikes which were 13 to 18 feet long, but many were shorter, only 12 feet long, for ease of transport and handling. They made movement slow and were unwieldy. The tallest and strongest men bore pikes and this was traditionally more prestigious than being a musketeer. In the 1640s the ratio of pikemen to musketeers in English armies was about 1 to 2, but was 1 to 3 by 1689. They could be used in a defensive role to ward off cavalry as the pike had a greater reach than the sword-armed horseman. Or they could be used aggressively against other infantry, particular enemy pikemen when soldiers engaged in a scrum known as the push of the pike.[52]

In conventional warfare, the pikemen were in the centre of the regiment with equal numbers of musketeers on each flank. The pikemen fought five deep, the musketeers six deep, though at Killiecrankie they were far thinner in ranks. Grenadier companies stood at the right of the regiment.[53]

It is possible to know how some of the units in Scotland in 1689 were armed. In February 1689 there was an order for Colonel Beveridge's regiment of English infantry to be supplied with 200 muskets and 100 pikes, suggesting

---

49 *Ibid.*, p.10.

50 Anthony Pollard and Neil Oliver, *Two Men in a Trench*, II (London: Michael Joseph, 2003), pp.95, 147; Roger Orrery, *Treatise of the Art of War* (London, 1677), p.26.

51 Childs, *The Nine Years War*, pp.75–76, 79.

52 Pollard and Oliver, *Two Men*, II, pp.96–97.

53 David Chandler (ed.), *Oxford History of the British Army* (Oxford: Oxford University Press, 2003), p.65.

a 2:1 ratio of men armed with each weapon.[54] Glencairn's and Kenmure's Scottish regiments were supplied with bayonets in June, the latter with 420.[55] Bargany's regiment was given 180 pikes and 280 muskets. Blantyre's were given 300 matchlocks but also needed 150 pikes.[56]

Many were not properly equipped for some time after they had been raised. Angus', on 3 July 1689, were in want of 800 bayonets, 400 swords and 400 bandoliers, and it is uncertain whether these were received in time for the battle they took part in in the following month.[57] They had received 600 muskets and 40 halberds (for sergeants) in May.[58] Therefore, some troops were armed with pikes and some with muskets. The bulk of the latter were matchlocks. Some of the musketeers had bayonets, too, but by no means all.

The infantry wore single-breasted red coats which reached to the knee and broad rimmed black felt hats with a low crown and a ribbon at its base. Their collars, cuffs and facing would be in another colour, often yellow or red. Officers were permitted some leeway in their dress and uniforms could be very ornate with gold and silver. Hastings' regiment had yellow facings and breeches and grey stockings.[59] In 1691 Mackay's regiment wore red coats lined with blue and Ramsay's red lined with white.[60]

Grenadiers were a relatively new type of soldier and recent writers have anachronistically likened them to the SAS, meaning that they were the army's elite. In 1678 Evelyn saw them in array at Hounslow Heath and described them thus:

> … now were brought into service a new sort of souldier called Granadiers, who were dextrous to fling hand Granados, every one having a pouch full, & had furr'd caps with coped crowns like Janizaries, which made them look very fierce, & some had long hoods hanging down behind as we picture fooles: their clothing being likewise py bald yellow & red.[61]

Orders for the equipping of Trelawney's regiment of infantry in 1684 saw each of the captain's companies issued with 20 pikes and 40 muskets. Thus, the standard ratio of 1 pike to 2 muskets that was the notional ideal in the 1640's was still in evidence 40 years later. Still the same weapon as used in the first half of the 17th century, the pike was on average some 16ft in length fitted with a spear head and protective languets. Used as a defensive weapon against cavalry attacks, the pike was also used offensively. (Artwork by Alan Turton © Helion & Company)

Grenadiers had been in action at Sedgemoor in 1685, but are not known to have used their grenades there. The grenade was an iron ball filled with gunpowder to which a fuse was attached. They were envisaged for use in sieges and in close combat as their range was limited. Grenades were more

54 TNA, WO5/5, p.63.
55 *RPCS* 13, pp.412, 414.
56 Thomson, *APS, Appendix*, IX, pp.63, 79, 28.
57 *RPCS*, 13, p.487.
58 Thomson, *APS, Appendix*, IX, pp.26, 36.
59 Grant, *From Pike to Shot*, pp.41, 48.
60 James Ferguson, 'Papers Illustrating the History of the Scots Brigade in the service of the United Netherlands, 1572–1697', *SHS*, I, vol. 32 (1898), p.570.
61 Evelyn, *Diary*, p.580.

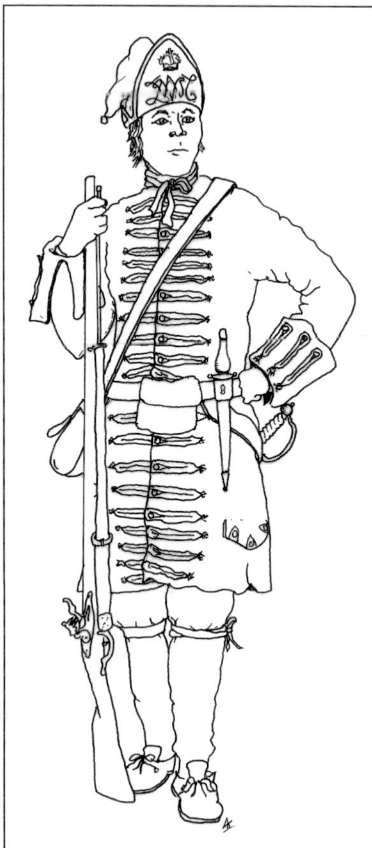

From the 1670's onwards, the armies of most countries organised their grenadiers into separate companies. Formed of the tallest and strongest of men, the Grenadier companies where to become recognised as the elite of the regiment, and as such frequently assigned the most dangerous task. An order of April 1678 makes for the raising of a company of Grenadiers for each of the first 8 regiments of the English army. Each of the companies was to be made up of a captain, 2 lieutenants, 3 sergeants and 3 corporals, and 100 grenadiers. (Artwork by Alan Turton © Helion & Company)

commonly used in naval warfare and siege work, and in April 1689 the Scottish government ordered 100 be made up for use in frigates.[62]

It seems that the colonel, as proprietor of his regiment once he had been given his commission, had to spend his own money to clothe and arm his men. Ludovick Grant in 1689 had to buy 600 muskets and bayonets costing £1,324 2s, as well as eight hundredweight of powder costing £6,480. George Clerk, an Edinburgh merchant, supplied these goods.[63] Officers would eventually be reimbursed by the government for this initial outlay.

There were a number of British military manuals published to guide officers in the art of war. Charles II had decreed that *An Abridgement of English Military Discipline* be used by his armies. It envisaged a leisurely advance to battle to avoid confusion by attempting to deploy from column of march to line of battle. Officers would march ahead to ensure the lines were in order, retiring before battle and before any shooting began. Men were expected to stand in line six paces apart, as musketeers needed space to load (flintlock-armed men needed but a pace on either side) and three paces in front of the next line. Assuming a regiment was 600 men strong and the men deployed six men deep, the frontage could be up to 200 metres and 10 metres deep. The firing pattern was that the first rank would fire, then reload; then the fifth rank would fire and so on. Once the first had fired, the men would peel off to the rear and the new first line would advance. The regiment thus discharged a sixth of its firepower at a time and so for much of the time most men would have loaded muskets. Silence was encouraged so the commands of the major and colonel could be heard; only they would be on horseback. Battles were slow as infantry exchanged fire.[64]

However another drill manual had other ideas. On the battlefield, fire was by platoon, in order that it would be continual. Each regiment was divided into platoons. The unit was six ranks deep, with grenadiers at the flanks. The front rank would kneel to fire; the men in the next two ranks, two paces behind the front rank, would then move up, fire and then their ranks opened. When standing, officers and sergeants would be to the rear. This was so that the officers could direct the men, leading them off the battlefield if need be or by advancing through the ranks if the unit needed to move forward. Orders were both verbal and by the beat of the drum. The sergeants were at the back so that they could prevent routs by threatening to kill any routers.[65] These manuals were, of course, theoretical and their strictures could dissolve in the heat of battle.

62 Balfour-Maitland, 'Estates', I, p.35–36.
63 *RPCS*, 13, p.544.
64 Childs, *Nine Years War*, pp.78–84.
65 John Mackay, *Rules to be observed by the body of Infantry* (Edinburgh, 1693), pp.3–5, 2.

Although new methods of company and regiment fire control where starting to be used by the 1680's, the salvo, harking back to the early part of the century was still in practise. In this drill motion, a large concentrated volley could be delivered by the majority of the formation's musketeers. (Artwork by Alan Turton © Helion & Company)

Cavalry were divided into two types; regiments of horse and dragoons, each type sub-divided into six troops, in theory 50 men strong in each. The horse were the elite of the armies, often armoured (back and breast plates), though helmets had been largely discarded for hats, armed with pistols and heavy swords. They would form up in two or three ranks with about six metres between each.[66] Their role on the campaign was to patrol and on the field to engage the enemy cavalry and to pursue fleeing enemies and so complete a victory, or cover their own army's retreat. The front rank would often loose off their pistols at close range and then charge with their swords. Dragoons were originally mounted infantry, able to fight on foot as well as on horseback, so were armed as infantry (with musket, bayonet and pistols, though no pikes) as well as cavalry, but only fought so occasionally; at Knockbrecht in June 1689 and later at Preston in 1715. They tended to be faster and lighter and were unarmoured. According to Mackay, 'hors is the great feare of the Highlanders'.[67] Conventionally, cavalry would make up about a third of an army's strength.[68] They were far more expensive to maintain than infantry, especially the horses in the way of having sufficient feed. Cavalry also engaged in scouting tasks.

Finally there was the artillery which was under the direction of the Board of Ordnance, rather than the War Office which dealt with the cavalry and infantry. There was no Royal Artillery as a permanent force until 1716. When guns were needed, they were taken from fortresses, castles and ships, and gunners found from these same places. Guns were often light enough that they only needed one horse and several men to pull them along. Civilians and infantry were also used in the deployment of guns to and on the field. In the field, these light guns, with two to four pound weight balls, were used to support the infantry battalions and had a range of about 800 yards. At a range of 200 yards, gunners would switch to 'partridge shot', loading the guns with a bag of iron balls which would burst shortly after leaving the muzzle and being devastating to a number of enemy troops. Larger guns were less commonly used because they were heavier and so difficult to transport over land. They tended to be used in siege warfare.[69]

66 Childs, *Nine Years War*, pp.85–86.
67 Mackay, *Memoirs*, p.277.
68 Grant, *From Pike to Shot*, p.11.
69 *Ibid*, p.13.

The Royal Regiment of Fuzileers was raised in 1685 by Lord Dartmouth, to protect and guard the artillery train. Matchlock muskets, with lit match cord were too much of a danger amongst the barrels of gunpowder used by the big guns, so this new regiment was issued with flintlock muskets. (Artwork by Alan Turton © Helion & Company)

At Killiecrankie Mackay had three 'leather guns'. These were lightweight artillery pieces with thin barrels clad with leather, reinforced with iron hoops. Their origin was in northern Europe in the Thirty Years' War (1618–1648) when there was a need to have light guns for battle use. They could be loaded with stone balls or grape shot. However they had many drawbacks; limited range, fragile and liable to be easily damaged, complex and costly to make and their barrels became very hot very quickly in battle, after only a little use, due to being thickly insulated. By the end of the 1630s they had passed their use-by date. Yet a Scottish soldier in Germany, James Wemyss, was interested in their use and as Charles I's Master Gunner, he had several made. Some were used in Scotland in 1675 and by 1688 a few were at his castle. They were two feet five inches long and 1.7–3.6 inches in calibre. A recent historian described them as being 'crude, ineffective and eccentric'.[70]

William's forces were a polygot of nationalities. There is a popular tendency to see the Jacobite campaigns as being a war between the English and the Scots, often specifically the Highlanders, but this is misleading and nowhere more so than in 1689–1690. This is better seen as a Scottish civil war, with some input from Dutch, Irish and English interlopers, to decide who sat on the throne in Scotland and what form of religion and government would hold sway there.

Despite substantial increases in the size of the standing armies in Britain under James II, from 1685–1688 (nine additional infantry regiments and seven of cavalry being raised in 1685 alone, along with two more Scottish units), it was not a force which had much experience of warfare, compared to many of its Continental counterparts who had been in conflict in the Low Countries, in northern Europe and against the Turks in the Balkans. Britain's only significant conflict overseas on land between 1660 and 1688 had been the ongoing war in Tangier, and even then, by the late 1680s only a small proportion of the English standing army had served there. Scottish and English troops had not seen much active military service in the field of battle at home. There had been the battle of Bothwell Bridge in 1679 and that of Sedgemoor of 1685, but again, only a minority of men had taken part in these relatively small scale engagements.

Yet English and Scots soldiers had served with the French and Dutch armies since the late sixteenth century, perhaps out or a mixture of economic and religious reasons when Holland had employed a British Brigade of volunteers and this persisted until the end of the eighteenth century. Foreign units serving as part of a wider national army were not uncommon at this time; the French and Spanish employed Irish units and the former Swiss, too. In the 1660s and 1670s with Britain and Holland at war there was a lack

70 David Stevenson, 'Scotland's Leather Guns', *History Scotland*, 2/6, Nov./Dec. 2002, pp.12–18.

of Britons in these 'Dutch' units but this was rectified by active recruiting in 1675 when hostilities between the two ceased. We have already noted that some of William's officers had served in these forces. In 1685 William of Orange had volunteered their services to his father in law, James, in the course of the Monmouth Rebellion. They had been accepted and arrived in England by early July 1685, just too late, as it happened, to help in the defeat of the rebellion. James II had been impressed with them as had Blaythwayt, who remarked 'They are the best men and best prepared for service, that ever were seen'.[71]

They returned without having seen any action, but in March 1688, with the knowledge that William was about to invade, their presence was needed again. James summoned them over but William, not wanting to increase his enemies, refused, but later allowed any officers to resign their commissions and return to Britain. A total of 104 out of 213 did so, including some Catholics, and these almost included Mackay, but he relented at the last moment. Very few of the rank and file left; these latter were all Catholics. William replaced the losses with Irish Protestants and Huguenot refugees who were far more politically reliable.[72]

When William's armada set sail in the autumn of 1688, his forces included these regiments. Three of these were sent to Scotland in March 1689, led by Mackay. Mackay's and Balfour's regiments were made up of 12 companies of 53 men each in November 1688.[73] Although these regiments were titled as British, they did include some Dutchmen as well. This was not uncommon among nominally foreign regiments.

These regiments were the most experienced units in the fight against James in Scotland, having served in the War of the Dutch in 1672–1678. Compared to their colleagues, many were relatively battle hardened veterans indeed. The three regiments from the Brigade who fought at Killiecrankie – Balfour's, Mackay's and Ramsay's – were, by the time they reached Scotland in March 1689, considerably weaker than at the time of their arrival in England in November 1688. This was because, as Mackay wrote, 'the king having taken away their old Dutch souldiers out of these three regiments'. This was because William saw the key theatre of operations as being Ireland and the Low Countries, not without justification as that was where James was with the bulk of his support. It did mean, though, that these three regiments had been denuded of the veterans among them. Yet elsewhere in his memoirs Mackay refers to him leading 200 'old foot' in Scotland.[74] The men then, were 'mostly new levied men'; but not all were.[75] The men wore red coats, with trumpeters and drummers wearing grey.[76]

Then there was the small Scottish army, founded in 1660, which had been increased by James II and had been ordered southwards in October 1688 to

71 Ferguson, 'Papers Illustrating the History', I, p.476n.
72 Childs, *The Army, James II*, pp.132–134.
73 *London Gazette*, 2397, 5–8 Nov. 1688.
74 Mackay, *Memoirs*, pp.3, 15, 59.
75 *Ibid.*, p.59.
76 Ferguson, 'Papers illustrating the History', I, p.210.

join the rest of James II's forces. Following his departure, some of the officers therein resigned their commissions rather than serve William and had been mostly disbanded in late 1688 after James' flight. Apart from one regiment of cavalry, none served in this campaign in Scotland, possibly because their political reliability was suspect.

New regiments were raised in Scotland in the spring of 1689 in order to deal with the threat posed by James' supporters there. Commissions were given to men who were known supporters of William of Orange, such as the Earls of Argyll and Melville. Leven's infantry regiment had been raised in March 1689; 800 men had enlisted in the space of merely two hours.[77] They had very little training, as Mackay wrote, 'I had no tyme all this campaigne to look after the modelling of them, or bringing them to a better forme, so they are very raw and new as yet'.[78] This was because, 'being continually ingadged against the rebells since I came to Scotland except for a few weeks the beginning' he was unable to do so.[79] On the eve of Killiecrankie, Mackay wrote, 'The Foot Regiments which I see at Stirling are in bad condition, but Blantyre the worst of all for the half of his regiment is little boys and old tired men'.[80] The following comment concerns newly raised troops in Ireland in 1689 but was probably apposite for many of Mackay's men in Scotland that year, too, 'A great many of the new men who had matchlocks had so little skill in placing of their matchlocks true and scarce one in four could fire their pieces off, and those that did thought they had done a great feat if the gun fired, not minding what they shot at'.[81]

However, this was not universally the case as Cleland wrote in late July 1689 of the men in his battalion, 'I have brought on of the battalions that hath still ben quartered with me to a verie good condition. They doe there exercises and fiere all well as many old regiments'.[82] Mackay had confidence in his cavalry, though with some more than others, writing on 26 July that Belhaven's Troop was 'composed of very good men and horses and well cloath'd and which is most of all use, of their zeale for the cause. I have not seen Annandale's yt the troops are generally in better order than the foot according to their number'.[83]

Roger Orrery had this to say about recruits: 'When we raise men … both generally unexpert in the use of Arms, and unaccustomed to the hardships of war, hereby, if suddenly after their being listed, they should be led on service, they would be expos'd to Defeats.'

If the men were volunteers, then he stated they were 'too frequently debauched, idle Persons, who having lived in Excess and Laziness are the less capable of undergoing the life of soldiers' and if pressed men 'they have still hankering to return, are commonly grumbling that they have been presst'.[84]

77 Balfour-Maitland, 'Estates', I, p.8.
78 Mackay, *Memoirs*, p.278.
79 *Ibid.*, p.286.
80 NRS, GD406/1/3609.
81 G. Storey, *An Impartial History of Affairs of Ireland during the last two years* (London, 1691), p.15.
82 Fraser, *Melville and Leslies*, III, p.115.
83 NRS, GD406/1/3609.
84 Orrery, *Treatise*, p.6.

Some men were motivated by means other than money and in Angus' regiment, Cleland could note that despite difficulties with money, 'our sogers radie to desert, except such as will not desert from a principle of love to the cause and there Majesties, of which sort my regiment is mostlie made up'.[85]

Not all the men in the Scottish regiments were Scottish, Mackay writing that 'Bargeny's is composed of good men, but most of the Scots Irish who came over the last somer'. Glencairn's regiment was also mostly composed of Irishmen, perhaps these were Protestant Irishmen who had fled from Ireland.[86] Captain James Donaldson brought himself and his company of infantry from Ireland in March 1689 to join Kenmure's regiment, 'out of zeale and affection to the Protestant religion and their Majesties' service', as had three officers who joined Bargany's, namely Samuel Moor and John Pirrie, lieutenants, and Ensign William Bartone.[87]

Men were often recruited on a geographical basis were the officers had local influence and power over the common men. The 10 troops of Scottish cavalry raised in 1689 were recruited thus:[88]

Troop	Districts
Annandale's	Wigton and Dumfries
Belhaven's	Lanark, Striveling and Clackmannanshire
Blair's	Perth
Eglington's	Ayr and Renfrew
Sir Charles Hackett's	Fife
Earl Marshall's	Aberdeen, Banff, Murray, Nairn and Inverness
Lord Newbottle's	Roxburgh and Selkirk
Lord Rollo's	Forfar and Kincardine
Lord Ross's	Peebles, Linlithgow and Edinburgh
Lord Tester's	Haddington and Berwickshire

Troops were taken from distinct districts of Scotland, judging by the surnames of their officers. Mackay's were recruited from northern Scotland; Balfour's from north-east Scotland and Ramsay's from southern Scotland.[89]

Although the English army was far larger than the Scottish army, few English battalions were employed in Scotland; most were sent to Ireland and the Low Countries or remained in England. The only English battalion at Killiecrankie was Hastings' Foot. It had been raised by Theophilus, Earl of Huntingdon in June 1685, in response to the Monmouth Rebellion, but like those other units raised at that time, not disbanded when the emergency was over. Huntingdon ceased to command with James' fall (he and several other officers had been dismissed because they were Catholics) and command passed in December 1688 to Ferdinando Hastings, hence the

85 Fraser, *Melvilles and Leslies*, III, p.115.
86 Mackay, *Memoirs*, pp.290, 298.
87 *RPCS*, 14, pp.181–2.
88 Balfour-Maitland, 'Estates, I', pp.49–50.
89 Reid, *The Last Scots Army*, pp.47–48.

unit's name.[90] The regiment had seen no military service whatsoever, though by the campaign's onset had been in existence for nearly four years. Mackay thought favourably of it, despite being a Scot, writing 'I prefer the English commonality in my judgement in matter of courage to the Scots'.[91]

The English cavalry (Berkeley's and Colchester's) had the difficulty that the horses suffered much due to the climate and so presumably some fell ill or died. Certainly towards the autumn of 1689 they had suffered serious losses. Mackay was impressed with their performance in the campaign, however, 'I found them very well inclined and ready for their Majesties' service, as all the English forces which served me this yeare have showen themselvs'.[92]

Artillery was the arm least employed in this campaign. This was partly due to the lack of guns in Scotland, except for in the garrisoned castles. It was also because their movement would be very slow and such would not be useful in a fast moving campaign. In fact there was only one instance of artillery being employed by the government's forces and that was at Killiecrankie. These were not provided by official means. On 14 July the Privy Council ordered Lady Weymes, 'lend some of your leather gunnes to General Mackay for this present expedition to the Highlands, wher no other artileiarie can be carried. Such guns as shall be lent wil be cairfuly restored, and in caise they be damnified the damage shall be repaired'.[93] These were provided.

One major drawback for the troops was outlined by Mackay, as was his remedy, for he was probably caught out as much as they:

> All our officers and souldiers were strangers to the Highlanders way of fighting and embattailling, which mainly occasioned the consternations many of them were in; which to remedy for the ensuing year, having taken notice on this occasion that the Highlanders are of such quick motion, that if a battalion keep up his fire till they be near to make sure of them, they are upon it before our men can come to their second defence, which is the bayonet in the muzzle of the musket … the General having observed this method of the enemy, he invented the way to fasten the bayonet to the musket without, by two rings that the soldiers may safely keep their fire till they pour it into their breasts, and then have no other motion to make but to push as with a pick.[94]

The other issue to consider is political reliability. Discontent in the army in the autumn of 1688 had helped to lead to James' mental collapse, but had he decided to fight many, if not most of his army would probably have followed his lead. Dumbarton's regiment of foot mutinied in 1689 over being posted overseas and Dundee was not the only army officer to throw in his lot with the deposed monarch; others from his regiment also doing so. Several officers and men of Livingstone's dragoons were, in 1689, conspiring against

90 Dalton, *Army Lists*, III, p.6.
91 Mackay, *Memoirs*, p.59.
92 *Ibid.*, p.267.
93 *RPCS*, 13, p.516.
94 Mackay, *Memoirs*, p.52.

Mackay. The plot was discovered and the miscreants gaoled. Mackay took it very seriously indeed and wrote on 27 June:

> It were necessary that fellow, with the other dragowns, were put to torture, and Lieutenant Murray deserves it by the confession of the serjent and one of the dragoons. If torture be just in any case it is in this: and since the law allows it, why should it not be used in a matter so essential to the service, and of such a pernicious consequence if it had taken intended effect'.[95]

Loyalty of other officers was questionable in these years; Lanier, Marlborough and others (though not Mackay) were ambivalent in their loyalty towards William. This led to their conduct of warfare being half-hearted. This was presumably due to them being understandably uncertain as to who would win and they did not want to find themselves on the losing side, with all the losses to themselves that that would entail in terms of wealth and position.[96]

At the outset of the campaign in 1689, both armies were relatively inexperienced, but both were led by veteran soldiers. The forces of William and Mary were conventionally armed with pikes and muskets, but had limited cavalry and artillery. It was a diverse force of Scots, English and Dutch. Yet many of these troops were new levied and/or inexperienced. The Scottish cavalry and infantry had had minimal training in 1689, and regular troops needed that in order to perform complex drill and firing in battle. Their generals as well as the men were not experienced in Highland warfare against the irregulars they were about to face. They were about to be put to the ultimate test.

---

95 *Ibid.*, pp.28–29, 240.

96 Childs, *Williamite War*, p.293.

5

The Battle of Killiecrankie

KILLIECRANKIE

Chorus
An ye had been whare I ha been,
Ye wad na been sae cantie, O!
An ye had seen what I hae seen
On the braes o' Killiecrankie, O!

1
Whare hae ye been sae braw, lad?
Whare hae ye been sae brankie, O?
Where hae ye been sae braw, lad?
Cane ye by Killiecrankie, O?

2
I faught at land, I faught at sea,
At hame I faught my auntie, O!
But I met the Devil and Dundee
On the braes o'Killiecrankie, O.

3
The bauld Pitcur fell in a furr,
An' Clavers got a Clankie, O.
Or I had fed an Athle gled
On the braes of Killiecrankie, O![1]

Killiecrankie is the best known battle of the campaign; having inspired poetry and song, possessing a National Trust for Scotland Visitor Centre and having been the subject of a sizeable booklet by a well known Scottish historian. Its fame also accrues from the fact that the victorious general was killed in the

1 Robert Burns, *Complete Poems and Songs* (Glasgow: Harper Collins, 1995), p.524.

moment of victory. The many biographies of Dundee also naturally feature the battle.

It was a 'good' day to fight a battle. It was the height of summer, which meant that there were many hours of daylight and an absence of rain which would otherwise make musketry and cannons useless. Visibility was good. Yet for the uniformed regular troops, the heat would be an added strain on a day that would be difficult enough, physically and emotionally.

Dundee arrived at Blair Castle on the morning of Saturday 27 July and learnt that Mackay's force, allegedly about 4,400–4,500 strong, was at Dunkeld, 16 miles away to the south and on their march to Blair. They would have to march through the Pass of Killiecrankie. This was a narrow path at the foot of a steep hill adjacent to the River Garry, where only three men can traverse at a time. A later traveller described it thus, 'a road made on the side of the hill over the river, there being no passage on the other side: the road is a mile long and the country opens again'. The road itself was, in actuality, a trackway where perhaps two or three men can march abreast; it would have been inaccessible for waggons and artillery. Although a handful of resolute men could have held up a far larger force there, there was no one to oppose him, at least not at that point.[2] According to Colonel Hector MacNeill, there was initially a Jacobite plan to march immediately towards the enemy with 400–500 men to attack them in the pass. Many officers supported this idea as they believed the army was not strong enough to defeat Mackay's complete force on other terrain. Yet this would take too much time and there was too little time to authorise it. The troops were too far distant and so an order was given 'to our little army to come up att all expedition imaginable'.[3] It is also possible that to attack a force in the pass would have been seen as dishonourable.

That morning, at daybreak, Mackay sent despatches to Perth to hurry up the six troops of dragoons and horse which were part of his command, though they were never to arrive, leaving his force pitifully short of cavalry. Major George Lauder was sent ahead with '200 choice fusiliers', 'the choice of our army' to secure the pass ahead of the main force 'and to send back what advertisement they could have of the enemy'. It is possible that these 200 men were armed with flintlock muskets and may have been the more experienced of the troops, quite possibly either taken from Balfour's regiment (which Lauder served in). Or they may have been grenadiers, taken from all the regiments of the army. The latter were certainly the elite and were often sent ahead of the main force in siege warfare or in other especially dangerous attacks, but if they were, it is a pity that Mackay was not more explicit. They left Dunkeld at four in the morning, arriving at the pass at Killiecrankie apparently at six, but almost certainly later. He then marched his main body of troops towards them. It was an 11 mile march, accomplished by 10:00 that morning. The troops were then allowed two hours to refresh themselves. Mackay met Lord Murray before the pass, and asked him how many of his

2 NRS, CH12/12/1717; Cameron, *Memoirs*, p.258; Daniel Kemp (ed.), 'Pococke's Tours in Scotland', *SHS*, 1, 1, (1887), p.229.

3 NRS, CH12/12/1717.

Atholl men were with him. Only 200–300, came the answer. Apparently most had left to save their cattle. Mackay thought that this was 'reasonable as well as customary' and he did not think ill of Murray. [4]

Lauder had investigated the pass and having sent his force through it, found that it was clear. The army marched through it in the following order: Balfour's, Ramsay's and Kenmure's infantry regiments were first, then Belhaven's troop, followed by Leven's and Mackay's infantry. The baggage train of 1,200 horses was next. Hastings' regiment and Annandale's troop brought up the rear. This latter regiment was then initially assigned to guard the baggage for Mackay believed that the Jacobites might detach men to attack it or that the country people, seeing it was undefended, might plunder.[5] The baggage was also guarded by 100 men sent from the laird of Weemys.[6]

Pass at Killiecrankie. (Author, 2017)

According to Iain Ban Beag Macreith, one of the Jacobite poets, a sole Highlander shot and killed a cavalryman whilst in the pass, but there is no other evidence to support the tale. Balcarres was explicit: 'Mackay entered the pass without any resistance'.[7] Yet it would have been possible for a man with a musket to have fired across the river and troops unscreened by trees and to fire into a slow moving target and to hit a man, and if the victim was not an officer, there is no reason why a contemporary would have noted it.

Meanwhile, a few miles to the north west, Dundee called a council of war in or near Blair Castle; a not unusual practice at that time, for he 'haveing thought it proper to have the advice of his council, and called all his principall officers together'. He told them of the proximity of the enemy and then proceeded to discuss what they should do next. Their march had been to secure the

4 Mackay, *Memoirs*, pp.56, 263–264; Edinburgh University Library, Laing MSS II 89/338.
5 *Ibid.*, pp.49–50.
6 EUL Laing MSS II, 89/338.
7 *Killiecrankie Story*, p.5; NLS, MS 3738, f28r.

castle and to preserve it. They could wait there for the additional men which they were expecting. Or should they take the offensive immediately and march directly towards MacKay to give battle?[8]

Battles are extremely risky military undertakings. As Roger Orrery noted, 'No one act of war, is so great in itself, or in the consequences of it, as fighting a battle.' He advised caution in making what would be a momentous decision, 'But as to the advantages are eminent to him who wins it, so the prejudices are no less to him whom loses it; and therefore nothing ought to be more exactly consider'd and weigh'd in war than whether a decision to battle shall be given, before the resolution to fight is taken.'[9]

Those who had seen service in the regular army, including presumably the officers recently arrived from Ireland, told Dundee, to a man, that it was risky engaging in battle at this juncture. Mackay's army was better disciplined than theirs and outnumbered theirs by half again, so they thought. There had not been a battle in this campaign and the men had therefore not been blooded, though there had been the fighting at Loup and the MacLeans had fought at Knockbrecht a few weeks ago. It would be better to have the men engage in a skirmish first. Gaining a small victory would raise their morale and make success in a larger battle more likely. It would be better if they waited for more men. They believed that their enemy was efficient and well led. Their arguments seemed strong and there was silence in the council room.[10]

Then Alexander MacDonald of Glengarry broke it. He 'differed in opinion from the officers.' Although admitting that the men were tired from hard marching and hungry due to lack of provisions, 'yet these hardships did not affect them in the same manner that they commonly did souldiers who are bred in an easyer and more plentifull course of life.' Rather, Dundee would 'find them both ready and able to engage, and perhaps defeat ane equal number of the enemy's best troops.'[11]

MacDonald then put reasoning behind his assertions. Highlanders liked nothing more than 'hardy and adventurous exploits.' He urged they attack the enemy immediately before they had marched through the pass, and hold them there. Waiting for them to deploy in front of the pass 'would discourage their men, that they would soon grow of no value, and lose that spirite and resolution which accompanies agressors.' He also suggested that their men keep the enemy in sight and stay on the high ground so they would be alert to any attack or could engage them in skirmishes when opportunity arose.[12]

The chiefs generally agreed but Dundee noted that Cameron had remained aloof to date. The former stated that the latter was so experienced that he should make his feelings known, 'he cannot miss to make a right judgement of the matter, and therefore, his shall determine mine.' Cameron was modest, pointing to his limited experience of warfare and that he would submit to Dundee's judgement. His opinion was 'to fight immediately, for

8 Cameron, *Memoirs*, p.258.

9 Orrery, *Treatise*, p.149.

10 Cameron, *Memoirs*, pp.258–259.

11 *Ibid.*, pp.259–262.

12 *Ibid.*, p.262.

our men are in heart; they are so far from being afraid of their enemy, that they are eager and keen to engage them'. To delay fighting meant that Mackay would be able to bring additional troops to join his army, especially horse and dragoons. Waiting would also mean that hunger would increase in their own ranks and it would be impossible to send out foraging parties with the enemy so near. Retreat would also be disastrous. Victory would bring credit to their cause and would encourage additional support.[13]

Dundee seemed pleased, 'His looks seemed to brighten with ane air of delight and satisfaction'. When Cameron had finished his speech, Dundee told the others of his pleasure. 'Not one in the company offering to contradict their General, it was unanimously agreed to fight'. This had a morale boosting effect on the rank and file, 'When the news of this vigorous resolution spread through the army, nothing was heard but acclamations of joy'.[14]

However, before the council of war ended, there was an exchange, the outcome of which, was to have decisive results for the outcome of the day's fighting and would arguably resonate throughout the entire campaign. Cameron informed Dundee that he spoke for the whole company that he submitted to his superior's judgement in all matters, except on one. 'It is the voice of your council, and their orders are, that you doe not engage personally … On your lordship depends the fate not onely of this little brave army, but also of our King and Country.' Cameron argued that a general's role was to 'have ane eye on all parts, and to issue out your commands as you shall think proper': their role was to obey him. The council all backed him up.[15]

Dundee then made his fateful reply:

> Gentlemen as I am absolutely convinced, and have had repeated proofs of your zeale for the King's service, and of your affection for me, as his General and your Friend, so I am fully sensible that my engageing personally this day may be of some loss if I shall chance to be killed; but I beg leave of you … that I may have ane opportunity of convincing the brave Clans that I can hazard my life in that service as freely as the meanest of them … if they doe not think I have personal courage enough, they will not esteem me hereafter, nor obey my commands with chearfulness.[16]

Dundee was brave but was taking a calculated risk, though it was not unknown for commanders in the seventeenth century to put themselves in danger in battle; sometimes with fatal results. There was another way in which the decision to fight was a gambler's throw. More men were marching to his banner. A list of troops made, presumably before the battle is as follows: Lochiel, 600 men, Glengarry, 400, Keppoch, 300, Frasers, 120, Clanranalds, 400, Glencoe and Appin Stewarts, 500, Badenoch men, 200, Glenmoriston's, 60, (totalling 2,580) as well as MacLean's and Mar's who were yet to arrive.[17]

13 *Ibid.*, pp.262–263.
14 *Ibid.*, p.264.
15 *Ibid.*
16 *Ibid.*, pp.264–5.
17 NRS, GD26/8/71.

Yet he did not want to wait before they had all arrived. This was because 'he would never have such a fair opportunity, Mackay then only having two troops of Horse with him, but if he delayed he would quickly bring up the English dragoons, which is the only thing the Highlanders are afraid of'.[18] Had Dundee been defeated, his rashness in not awaiting reinforcements would have been held against him. The Jacobites were taking a risk, therefore.

The die was now cast and the council could do no more. The army marched for the Pass of Killiecrankie and formed up on 'a rugged uneven, but not very high mountain'. Mackay's force had already cleared the pass and were forming up on the plain which extends along the river. Clearly, Cameron believed that Mackay wished to use his superior numbers to outflank Dundee, so Dundee drew up his regiments in just one line, without any reserve. Mackay's men stood in ranks of three. Since they were tired by their rapid march in order to get through the pass without being attacked, they were allowed to sit on the ground where they would otherwise have stood.[19]

Once Mackay's first five regiments and Belhaven's troop had reached the other side of the pass, they halted in a corn field on the banks of the River Garry in order to allow the slower moving rearguard to catch up. Mackay may now have been roughly where the 'Claverhouse stone' now stands. Mackay ordered Lauder to advance with 200 fusiliers and a troop of horse, unnamed but presumably Belhaven's, in order to locate the Jacobite army. They advanced some hundreds of paces up the hill. Advance parties of the Jacobite army came into view. Mackay galloped to where the viewpoint was. He ordered Balfour to have the ammunition, presumably hitherto carried by the pack mules, distributed and to put the soldiers under arms.[20] Mackay had clearly calculated that ammunition would not have been needed immediately, so it was fortunate that there was no immediate Jacobite attack.

Mackay could see some small groups of Jacobites about a mile away. They were marching slowly along the foot of a hill near Blair, towards where his army was. Yet this may well have been a feint, allowing themselves to be seen and for Mackay to react to them, whilst the bulk of the Jacobites marched around the hill of Lude to occupy the high ground to the north of the pass, not far from Creag Eallaich. Before refreshing himself, he sent orders to Balfour to march towards where he was, with all the infantry. Yet ahead was 'an eminence just above the ground … of a steep and difficult ascent, full of trees and shrubs, and within a carbine shot' of where his men were. Mackay believed that this terrain would be advantageous to his enemy, reasoning that from it 'they could undoubtedly force us with their fire in confusion over the river'.[21]

In order to counter this, he had each regiment form by a *Quart de Conversion* (wheeling the men one quarter of a complete evolution) to the right of the ground on which they stood. So instead of facing their

18 NLS, MS 3738, f28r.

19 Cameron, *Memoirs*, p.265.

20 Mackay, *Memoirs*, p.50.

21 *Ibid.*, p.51.

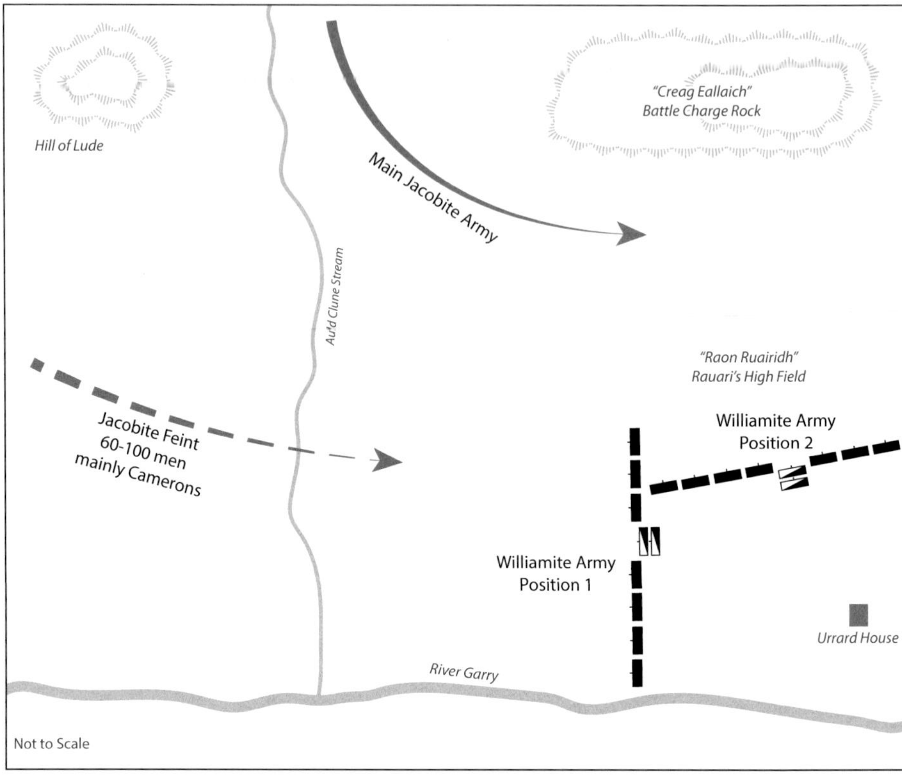

Map 1 The marches of both armies to Killiecrankie, 27 July 1689.

N.B. No contemporary map exists so this is an estimate based on contemporary written accounts. This map was based on one drawn by Rulzion Rattray.

original line of march, to the north, they now faced to the east. They then marched up the hill, though only a little and had probably Urrard House to their immediate rear, and avoided the difficulty just foreseen. Their new position meant that they 'got a ground fair enough to receive the enemy', but were not in a position to attack them, for within musket shot there was another contour before them. His army, therefore were on the lowest contour whereas the Jacobites were above them, with their backs to the very high hill. This, Mackay believed, was the natural position of the Highlanders, who preferred to have a sure retreat behind them, especially if their enemy included cavalry.[22]

By now the five regiments of infantry and one troop of horse were in position. Hastings' regiment was still marching through the pass. The Jacobites were visible on the slopes above them. Mackay resolved to have his troops remain where they were, rather than 'to put his men out of breath and in disorder by attacking the enemy against the hill'. He had his regiments move in order that only a little distance remained between each one. The 200 fusiliers that Lauder had led through the pass remained together (thus denuding the regiments the benefit of these elite troops) 'posted advantageously upon the left of all, on a little hill wreathed with trees'. Each of the regiments was then divided into two and then each arranged so that it was three men deep. In the middle of the battle line there was a great opening and it was here that

22 *Ibid.*

he placed his two troops of horse. By now both were together and Hastings' regiment had arrived as well and the latter were now on the right of his line. Mackay also placed a 'detachment of firelocks from each regiment to the right hand to fortify Hastings' [understrength] regiment'. It is not known how large this collection of men was, nor who led it. To their immediate right was the Girnaig Burn, a fairly substantial tributary of the Garry, but was fairly shallow and so would have done little to have protected their right flank. The Garry ran parallel to the army's line a few hundred yards to their rear. Mackay intended, when the Jacobites attacked, and after his infantry had fired, to have the cavalry flank the enemy on either side, as he did not want to expose his cavalry to the enemy's, believing the latter's to be superior in quality, composed as they were largely of veteran troops against Mackay's newly raised horsemen. These men also included gentry, such as James Rattray of Corb.[23]

We now turn to the composition of each army, beginning with the Jacobite Army.

Historians have differed as to Jacobite numbers, though it is generally concluded that they were outnumbered by their foes. Pollard and Oliver give an approximate figure of 2,500.[24] Reid gives them as 2,500 infantry and 40 cavalry.[25] Catriona Fforde gives a lesser figure of 2,000.[26]

There are varying figures given by contemporaries for the Jacobite army. One was that Dundee had 2,500 infantry and a troop of cavalry.[27] Another states there were but 1,800 infantry and 45 cavalry.[28] MacNeill gave the figure of but 1,600 and also one of 1,900.[29] Captain John Creighton, who was not present, states that there were 1,700 infantry, including 300 Irish, and 45 cavalry.[30] The total number '[did] not fully amount fully to two thousand men', according to Cameron.[31]

Individual unit strengths given by contemporaries are as follows:

Order of battle from right to left:

MacLeans under Sir John MacLean, 200–500
Irish regiment under Colonel Nicholas Purcell, 300 men
Clanranalds, 400–600
Glengarrys, 300
Cavalry troop, 40–50 men (initially on the left flank)
Camerons, 240 strong, but 40 detached as advance guard
Sir Donald MacDonald's regiment, 500–700[32]
The total strength was about 1,980–2,700.

23 *Ibid.*, pp.52, 53, 56.
24 Pollard and Oliver, *Two Men*, II, p.189.
25 Reid, *Killiecrankie*, p.15.
26 Fforde, *Summer in Lochaber*, p.145.
27 James MacPherson (ed.), *Original Papers, containing the Secret history of Great Britain* (London, 1775), p.369.
28 Anon, *Memoir of Lord Dundee* (London, 1711), p.31.
29 NRS, CH12/12/1717.
30 John Creighton, *Memoirs*, p.268.
31 Cameron, *Memoirs*, p.268.
32 Cameron, *Memoirs*, p.266; Murdoch, 'Grameid', pp.128, 122–123; NRS, GD26/8/71.

View of Jacobites looking towards Mackay's army. (Author, 2017)

Not all Dundee's men had arrived. Cameron had 24 miles to march in one day so did not arrive with the bulk of his clan in time for the battle, and as noted, there were others marching towards Blair.[33]

William's Army

It is generally agreed by historians that Mackay had a numerical advantage. Pollard and Oliver give him a rough figure of 4,000 men.[34] Catherine Fforde agrees with this number.[35] Reid gives 3,500 infantry and 100 cavalry.[36] Highest is Grant's figures of 4,560 infantry and 110 cavalry.[37] Oddly enough, a recent biographer of Dundee wrote that 'Mackay's army on this occasion largely consisted of irregulars'.[38]

As to contemporaries, Cameron believed that Mackay had 3,500 infantry and two troops of horse.[39] Another Jacobite source listed him as having eight regiments of foot, totalling 4,500, with two troops of horse.[40] Highest is Creighton's estimate of 5,000 men.[41] Hamilton put his numbers at 4,000 infantry and thought he had four troops of horse.[42] Mackay wrote that he had 3,000 infantry at most and the cavalry.[43] As he was in actual command of these troops it would seem that he was probably best placed to know the most accurate figure. Lanier wrote a few days later that Mackay had 3,000 men, too.[44] An anonymous contemporary source agrees with Mackay that he had 3,000 foot and two troops of horse.[45]

Five of his regiments were officered as below:

Regiment Rank	**Kenmure's**	**Mackay's**	**Leven's**	**Balfour's**
Colonel	Viscount Kenmure	James Mackay	Earl of Leven	Barthold Balfour
Lieut. Colonel	John Ferguson	David Collyart	William Arnot	Thomas Livingstone
Major		Johnan Brouchan	Robert Bruce	George Lauder
Captain	James Donaldson	Walterus Boye	Archibald Patoun	Barthold Balfour
Captain	Alexander Gordon	George Canocke	Sir Robert Hamilton	Thomas Ersksine
Captain	James Gordon	Petrus Watkin	Henry Verrier	Ferdinand Cunningham

33 EUL, Laing MSS II, 89/338.
34 Pollard and Oliver, *Two Men*, II, p.189.
35 Fforde, *Summer in Lochaber*, p.145.
36 Reid, *Killiecrankie*, p.12.
37 Grant, *From Pike to Shot*, p.58.
38 Scott, *Bonnie Dundee*, p.215.
39 Cameron, *Memoirs*, p.265.
40 MacPherson, *Original Papers*, p.369.
41 Creighton, *Memoirs*, p.268.
42 Mackay, *Memoir*, p.248.
43 *Ibid.*, p.46.
44 NLS, MS 3740, 96.
45 EUL, Laing MSS II, 89/338.

Regiment Rank	Kenmure's	Mackay's	Leven's	Balfour's
Captain	John McCulloch	Charles Graham	William Hill	Alexander Livingstone
Captain	Patrick Dunbar	Everard Hasquet	James Denholme	William Manning
Captain	Thomas Kennedy		John Fullerton	Richard Cunningham
Captain	William Gordon		James Bruce	
Captain			James Lundie	
Captain			Charles Arcskin	
Captain			John Moncrief	
Captain		Mr Mackenzie		
Captain		Angus Mackay		
Lieutenant	John Nisbet	Robert Mackay		Mr Arnault
Lieutenant		Mr Campbell		Mr Chambers
Lieutenant			Waddell	

Hastings' Regiment

Captains	Lieutenants	Ensigns
	Thomas Carlton	William Delawall
Fernando Hastings	William Rhodesby	Ralph Cudworth
Robert Ingram	John Hooks	Deacon Garnett
Wolfstan Dixie	John Fry	Henry Tern
Joseph Tidcomb	John Sheldon	John Orefeur
Charles Hatton	George Comly	Hussey Hastings
Joseph Jacob	Michael Dunkin	Joseph Byerly
Thomas Condon	George Keyworth	Thomas Kniveton
Charnock Heron	Henry Waland	William Callow
Christopher Hatton (Grenadiers)	Bernard Ellis	

Chaplain Gabriel Hastings, Adjutant Talbott Lascels, surgeon Claudius Gillett, Quartermaster John Eams.

Cavalry – Independent Troops of Scottish Horse[46]

Troop Rank	Belhaven's	Annandale's
Captain	Sir John Hamilton	William Johnstone (absent)
Lieutenant	William Hamilton	William Lockhart
Ensign	Weir of Kirkfield	John Johnstone

Artillery: three 'leather guns', in charge of Master Gunner James Smith and 2nd Lieutenant Theodore Drury.[47]

It is impossible to be sure of the numbers of each unit, though these are stated in Grant's book, for there are no surviving muster rolls or lists

46 Dalton, *English Army Lists*, Vol. I, pp.38, 85, 94; Vol. II, pp.143, 232, 234.
47 RPCS, 14, pp.351, 421.

of numbers. In theory each infantry regiments should have been 780 men strong, but the reality is likely to have been far different.

The total strength of Dutch-Scottish regiments, Ramsay's, Mackay's and Balfour's, was 1,960 in 1688, but this had plummeted to 1,100 in March 1689 as William had creamed off the best men for service elsewhere, and though more may have been recruited thereafter as ordered, there may also have been losses due to illness, desertion, wounds and death. In May there is a reference to Balfour's regiment being supplied with 400 pikes and 400 muskets (suggesting a strength of 800, perhaps) and later that month that Ramsay's having 600 veterans. Ramsay's had 624 men in April 1689 judging by its order for uniforms.[48] One contemporary source noted that in sum these three regiments consisted at the battle at 1,500 men.[49]

Leven's regiment began its existence in March with 800 men, and by July had a depleted strength due to 200 men being at Inverness and similarly, Hastings' regiment, having 500 men in 1688, then 780 men in early 1689 (in 1690 it is cited as being 606 men strong), lacked 100 men who were at Inverness.[50] The source listed at the end of the last paragraph gives Leven 600 men at least and Hastings with 500.[51] Annandale's troop and Belhaven's troop numbered 'about a hundert hors'.[52] There were also 100 Highlanders led by Lord Weemys' son, perhaps baggage guards.[53] It would seem that Mackay outnumbered Dundee but at most by 3:2.

These numbers may seem small by contemporary standards: at the battle of Aughrim in Ireland 1691 there were approximately 20,000 men involved on each side and at Waldeck in the Spanish Netherlands 1695 there were almost 60,000 men. However, we should bear in mind that in both cases these were multinational armies. At Sedgemoor in 1685 the total numbers involved, perhaps about 7,000, were not much larger than those engaged at this battle.[54]

What was perhaps significant about this army's composition was its lack of cavalry; whereas conventionally cavalry might make up a quarter to a third of an army, as had been the case at Sedgemoor, here with only about 100 cavalrymen and 3,000 infantry, the proportion was a thirtieth. If Mackay had been facing a regular army he would have had serious problems as his cavalry would not have been able to prevent the enemy's from combining attacks with their infantry on his infantry. As it was, the Jacobite cavalry was even numerically weaker than his and formed an even smaller proportion of their army. Yet a more substantial cavalry force could have given the advantage to him. He thus went into battle lacking such; perhaps he believed that he could win without them. Yet it is difficult for substantial numbers of cavalry to subsist in one place, as had been found with the regiments of English cavalry summoned to Scotland.

48 Mackay, *Memoirs*, p.3; Balfour-Maitland, 'Estates' I, pp.95, 114.
49 EUL, Laing MSS II, 89/338.
50 Grant, *From Pike to shot*, pp.32; Storey, *Impartial Relation*, p.96.
51 EUL, Laing MSS II, 89/338.
52 Mackay, *Memoirs*, p.263.
53 *Ibid.*, p.61.
54 Chandler, *Marlborough*, pp.334–335; Barratt, *Battles*, p.169.

It is also worth noting that this was largely an inexperienced army whose training was limited. Leven's and Kenmure's regiments and the two troops of Horse had only been in existence for four months. Hastings' was formed four years ago but had probably not heard a shot fired in anger. Although the three Dutch regiments had been in existence far longer, the majority of the men in these units had limited experience of war as William had creamed off the veterans for conflict elsewhere. The troops had a mixture of weapons: mostly matchlocks, but some with flintlocks, some with bayonets but many not, and some had pikes not firearms. Apparently on 20 July all of Kenmure's musketeers, perhaps 450, were provided with bayonets, but the regiment's pikemen retained their unwieldly weapons.[55] Leven's musketeers were all matchlock armed.[56]

They were arrayed from left to right as follows:

Lauder's detachment of 200 fusiliers
Balfour's regiment
Kenmure's regiment
Ramsay's regiment
Annandale's troop
Belhaven's troop
Leven's regiment
Mackay's regiment
Hastings' regiment

Assorted troops from all regiments. It is impossible to ascertain numbers for most of the above infantry units.

It has been estimated that a 760 man regiment which is three men (nine feet) deep will have a frontage of 810 feet, so Mackay's line would have been about 3,200 feet plus intervals (each about 30 yards apart) between regiments; perhaps twice that, therefore.[57] The baggage was naturally to the rear, behind some houses and gardens.[58] The distance from the stream to the hill where Lauder's men were is 1,500 yards, so each unit would have been, on average, about 29 yards from each other, but the gap in the centre between Ramsay's and Leven's, where the cavalry were would have been over 100, so that neither could have supported one another.

Mackay's forces were strung out in a thin line to maximise firepower at the expense of reducing its morale and melee value. Placing the elite infantry at the left risked reducing the morale and strength of the other regiments. Whilst it was understandable that the best troops be pushed forward through the pass, not returning these men to their units thereafter was taking a risk.

Dundee had sent out advance guards to find out where his enemy was, but they could not initially see their seated enemies. It was only when they moved nearer did Mackay's men rise to their feet to await attack, that they were seen.

55 RPCS, 13, p.542.
56 *Ibid.*, 14, p.20.
57 Grant, *From Pike to Shot*, p.154.
58 NRS, CH12/12/1717.

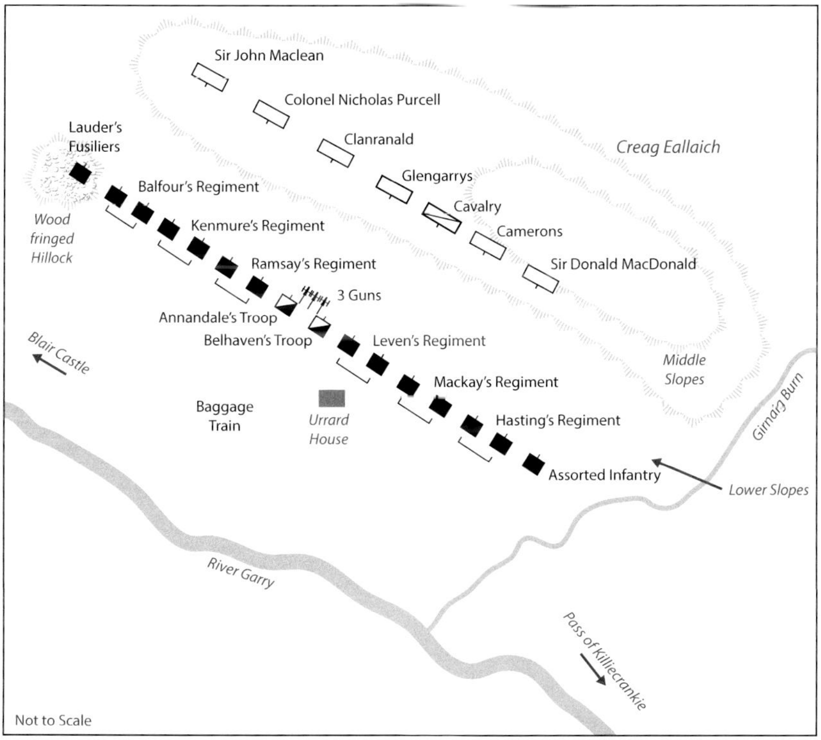

Map 2 Position of the armies at the battle of Killiecrankie, 27 July 1689.

N.B. No contemporary map exists so this is an estimate based on contemporary written accounts.

Dundee had his men stand on the brow of the hill opposite to them. Having seen Mackay's order of battle, he chose to counter any possible out flanking by extending the gaps between his own units. It was late afternoon when this manoeuvre had been completed, as both sides extended their lines which 'consumed a good part of the afternoon'.[59] Dunfermline later wrote that they 'possessed themselves on a strong ground'.[60]

The Jacobites extended their line of battle towards their left wing. Mackay was concerned that this might be an attempt to outflank his force to its own right. It might even be an effort to get between his army and the pass, 'which would be a very advantageous post for them, whereby they could cut all communication betwixt us and Perth'. This was worrying because Mackay expected six troops of horse and dragoons, as well as additional supplies. Furthermore, any Jacobites who did so, might be able to raise the Atholl men to their cause. This manoeuvre 'brought the enemy, whatever his design might have been, to a stand, and so we lookt upon one another for at least two hours'.[61]

According to Cameron, the first shots of the battle were fired by Mackay's men, whilst Dundee was altering his army's dispositions. Yet Mackay thought otherwise. He claimed that because he was so obvious a target and the Jacobites were so close, they fired at him 'all over where he moved'. Firing at a single individual at long range with notoriously unreliable muskets led

59 Cameron, *Memoirs*, p.265; NLS MS 3738, f28r.
60 NRS, GD112/39/145/11.
61 Mackay, *Memoirs*, p.54.

not to Mackay being hit, but rather several of his men being wounded at the very onset of the battle. Meanwhile, Balfour's regiment had advanced too rapidly and were out of line. The Jacobites made no attempt to attack them, so Mackay, fearing that they might be outflanked, had them retire to be in alignment with the other regiments.[62]

As was not unusual in warfare at this time, Mackay made a short speech to the men nearest to him. He told them that their cause was just, that they were fighting for Protestantism, not only in Britain, but in the world. The happiness of their country and the maintenance of their laws, depended on their successful defence of them on that day. They must not betray such by any faintheartedness on their part. He also reminded them of their own safety:

> … assuring them that if they kept firm and close they should quickly see their enemy's take the hills for their refuge … but on the other hand, if they happened to give way (as he should not expect) before that rabble of the Highlanders, they might freely conclude few or none of them should escape those naked pursuers far speedier of foot than they … stand to it like men fighting for their religion and liberty against the invaders of both.[63]

According to him, it had a positive effect for the men 'all answered with the greatest chearfullnesse imaginable, that none of them, should abandon me'.[64]

Not all commentators approved of these battlefield speeches, though were aware of their being referred to in the Classics. Orrery thought that they should not be given because a commander could not address more than one unit at a time. He recommended that the general give his speech to his senior officers and then they could cascade the message down to the junior officers and then to the men.[65]

Mackay had no desire to advance, for reasons already explained. He feared that the Jacobites might attack and this could unsettle his men, unaccustomed to their way of fighting. Yet he could not pass the river with his enemy in such close proximity. Therefore, 'He resolved then to stand it out, tho' with great impatience, to see the enemie come to a resolution, either of attacking or retiring, whereof they had more choice than he'. This was to pass the initiative to the Jacobites. However, the government army did possess artillery and so Mackay ordered that the three guns, which had been carried on horseback, to open fire, in order to provoke an attack.[66] They continued to do so, according to one eye witness, for an hour, presumably ceasing when the cannonballs were all fired. According to McBane, 'when they Advanc'd we played our Cannon for an Hour on them'.[67] However, other observers thought the cannon fire was of only limited duration. Mackay

---

62 *Ibid.*, p.53.

63 *Ibid.*, pp.53–54.

64 *Ibid.*, p.267.

65 Orrery, *Treatise*, p.186.

66 Mackay, *Memoirs*, pp.54–55.

67 Mark Napier, *Memorials and letters illustrative of the life and times of John Graham of Claverhouse, Viscount Dundee*, 3 vols. (Edinburgh: T.G. Stevenson, 1862), 3, p.724; McBane, *The Expert Sword-Man's Companion*, p.78.

wrote that the guns 'proved of little use, because the carriages being made too high to be more conveniently carried, broke with the third firing'.[68] What all could agree on, though, was that the guns, creating noise and smoke, did very little damage to the Jacobites.

Even so, perhaps to counter this, there was more Jacobite musketry aimed at Mackay as he stood or rode in front of his army. A few of his men were wounded, though the firers missed their principal target. In order to facilitate their aim, some Jacobites stationed themselves in the few houses which stood on the slope, or possibly in the one house with walls and sheds as described by MacNeill. Annoyed by this, Mackay ordered his brother, Colonel Mackay, to send a captain and some musketeers out of his own regiment to dislodge them. He hoped that this skirmish might lead to a more general battle which he was wanting before night fell. The party (presumably a company) of 50 men, led by Captain Angus Mackay, went to the houses and chased the Jacobites there away, having caused them a few casualties.[69] According to one source, the skirmishers were from MacLean's regiment, and they lost five men but inflicted higher casualties on their enemy.[70] Another source states that the Jacobites fled to another house and then Mackay went to dislodge them from there as well, but never returned. This suggests that the main action took place shortly afterwards and the combatants in this skirmish were enveloped in the larger battle.[71] Mackay wrote that half an hour after this skirmish the battle began in earnest.[72]

Private McBane, standing with Mackay's army, described the scene thus: 'we then gave a shout, Daring them as it were to advance, which they quickly did to our great loss.'[73] The fire was annoying but only occasionally deadly as Cameron wrote, 'The continual fire of the enemy from the lower ground covered them, by a thick cloud of smoke, from the view of the Highlanders, whereof several dropping from time to time, and many being wounded'.[74]

Such firing led to some of the Jacobites demanding that they attack, but with the sun beating down in their faces, Dundee urged patience until the sun began to set and was no longer an impediment to their sight. Cameron realised that the men needed something to divert them from being immobile targets. He commanded his men to shout and this was echoed by the remainder of the army; by those adjacent and then extending throughout the whole. There was also the sound of musketry, cannon and the enemy's shouts, echoing along the hills, rocks and caverns. Apparently '[The] Highlanders fancy that their shouts were much brisker and louder than that of the enemy.' The high pitched scream/cry, known as 'Gaoir Catha' was typical of Highland warfare, having been heard at Tippermuir in 1644 and in later wars in which the Highlanders served.[75]

68 Mackay, *Memoirs*, p.55.
69 Mackay, *Memoirs*, p.55; NRS, CH12/12/1717.
70 MacPherson, *Original Papers*, p.369.
71 EUL, Laing MSS II, 89/338.
72 Mackay, *Memoirs*, p.55.
73 McBane, *The Expert Sword-Man's Companion*, p.78.
74 Cameron, *Memoirs*, p.266.
75 *Ibid.*, p.267.

Cameron then gave his men a speech, complimenting them on their noise and declaring that their vigorous shouting was a good omen, in contrast to that of their enemy, which he told them was 'low, lifeless and dead'. He claimed that his words spread through the army and 'how wounderfully they were incouraged and animated by them'.[76]

The Rev. Robert Patten later recorded that in 1715 one William Irwine, a Scottish non-juring clergyman 'preach'd a Sermon full of Exhortations to his Hearers, to be Zealous and Steady in the Cause', which 'was very well digested and suited fitly for the Men that heard it'. Apparently he had preached likewise at Killiecrankie.[77] It is possible, as in the prelude to an anticipated battle, 'they cast their brogues of bull's hide, and make a pile of their plaids, and then stripped, prepare for the battle'.[78]

There was some movement among the Jacobite cavalry, initially posted to the left of their line before Dundee had it moved to the centre. He was concerned that Mackay's cavalry might march around the rear of the Jacobite army in order to hinder its retreat.[79]

A late twentieth-century military analysis of Dundee's tactics so far was very favourable, 'Dundee's strength lay in his ability to combine the pre-battle movement and psychology of an O'Neill with the primal Celtic charge of an MacColla'. By securing the high ground he had had given his men the bonus of the value of shock when it came to a charge. By forcing his enemy to wait he had given them a psychological handicap. He had his men grouped in column-like formations. The enemy may have dreaded the Highlander; Defoe wrote that such 'made an uncouth figure. The oddness and barbarity of their Garb and Arms seemed to have something in it remarkable … proud, arrogant vain glorious boasters, bloody barbarous and inhuman butchers'.[80] Given that most of Mackay's army were Lowland Scots, Dutch or English, the Highlanders would have seemed alien indeed, given the differences in costume and appearance between them and this would have been unsettling.

It was about a half hour before sunset when the attack came; Dunfermline, in charge of the Jacobite cavalry, put it at seven in the evening. Mackay had already commanded the regimental officers to begin their regiments' fire when the Jacobites were about a hundred paces away. They would fire by platoon 'to discourage the Highlanders meeting with continual fire'.[81]

According to McBane, 'the sun going down caused the Highlandmen to Advance on us like Mad Men, without shoe or stocking, covering themselves from our Fire with their Targes'.[82] An anonymous Jacobite officer claimed the Highlanders threw away their plaids, haversacks, and other 'utensils' to fight in shirts and doublets only.[83] Cameron wrote:

76 *Ibid.*
77 Robert Patten, *History of the Rebellion of 1715* (London: James Roberts, 1745), p.31.
78 Murdoch, 'Grameid', p.183.
79 NRS, CH12/12/1717.
80 James Hill, *Celtic Warfare, 1595–1763* (Edinburgh: John Donald, 1986), pp.64–74.
81 NRS, GD112/39/145/11; Mackay, *Memoirs*, p.55.
82 McBane, *The Expert Sword-Man's Companion*, p.78.
83 *Memoir of Lord Dundee*, pp.31–2.

View of Mackay's army facing Jacobites. (Author, 2017)

> Dundee gave orders for the attack, and commanded, that so soon as the McLeans began to move from the right, that the whole body should, att the same instant of time, advance upon the Enemy. It is incredible with what intrepidity the Highlanders endured the Enemy's fire; and though it grew more terrible upon their nearer approach, yet they, with a wonderful resolution, kept up their own, as they were commanded.[84]

It is uncertain how many volleys were fired against the Jacobite army as the two accounts which mention the number vary. A Jacobite contemporary wrote that melee occurred 'before we could fire three shots apiece', which suggests two being fired.[85] Yet McBane wrote, 'we could [only] Fire three shots a-piece'.[86] Writing over half a century later, General Henry Hawley (son of the Colonel Francis Hawley mentioned in chapter 2) wrote that a volley at a distance was useless 'for you never get time to load a second cartridge' and so volley fire should not begin until the Jacobites were 'within 10 or 12 paces'.[87] It should be remembered that troops did not all fire at once, but by platoon, but with three ranks there was the potential for all the musketeers to fire one shot before melee and it is possible that that was confused with the suggestion that

84 Cameron, *Memoirs*, p.267.
85 *Memoir of Lord Dundee*, p.32; Napier, *Memorials*, 3, p.724.
86 McBane, *The Expert Sword-Man's Companion*, p.79.
87 Lord Elcho, *Short Account of the Affairs of Scotland, 1744–1746* (Edinburgh: David Douglas, 1907), p.460.

each man fired three times, which would have been impossible in the time that the Highlanders would have taken to charge home.

Musket fire was the crux of the battle. If Mackay's musketeers could inflict sufficient casualties on the charging Jacobites, they could either stop them or kill/wound sufficient that those who reached their ranks would be inadequate in number or/and dispirited to win a hand-to-hand fight. The cavalry could then attack the Jacobites in the flank and rear and so complete the victory. Dundee had no reserves and so a reverse left him with no second chance to change the battle's course. To maximise his firepower Mackay had deployed his regiments in three ranks rather than the conventional six, so doubling his fire power. This meant that all the men in all three ranks could fire. Men fired in platoon, one at a time, so volleys were continual; men not firing would be reloading.[88] The weakness in Mackay's disposition was that the lines were thin and so vulnerable to an enemy that was able to charge home; secondly he had no reserve, so any break through would be fatal. As with Dundee, he was taking a risk that line would defeat charging column. Yet it had happened in the Thirty Years' War (1618–1648); the charging Swedes at Lützen and Rocroi in 1632 and 1643 had been held at bay by Spanish musketry.

Dundee had his troops in small compact units, 'separate bans like wedges condensed and firm'.[89] As with the column tactics employed by the French in the Revolutionary and Napoleonic battles over a century later, this was ideal for little-trained and inexperienced troops, as it did not require drill and exercise by experienced NCOs or any tactical finesse. It needed speed and bravery; troops in column moving rapidly forward, especially downhill, can cut through thin lines of the enemy especially those unaccustomed such aggression; casualties caused by defensive musketry can be ignored by their fast moving colleagues.

Mackay lost his gamble. Musketry, on this occasion, was insufficient to stop their advance. If Mackay had 2,000 musket armed troops, then that would mean, 2,000 potential casualties, but there are other factors which would lead to it being far less so. Firstly about half of the infantry were relatively inexperienced, two regiments having only been raised earlier that year and another only in 1685 and had no experience of battle. Secondly the troops were firing uphill and would be less accurate as shots would naturally fire too high. Thirdly the Jacobites were advancing down terraces which meant that most would be out of view for part of the time they were charging. We could also add that the three guns were now of no use, either, so there was no canister to be used against the massed enemy chargers.[90]

The extent and effectiveness of the musketry was variable, too. Mackay wrote 'that of my regiment, my Lord Levens, and Kenmore with the half of Ramsay's battalion made pretty good fire'. Mackay claimed that his own regiment 'made great fire … being well exercised thereto by my brother', and

88 David Blackmore, *Destructive and Formidable Fire: British infantry firepower, 1642–1765* (London: Frontline Books, 2014), pp.37, 49–53.

89 Dalrymple, *Memoirs*, II, p.82.

90 Pollard and Oliver, *Two Men in a Trench*, II, pp.233–234.

though this made 'execution' among the Jacobites, was not enough. However, 'the other half of Ramsays, with Balfours whole regiment, and Lauder's detachment of 200 men gave ground, or rather fled without any firing'.[91] However, it is not known how many this fire killed.

Lauder's men on the far left of Mackay's army, though he had '200 of the choice of our army, but did as little as the rest of that hand'. It was uncertain whether the latter's inaction was due to Lauder's fault or that of his men (or whether either were, as Mackay was not in a position to view the effect of the firing).[92] Archaeological evidence suggests that the weight of fire from these battalions on the left was less than elsewhere (32 percent of projectiles found here compared to 58 percent in the centre), though was still not wholly insignificant.[93] Recent findings suggest that one grenadier in Mackay's army threw a grenade at the attackers. This is the first time that such a weapon was used in Britain, though grenades were allegedly used in siege warfare at Bristol in 1644, so Killiecrankie may have seen the first use in a British battle. No contemporary makes a note of this, which suggests its value was limited.[94]

Yet the Jacobites would have presented an easy target, being 12 to 14 men deep according to Hawley. The musketry had not been ineffectual, as Cameron later noted, 'the greatest part of them [the Jacobites] fell within a few paces of their enemy when they received their last fire'.[95] But it was, overall, insufficient to prevent the Jacobite advance.

The Jacobites also fired at close range, too, 'like one great Clapp of thounder'.[96] Three officers of Mackay's regiment; Captains Lamy and Angus Mackay were shot as was their lieutenant colonel, though none fatally.[97] Yet MacNeill wrote of there 'being a perpetuall running fyre till we came to their very breast'.[98] However, Mackay stated that the Jacobite fire was 'ragged'.[99] MacNeill later wrote that there was 'but smale loss on either syde'.[100] It is possible that there may have been some archery on the Jacobites' part: bows have already being mentioned as being carried by some and another poet noted that on the battlefield, 'not an arrow was discharged that day needlessly'.[101]

According to McBane, 'At last they threw away their Musquetts, drew their Broad Swords advanced furiously upon us, and were in the middle of us'.[102] The Jacobites 'fell in pell-mell among the thick of them with the broad swords. After this the noise seem'd hushed; and the fireing ceasing on both sides, nothing was heard for some moments but the sullen and hollow clashes of broad-swords, with the dismall groans and crys of dyeing and

91 Mackay, *Memoirs*, pp.264–5.
92 *Ibid.*, p.56.
93 *Archaeological Metal Detecting Survey*, 2015, p.17.
94 Pollard and Oliver, *Two Men*, II, p.234.
95 Elcho, *Short Account*, p.460.
96 Cameron, *Memoirs*, p.271.
97 *Ibid.*, p.267.
98 Mackay, *Memoirs*, p.281.
99 NRS, CH12/12/1717.
100 *Ibid.*
101 Mackay, *Memoirs*, p.264.
102 NRS, CH12/12/1717.

wounded men'.[103] A Jacobite poet wrote, 'In spite of their thrusting, though stubborn their will, they lost their ground and their lives to boot'. Another wrote, 'No sword was in scabbard and no dirk was in sheath there, was there not smashing of skulls and tearing of shoulders, giving their enemy strokes to the red cassocked folk'.[104]

MacLean's fought Mackay's and routed them.[105] The lieutenant colonel, Mackay's brother, already injured, was killed, fighting among a handful of his veteran pikemen. Captains Lamy and Angus Mackay, having been already wounded by musket balls, were killed by broadsword-wielding Highlanders, having been abandoned by most of their men; the musketeers were the first to flee. Apparently Angus Mackay 'fought stoutly for his lfy, and disingadged himself, having received four considerable wounds of broadswords in his head and body'. Lord Leven saw him and gave him his own horse to carry him away. Captain Lieutenant Mackenzie was left mortally wounded among the dead. Five lieutenants were killed; another two captains were left wounded, so, 'all the captains of the battalion … were either killed or doe bear the marks of their good behaviour'. According to Mackay, it was this regiment on which 'the greatest force of that side was poured upon'. He thought that this was because some of the Jacobite officers had served in it when on the Continent and 'were of the opinion if it were beat that it would facilitate the rest of the work'.[106]

There was 'a hideous noise which made Kenmure's whole regiment run and they being placed in the middle the Highlanders came upon the middle', presumably attacking other battalions in the flanks.[107] Kenmure's regiment had also taken severe losses. The captain of the company including Lieutenant David Stewart was killed and he was taken prisoner. Captain James Donaldson received seven wounds, though lived and was taken prisoner, losing £100 to his captors.[108] The regiment's lieutenant colonel, John Ferguson, was also killed.[109]

It has also been suggested that there was another reason why the line collapsed so quickly. Atholl men began to fall on the baggage in the rear. Men in Mackay's regiment 'cryed treachery and ran'. This had potentially crucial results as it was claimed, 'Dundee would certainly have been routed if the Atholl men had lyen by and Mackay's men had stood to it'.[110]

It seems that the Jacobites attacked on their enemy's left first. Indeed the men on Mackay's right were still standing in their initial positions whilst the Jacobite right was engaging Mackay's men. Most of Balfour's regiment fled. Thus abandoned, their commander, together with a few other men, were killed. According to the poet:

103 Miller, 'Killiecrankie', p.67.
104 McBane, *The Expert Sword-Man's Companion*, p.78.
105 Cameron, *Memoirs*, pp.267–8.
106 MacPherson, *Original Papers*, p.370.
107 Mackay, *Memoirs*, pp. 281–2.
108 EUL, Laing, MSS II, 89/338.
109 *RPCS*, 15, pp.307, 181, 308.
110 Mackay, *Memoirs*, pp.59–60.

'O Colonel Balfour, worthless man,
I think you got all you wanted of warfare:
They smashed your crown and brought your hat over your ears,
And they cut your boots at the back'.[111]

Lieutenant Chambers, 'a resolute man according to the testimony of his officers', was cut down. Lauder tried to rally his men, but without success. Ramsay had no initial success in rallying his men, either.[112] That there was some fighting on Mackay's left is further evidenced by the fact that a Jacobite officer's targe shield was found there, damaged in melee, but the fewer musket balls found there does suggest that firing by the left wing regiments was limited compared to the fire elsewhere in the battlefield.[113]

Seeing the Jacobite attack, and now that the firing on both sides was over, Mackay called on Belhaven's horse to march forward to attack the right flank of the enemy, with Annandale's troop 'ordering him to flank to the left hand the enemy'. This could have 'been of such effect had they the resolution to obey their orders, and wold have so encouraged he foot that in all appearance the Highlanders would have soon run for it'. Belhaven's did not move forward, so Mackay led them himself and once Belhaven 'commanded them did behave very honestly'. They were now to the right of Kenmure's infantry and disordered some of them, 'and so began the first break so neere as I can remarque'.[114] This was countered by the Jacobites. Dundee was with his few cavalry in the centre of his army. The cavalry had been led by Dunfermline, but that morning he had been superseded by Sir William Wallace of Craigie, to Dundee's displeasure. When the cavalry advanced, with Dundee at their head, Wallace 'either his courage failing him, or some accident interposing', ordered the horsemen to wheel to the left. This halted the cavalry and brought them into a confused state. Unaware of this, Dundee continued to ride forwards, towards Mackay's two troops of cavalry, stationed at the centre, near to the artillery. He rode into the smoke. Following him were Dunfermline and 16 cavalrymen. Despite Wallace's orders, the men followed Dundee. He raised himself on his stirrups, waving his hat to urge his followers on. Mackay's cavalry 'made but little resistance. They were routed and warmly pursued by those few gentlemen'. Wallace and those with him took no further part in the action.[115]

However, another claim is that Belhaven's stood one fire, suggesting the Jacobite cavalry fired their pistols before making as if to go in with the sword, before their opponents fled, 'but could not be persuaded to return', whilst Annandale's stayed and fought, at least for a while.[116] A number of carbine and pistol balls were found by a recent archaeological survey, though these may have been fired at both Mackay's infantry or his cavalry.[117] The Jacobite

111 EUL, Laing MSS II, 89/338.
112 Miller, 'Killiecrankie', p,67.
113 Mackay, *Memoirs*, pp.266, 282.
114 Pollard and Oliver, *Two Men*, II, pp. 232, 234.
115 Mackay, *Memoirs*, pp.56, 265.
116 Cameron, *Memoirs*, p.268.
117 EUL Laing MSS II, 89/338.

cavalry pushed back their opposite number, 'who, in fleeing in the confusion they were in some of them brock in upon their left wing of their own foot'.[118]

Incidentally, there is a claim that the guns which might have been long silent, fired on Dundee's cavalry, presumably to little or no effect, though.[119] This could account for the Jacobite cavalry turning on them after having seen the back of Mackay's cavalry. Sir William Wallace was opposed to this but Dunfermline attacked the men with the guns with 16 horsemen and 'beat the enemies from their cannon and took them before the rest of the horse came up'.[120] James Smith, master gunner in charge of the artillery, 'received many wounds in his head and body'.[121]

Mackay was unaware that his cavalry were not following him against the Jacobites. Calling their officers to follow him, 'he spurr'd his horse through the enemy'. He was shocked to find 'no body nevertheless followed him, but one of his servants, whose horse was shot in passing'. Alone, Mackay wished that he had had 50 reliable troopers (such as Colchester's Horse) with him, for he believed that if this had been so, 'he had certainly, by all human appearance recovered all'.[122]

In the confusion of battle, Mackay was able to pass through a crowd of advancing Jacobites. Having done so, he viewed the battlefield. He saw that 'all his left had given way and got down the hill ... so that in the twinkling of an eye in a manner, our men, as well as the enemy were out of sight, being got doun pall mall to the river where our baggage stood'. He found this a sad spectacle and was initially surprised to see himself alone on the field. He later wrote, 'that resolution and presence of mind in a battle being certainly a singular mercy of God, he denyeth and giveth it when and to whom he will, for there are seasons and occasions, that the most firm and stout hearted do quake and fear'.[123] He wrote, two days later, 'there was no regiment or troop with me, but behaved lyck the vilest coward in nature [except two]'.[124]

Meanwhile, the Jacobites were getting the best of the melee. Their casualties during the hand-to-hand fighting were light, 'few or none of them were killed after they drew their swords'.[125]

According to Balcarres, 'they [Mackay's men] defended themselves but faintly'.[126] The poet wrote of Mackay's men, 'In spite of their thrusting, and though their hopes were strong, They lost their ground, and their souls after it'.[127] A Jacobite officer claimed 'the enemy ... did not maintain their grounds two minutes after the Highlanders were amongst them'. It seems to have been a one-sided fight. The same officer wrote, 'Many of General Mackay's officers and soldiers were cut down through the skull and necks to the very breasts;

118 Archaeological Metal Detecting Survey, p.16.
119 NRS, CH12/12/1717.
120 EUL, Laing MSS II, 89/338.
121 NLS MS 3738, f28v.
122 *RPCS*, 14, p.351.
123 Mackay, *Memoirs*, p.56.
124 *Ibid.*, p.57.
125 *Ibid.*, p.255.
126 Cameron, *Memoirs*, p.271.
127 NLS, MS 3738, f28v.

Generals and staff from the opposing armies.

(Illustration by Mark Allen © Helion & Company)

See Colour Plate Commentaries for further information.

Jacobite regulars.

(Illustration by Mark Allen © Helion & Company)
See Colour Plate Commentaries for further information.

Jacobite clansmen and clan colours.

(Illustration by Mark Allen © Helion & Company)

See Colour Plate Commentaries for further information.

Soldiers of the Scots Brigade and regimental colours.

(Illustration by Mark Allen © Helion & Company)

See Colour Plate Commentaries for further information.

Other Scottish regiments that fought in the battle.

(Illustration by Mark Allen © Helion & Company)

See Colour Plate Commentaries for further information.

Hasting's regiment, Government cavalry and artillery crew.

(Illustration by Mark Allen © Helion & Company)
See Colour Plate Commentaries for further information.

The Cameronians at Dunkeld.

(Illustration by Mark Allen © Helion & Company)
See Colour Plate Commentaries for further information.

Regiments involved in the fighting at Cromdale and that operated in Scotland during the rebellion.

(Illustration by Mark Allen © Helion & Company)
See Colour Plate Commentaries for further information.

others had skulls cut off above their ears like night caps, some soldiers had both their bodies and cross belts cut through at one blow; pikes and small swords were cut like willows'.[128] The melee was over quickly and the redcoats soon broke off, according to Macneill.[129]

The retreat was startling, the Jacobites having 'oblig'd us to Retreat, some fled to the water, and some another way, (We were for the most part New Men)'.[130] The poet wrote, 'But dispersed like flies are King William's men, And we are in grief though we chased them away'.[131] According to Cameron, 'The Highlanders had ane absolute and compleat victory. The pursute was so warm that few of the enemy escaped'.[132] There was another Jacobite account of those, 'who followed the slaughter for a good way'.[133] The Jacobite poet talks of their lust for killing, with lines such as, 'Little rest will we take until we slaughter Lowlanders' and 'We were so wicked, and venomous towards our enemies, That we wouldn't let go our hold of a single Lowlander'.[134] One report was that 'the slaughter in the battle was equall but after the battle most of Mackay's men were killed by the Athollmen and by the country men and such as they killed not they robbed ym of their money and stript them to the shirt'.[135]

Lieutenant Waddell of Leven's regiment was later accused of cowardice. Sergeant George Fairlie recalled that 'he did see Lieutenant Waddell deserting his post severall tyms in the heat of service' and 'he came away with severall of the common souldiers who the enimie at that instant did depart from the regiment'. Robert Lawson, a soldier of the colonel's company, noted, 'that Waddell left his men on several occasions during the battle, 'did see the said lieutenant hid after going about to keep the men together, but as he had heard Captain Archibald Patoun call for lieutenant Waddell he did not see him thereafter'. Sergeant Prengald thought that he had not seen the officer after the first volley had been fired at the Jacobites. Yet two other lieutenants thought that Waddell 'behaved himself well in the hottest of the action'. Two other officers thought that he had separated from the regiment but only by trying to keep the platoon together and that although he did leave the field with the regiment's right wing, he was not guilty of cowardice.[136]

It was not only the Highlanders who were able to defeat the soldiers before them. According to Cameron the Irish troops 'defeated ane intear battalion of disciplined troops'.[137] Orrery, when writing his military treatise, gives reasons why regular troops could be beaten when fighting came to close quarters. He cited an example in the sixteenth century when buckler and sword-armed infantry (as the front lines of the Jacobite army were) were victorious: 'Targets,

128 Miller, 'Killiecrankie', p.67.
129 *Memoir of Lord Dundee*, p.32.
130 NRS, CH12/12/1717.
131 McBane, *The Expert Sword-Man's Companion*, p.79.
132 Miller, 'Killiecrankie', p.67.
133 Cameron, *Memoirs*, p.268.
134 MacPherson, *Original Papers*, p.370.
135 Miller, 'Killiecrankie', pp.66–67.
136 EUL, Laing MSS, II, 89/338.
137 NRS, GD26/9/4/3.

though very flippent ones, have not only resisted the push of the pikes, but also that half the number of targeteers, have entered into the ranks of double their number of pikes, without targets, and have routed them.'

The other difficulty for the pikemen was that the points of the pikes could be chopped off by sword-wielding men unless there was a four feet length of iron casing the end of the pike's wooden shaft.[138]

As to the musket armed troops, Orrery noted that '[they] shift for themselves, if that volley does not work; for then they do it in haste and often too timerously, for even while they are firing, they are looking which is the best way to flee, when they have done firing.'[139]

The shock of troops charging downhill against foes who are unaccustomed to that method of warfare also contributed to the defeat. Similar results were to occur at Prestonpans in 1745 and to a lesser extent at Sheriffmuir in 1715 and at Falkirk in 1746.

It is often noted in books about the battle, that a major reason for Mackay's defeat was that his infantrymen, armed with muskets and plug bayonets, were unable to put their bayonets onto their muskets in time for them to be effective against their enemies. Yet no contemporary mentions this and in any case, many of the infantry were not equipped with bayonets (many units retained pikemen). Of course an absence of evidence does not mean to say that bayonets were not an issue in the battle's outcome, but at best it is an unproven hypothesis; at worst a hoary piece of battlefield mythology which only gains from unreflective repetition.

A rout was fatal to the defeated troops, as Kane noted, 'if they are broke, not a man in 10 escapes … for, upon all warm Pursuits, there is but little quarter to be expected'.[140]

During the latter stages of the battle there are two accounts of individual action by soldiers of the bested army. Defoe recounts the following duel:

> An English soldier pressed hard by a Highlander, the regiment being in disorder, for the English had the worst of it; the English soldier was singled out in the pursuit by one particular Highlander, and found himself in great danger, he defended himself with the club of his musket as long as he was able, his shot being spent before, after which they came to their swords, the Englishman understood the broadsword very well, but the Scots man received all the blows upon his targe; so that the Englishman could not come in with him, and at the same time he laid hard at the English man with his broadsword, and had cut him in two or three places, at which the Englishman enraged, rather than discouraged, cried out to him, you dog says he, come out from behind the door and fight like a man, meaning from behind his great target; but the Scots man though as brave as the other, knew better things than that, and laying hard at him had cut him down, and was just going to kill him, when some of the regiment that saw him distressed, came up to him and rescued him, and took the Highlander prisoner.[141]

138 Cameron, *Memoirs*, p.297.

139 Orrery, *Treatise*, pp.27–28.

140 *Ibid.*, p.190.

141 R. Kane, *The Campaigns of King William and Queen Anne* (London: J. Millan, 1745) pp.120, 122.

Soldier's Leap. (Author, 2017)

McBane was also trying to escape, though lacked any comrades obligingly near enough to rescue him. He had to rely on his own exertions. According to him:

> I fled to the Baggage and took a horse, in order to Ride the water. There followed me a Highlandman with sword and targe, in order to take the horse and kill myself, you'd laugh to see how he and I scampered about; I kept always the horse between him and me. At length he drew his Pistol and I fled, he fired after me; I went above the Pass, where I met with another water, very deep, it was about eighteen feet over betwixt two Rocks, I resolved to jump it, so I laid down my Gun and hat, and jumped and lost one of my shoes on the jump [this was the Soldier's Leap] … The Enemy pursuing hard I made the best of my way to Dunkeld, where I stayed till what of our men was left came up.[142]

Many were lost in the rout as they tried to escape, either by drowning in the Garry to their rear or elsewhere; McBane recalling, 'many of our men was lost in that water and at the Pass'.[143] Some of the Athollmen 'after the fight they fell upon our men that were scattered, and killed divers of them'.[144] Fighting with a river to the army's back had undoubtedly increased casualties for the

142 Pat Rogers, *Daniel Defoe's Tour through the Whole Island of Great Britain* (Harmondsworth: Penguin, 1971), pp.676–677.

143 McBane, *The Expert Sword-Man's Companion*, p.79.

144 *Ibid.*

defeated army, as the French and Bavarians were to discover at Schellenburg in 1704 after Marlborough's army's successful assault on their position. The only ford was to the rear of Leven's and Hastings' regiments and this would be least accessible to the routers.

According to Balcarres, the survivors would have suffered even more casualties had not the Jacobites stopped to plunder. The baggage was behind Mackay's central part of his line. He wrote 'unluckily when they came to the enemies' baggage, it stopped their pursuit and lost them parts of the fruits of their victory'.[145] According to an army chaplain, they 'ran to the Plunder and it was to them a Prize more valuable than Victory'.[146] Cameron, though, disputed this as being unjust. According to him, 'severall gentlemen, and others, who lived in that neighbour hood, and who knew the most minute circumstances of that glorious action, and likeways with severall of the Chief, besides low country gentlemen and others who were eye witnesses to all that passed' refuted Balcarres' allegations. They stated that:

> The Highlanders pursued so far, that they could not distinguish friends from foes before they gave over, though the rout began about the setting if the sun: That they were so excessively fatigued, that they inclined to rest themselves there during the dead of the night: That it was midnight ere they returned, which gave opportunity for these troops to attempt their escape … And that they neither saw the enemy's baggage nor the field of battle, till the sun was some hours up next morning.

Apparently those who did escape were on horseback and so, 'unless several partys had been posted before hand in proper places, it was impossible to prevent their escape.[147]

Many of those who had fled were in a wretched state. When Mackay joined 'about two hundred of his broken troops', they were:

> … in such a miserable plight, and so gashed and deformed with their wounds that they moved the compassion of their greatest enemys. So great, however, was the fright of these wretches, that they travelled all that night, some of them bound with ropes, or supported by their comrades on their horses, and others trailing their limbs after them, and crying out with the smart of their wounds.[148]

According to Cameron, Mackay's actions after his men were in rout were those of shock and despair:

> … when he saw his army intearly broken and dispersed, he was in such a consternatioun that for some moments he remained, as it were, stupid and undetermined what to doe; but being afraid of falling into the enemy's hands, he made off with whip and spur, and never halted until he arrived at the Laird

145 *The London Gazette*, 2476, 1–5 Aug. 1689.

146 Balcarres, *Memoirs*, p.47.

147 Morer, *Short Account*, p.94.

148 Cameron, *Memoirs*, p.272.

of Weems his house in Apnadow, and the next night he came to Drummond Castle'.[149]

Yet Mackay's account is rather different, as we shall see.

The Jacobite attack was not universally successful, however. This was because Dundee's line was shorter than Mackay's due to the former being outnumbered. There were no Jacobites in front of Leven's regiment. Thus this newly raised Scottish regiment fired at Cameron's men in the flank; the latter lost 120 men 'which was just one half of his number, and was occasioned by a furious fire that he received in the flank'. Mackay put this down to 'the diligence and firmity of the said Earle and his lieutenant colonel, major and other officers'. Even so, the Camerons' target, Mackay's regiment were 'routed and destroyed in a manner that few of them ever returned to their colours'.[150]

The other point to note is that the slopes and terraces of the hillside are not uniform. Those to the front of Mackay's regiment, for example, known as Raon Ruairdh or Rory High Field, are ideal for screening charging troops. This would mean that troops on the defensive could not see their enemy and so might fire precipitately with little effect. Yet the slopes further to the south are more uniformly gradual and thus would give defenders the advantage in that they could see their enemy and so be able to anticipate their arrival and effectively prepare for it by well-timed volleys of defensive fire.

Mackay later wrote that Leven's regiment did so well because they were not so strenuously attacked. Secondly there was a greater proportion of officers to men than in the other regiments. He added that they were 'very good brisk gentlemen'. He considered that Hastings' regiment possessed the same advantages.[151] Lanier praised the latter thus, 'behaved themselves well that they were not broken'.[152] Another account stated that 150 of the Scottish soldiers rallied because they 'had been in service abroad and remembered the ill consequences of such a flight would expose 'em to the swords of persons nimbler than themselves'.[153]

Sir Donald MacDonald's attack also faltered; again this battalion was on the Jacobite army's left flank. His flank was exposed to the fire of Hastings' regiment. Several of the Highlanders began to fall under their musketry. Sir Donald, noticing both this and that there were houses and dykes which might provide his men with cover, had them take shelter there, seeking the safest option. Orders were sent to them, that they were needed to support Cameron's attack, but these were slow to be carried out because the men were scattered behind a variety of forms of cover and doubtless reluctant to emerge from it and risk their lives again.[154]

However, Hastings' regiment suffered casualties and was pushed back. Major Jacobs was wounded.[155] An anonymous report claimed 'Coll Hastings

149 *Ibid.*, p.299.
150 *Ibid.*, 298–299.
151 Cameron, *Memoirs*, p.271; Mackay, *Memoirs*, p.265.
152 Mackay, *Memoirs*, p.59.
153 NLS, MS 3740, 96.
154 Morer, *Short Account*, p.93.
155 Cameron, *Memoirs*, p.273.

behaved himself well but was beat off his ground and upon that retiring till he knew that Leven's men had stood'.[156] Likewise Major Robert Bruce of Leven's regiment with several lieutenants were killed.[157] It would seem that, contrary to the statements often made about both these units standing entirely firm, one half of both regiments fled after taking casualties in hand to hand fighting; Mackay had divided each regiment into two, after all, and as we shall note, the men from these two regiments who left the battlefield in good order amounted to only about 400.

Mackay, thinking he was alone on the battlefield, 'looking further to the right he espied a small hep of red coats'. He galloped over to them and found that it was part of Leven's regiment. Yet another version states that 'the General Mackay was missing till after ye business was over and they say was found in a thicket'.[158] Leven (now remounted by his servant bringing up another horse) and most of his officers were there. Mackay praised them for their valour. According to one account, Leven had recovered the regimental flag of Mackay's regiment and when the two met, 'Mackay lighted and embraced him, and kissed him many times, saying he had saved his honour, his life and the kingdome. He would never forgett it and he would represent it fully to the King'.[159] However, one account claimed 'The first officer that left his post from Mackay's army, was the Lord Leven; the glistening and clashing of the Highlanders' swords and targets scared his horse so much, that he ran six miles before he could draw back.'[160] Yet this seems unlikely; not only does Mackay contradict it but elsewhere in the same account there are known inaccuracies.

However Leven's men were in a confused state because there were men from other regiments with them. Mackay asked Leven and his officers to put the men in 'condition to receive the enemy, whom he minutely expected'. Mackay then rode off to see Hastings' regiment. The commanding officer there had been able to repel and pursue some of their enemy and was returning his men to their original position. His pikemen had deterred another attack. The Jacobites' plundering of the baggage allowed the remnant of his army some respite. Mackay sent Captain Mackay, his nephew, who was on horseback, to find any officers or men from the same battalion and to urge them 'back to joyn him, in which case he assured them of advantage'.[161]

Dundee's 16 cavalrymen, having chased Mackay's cavalry off the field, returned to the battlefield. They were surprised to find some of Leven's regiment and Hastings', still there and formed. Dunfermline wanted to attack, and so suggested gathering about 50–60 Highland infantry. These men were currently looking after the corpses of their dead comrades. Language differences were problematic as the Highlanders could only speak Gaelic. However, Drummond of Balhaldys, Cameron's son-in-law,

156 EUL, Laing MSS II, 89/338.
157 NRS, GD26/13/98.
158 EUL, Laing MSS, II, 89/338.
159 NRS, GD26/13/98; Mackay, Memoirs, p..
160 Fraser, *Melvilles and Leslies*, I, p.253.
161 *Memoir of Lord Dundee*, p.33.

began to gather some of the men together. They began to march against Hastings' regiment.[162]

Hastings' regiment was not wholly isolated. Seeing the Jacobites moving towards them, Leven's regiment advanced to their aid. The Jacobites refused to engage, partly because some of their number were 'rather followers of the army than souldiers'. Their officers decided they should retreat and in doing so came across, what was to them, a shocking and terrible sight. They 'discovered the body of their noble General, who was just breathing out his last'. Dundee had been shot and the fatal ball had entered his body on the lower part of his left side. They carried him off, possibly just about still living, but in doing so, received fire from Leven's regiment. Another casualty was Haliburton of Pitcur, who was shot and died two days later.[163]

Apparently when Dundee was shot, he was caught from falling off his horse by one Johnston. Then, 'the viscount then asking the said Johnston how the day went, and that he answered the day went well for the king (meaning king James), but that he was sorry for his lord: and that the viscount replied it was the less matter for him seeing that the day went well for his master'. His body was wrapped in highland plaids after the battle and was buried at Blair.[164]

Once they had got out of the range of their enemy's musketry, they began to be fearful. Some other Jacobites began to gather with them. Drummond found others. There was a desire to return to the fight against Leven's regiment. A total of 60 men agreed to do so. They marched ahead but found that the enemy were in possession of a large house, possibly Urrards and it would be an insurmountable task to have dislodged them from it. Although more Jacobites returned to the field by midnight, the would be defenders had already taken the opportunity to retreat under cover of darkness.[165]

According to Balcarres, Mackay's remaining regiments missed their opportunity to reverse the day's outcome. He was of the opinion that they had only been partly involved in the fighting and 'if these had had resolution they might easily fall upon the Highlanders whilst they were indeed about the spoil and so quite changed the fate of the day but neglected this opportunity … were in such a consternation they knew what to do'.[166]

Mackay expected that his men might be attacked at any moment. He had decided against stationing his men in the house and grounds of Urrards because he thought that if he was not relieved, then 'there was no hope of escaping out of the enemy's hands by defending an inclosure so far from new relief'. The return of his nephew brought no new hope that anything had gone well for him on the left. The nephew explained that he had seen 20 men formed at the edge of the wood where Lauder had initially been posted. He thought that these might be men of his own regiment. So he decided to exhort them to make at least one discharge if they were attacked. Galloping

162 Mackay, *Memoirs*, pp.57–58.
163 Cameron, *Memoirs*, p.269.
164 *Ibid.*
165 Thomson, *APS*, Appendix, IX, p.56.
166 Cameron, *Memoirs*, p.270.

Route of Mackay's men across the Garry after Killiecrankie. (Author, 2017)

over, he discovered that these were Jacobites. At this point he had some men with him, and being that they were apparently resolved to fight, the Jacobites there, unable to see their numbers, due to dusk falling, allowed them to withdraw unmolested.[167]

A few men of Mackay's regiment, finding the injured Captain Mackenzie, carried him with them and joined those remaining troops on the stricken field. Mackay led the remnant of his forces from the field, about 400 men (Lanier claimed there were 500 men, drawn from Hastings' and Leven's regiments), after taking one last look at the Jacobites to see whether they were going to approach the river after him. He was joined by a few men from Annadales' horse; two officers and four or five men, as well as Belhaven. These troopers then acted as scouts during the retreat. They crossed the River Garry unmolested, using the river's narrowest and shallowest point to do so, which can be done by wading through the water (elsewhere it is much deeper and faster and fugitives trying to cross there were drowned). There was no sign of any Jacobites in pursuit, so Mackay had to decide where they should retreat to. Some of his officers suggested that they should go to Dunkeld and thence to Perth, retracing the route that they had taken towards Killiecrankie earlier in the day. Instead, Mackay resolved to march several miles into the Highlands, then crossing the Strathspey, over to Castle Drummond, which

167 NLS, MS 3738, f28v.

was garrisoned, and then to Stirling. There he hoped to 'make all the speed possible to fall upon some present measures'.[168]

This course of action was still opposed by some of his officers. They told him that some of the men under their command were so demoralised that they would make no resistance if the Jacobites attacked. Mackay was 'very well satisfied of the truth of what they alledged'. Yet he was unbending because he thought that Dundee, whom he believed was still alive, would pursue with his cavalry, leaving the infantry to carry on with their plunder of the baggage. Therefore, he wanted to put his men in territory that would be unsuitable for cavalry to fight in. He also chose that route because it would mean they would not fall prey to the Athollmen who might otherwise 'run the whole night and next day upon the runnaways'. Two miles from the battlefield, he met Ramsay with 150–200 men, mostly men who had thrown away their weapons in flight. They joined forces and now there were 600–700 men, though it may have reached 800 by the day's end.[169]

Continuing by a little river, the men came to some houses, part of the estate of Lord Weemys, whose son was a captain who had served against the Jacobites. Travelling over hills and bogs, the men did not stop during the night. At the break of day they found themselves in Strathspey. However, the countrymen thought that they were Jacobites come to plunder, perhaps because of their less than regular appearance, and 'did raise a great noise and shout'. This alarmed Mackay's men, most of whom scattered to the hilly ground. Mackay and some of his mounted officers rode among them and with the aid of their pistols, threatened them back again. About 100 men, however, did not rejoin their comrades. Their fate was to be 'knockt in the head and stript, or taken prisoners'. The others continued without much halt, even though it was Sunday, arriving late that night at Castle Drummond. They reached Stirling on 29 July, allegedly but improbably, 1,500 strong.[170]

Historians customarily state that the casualties were high, on both sides. Pollard and Oliver state that though about half of the Jacobite army was killed, Mackay's army lost between half and two thirds dead.[171] These figures, if true, are exceptionally high.

Jacobite casualties

For the victors, the losses were serious. It was not unusual for senior officers to be wounded or killed. At the battle of the Boyne in 1690, the Duke of Schomberg lost his life and William III was injured.[172] General Ruth was killed at Aughrim in 1691 and Gustavus Adolphus was slain at Lützen in 1632. It was an occupational hazard, especially for generals who led from the front. Dundee was brave but also foolhardy.

168 Mackay, *Memoirs*, p.58.
169 *Ibid.*, p.266; NLS, MS 3740, 96.
170 *Ibid.*
171 *Ibid.*, p.61.; *The London Gazette*, 2476, 1–5 Aug. 1689.
172 Pollard and Oliver, *Two Men*, p.199.

Memorial plaque to John Graham of Claverhouse, at St. Bride's (redundant) chapel. (Author, 2017)

Despite routing their enemy, the Jacobites did not have 'it cheap bought … for they lossed very near a third of their number [about 600] '.[173] Apart from Dundee, a number of lesser officers were also slain; the laird of Largo, a MacDonald chieftain and several other MacDonald gentlemen, a brother of Glengarry's, several relatives of Sir Donald MacDonald, a number of MacLeans 'and a multitude of others whom it were tedious to recount'.[174] Mackay claimed 'The enemy lost on the field six for our one'. This cannot be true. Yet he agreed with Cameron that, apart from Dundee, 'several gentlemen of quality of the countys of Angus and Perth, but also many of the best gentlemen among the Highlanders, particularly among the MacDonalds of the Isles and Glengarie were killed'.[175] Among the officers, a Captain Grant was killed. The wounded included James Malcolm.[176] A letter allegedly written by Dundee after the battle gives Jacobite losses as 900.[177] Jacobite losses had been mostly caused by the lethal musketry, both as they charged towards Mackay's regiments and additional firing from Leven's and Hastings'

173 Kane, *Campaigns*, p.4.
174 Cameron, *Memoirs*, p.268.
175 *Ibid.*, p.280.
176 Mackay, *Memoirs*, p.59.
177 Thomson, *APS*, Appendix, IX, p.55.

men who stood. Firepower could have denied them the victory had they been equally deadly all along Mackay's line. Together with effective artillery and better cavalry, the Jacobites could have been defeated as occurred at Culloden in 1746.

Williamite casualties

Mackay's army suffered the higher casualties. Murray wrote on the day after the battle, 'I have no particular account yet of the losses, but sertenlay ye losses is grat'.[178] Melville wrote, 'ther wer so many of our friends safe though the loss we have is yet very considerable'.[179] According to Cameron, 'No less than eighteen hundred of them were computed to fall upon the field of battle' and he thought that this was a sixth of the total.[180] MacPherson put losses at between 1,500–2,000, with 500 prisoners taken.[181] MacNeill wrote of 2,000 dead and 500 prisoners; as did Balcarres.[182] Dunfermline wrote 'I does believe there was never a greater victory in soe short a time they left 1200 [dead] on the spot and I doubt not but there was as many in the flight we have about 400 prisoners and many of their officers are killed and we have 10 or 12 of their best officers prisoners'.[183] Lady Castlehaven wrote, 'many of our poor men ... [were] haried, broken and bruised ... [one of our friends] so badlie wounded that he cannot live'.[184]

Contemporary letters were concerned about officers who had died. The dead included Lieutenant Beverley Newcomen, son of Sir Thomas Newcomen, and Captain Tom Stanley of Hastings' regiment.[185] Although many men from Leven's regiment had survived, on 17 August the unit was clearly depleted, with Mackay writing to Leven 'your Lordship's regiment is render'd incapable to serve in haste'.[186] Lieutenant Ferguson's death left his family of a young widow and two children aged under five in dire straits. Apparently they were unable to access his estate worth £300 annually. There were debts to pay and she petitioned for immediate possession, invoking a custom dating back to James IV, stating that if a man died in battle, this would be granted.[187]

The Jacobite poet has much to say about the slaughter:

'Many a helmet and skull
Lay in splinters on the knolls
Blood ran in waves through the grass'

178 Dundee, *Letters*, p.84.
179 John Atholl, *Chronicles of the Atholl and Tullibardine Families*, vol. 2, (Edinburgh, 1908), p.303.
180 NRS, GD406/1/3644.
181 Cameron, *Memoirs*, p.270.
182 MacPherson, *Original Papers*, p.370.
183 NRS, CH12/12/1717; NLS MS 3738, f29r.
184 NRS, GD112/39/145/11.
185 NRS, GD26/13/26.
186 Rawdon Papers, p.311.
187 Mackay, *Memoirs*, p.262.

And

> 'On Killiecrankie of thickets
> Are many graves and stiff corpses.
> A thousand shovels and spades were requisitioned for covering them.'[188]

Since no official casualty rolls were compiled, it is impossible to know the scale of Mackay's losses. Mackay claimed that he brought between 600–700 men away from the stricken field, and as the man on the spot it is not unreasonable to suppose that this is probably the most accurate estimate. There were 500 prisoners. If we accept that Mackay had about 3,000 soldiers at the day's start, then the difference between the survivors under Mackay and the prisoners taken equates to 1,800–1,900 dead, but the true figure is probably a little less because some fugitives, such as McBane did not join Mackay and fled straight to Edinburgh via Dunkeld. Even so, we are probably looking at perhaps 1,600 dead; or just over 50 percent of the entire force, many of whom would have been killed in the pursuit following the collapse of the formed units of Mackay's, Balfour's, Kenmure's and Ramsay's. Individual unit casualties are unknown, and the two cavalry troops clearly had losses for there is a reference for them having to recruit in September, as had Leven's in August. By November some of the officer prisoners taken were exchanged.[189]

These were serious casualties indeed by contemporary standards. At the Boyne in the next year, the defeated Jacobites lost about 2,000 men or about 10 percent of their total and at Waldeck about 5,040 of 24,000 Frenchmen were lost. Mackay's losses outweighed in percentage terms the Jacobite dead at Culloden and that battle is often termed a massacre and Jacobite casualties are stressed. However, in Montrose's victories at Inverlochy, Auldearn and Kilsyth in 1645 the defeated Covenanters had lost over half their men due to the bloody routs.[190]

Mackay had lost so many because many of his soldiers routed and were pursued by a faster moving enemy who attacked them whilst they were virtually defenceless and in many cases unarmed. When an army can conduct an orderly retreat and/or has friendly forces nearby who can deter a rigorous pursuit this can be avoided, as occurred for the allies at Fontenoy in 1745. Such was not the fortunate lot of some of Cope's troops at Prestonpans in 1745, of Mar's at Sheriffmuir in 1715 and of the Jacobites at Culloden in 1746, where the luckless pursued troops were cut down in hundreds by their pursuers, whether lightly clad Highlanders or mounted dragoons. In the latter case alone this has been termed a war crime, though it was a commonplace if undoubtedly bloody part of battle.

There were many wounded as well as dead. Corporal Richard Robertson of Kenmure's regiment, sustained 22 wounds in his body and head, yet survived. Hugh Ross of Mackay's received two musket balls in his legs and

188 NRS, GD77/189.
189 Miller, 'Killiecrankie', p.68.
190 *RPCS*, 14, pp.180, 256, 38, 523.

was unable to walk thereafter without stilts. Captain James Donaldson of Kenmure's received seven wounds and was robbed of £100.[191]

Care for the wounded was limited. Hospital and medical care on a large scale for soldiers was poor, as the campaign in Ireland also showed. Apparently there were no army surgeons present with Mackay's men at Stirling, though there was meant to be one per regiment. However, David Mure or Muir, a Stirling surgeon who had been employed at the castle for four years, was on hand to assist. He tended to the wounded from the regiments of Leven, Mackay, Hastings and Kenmure; in all about 250 men. He sent to Edinburgh for medicine and used claret to bathe and foment wounds. On January 1691 he had to apply to the Privy Council for reimbursement.[192] It seems this plea fell on deaf ears for in a letter of 1708 he wrote of his services, adding, 'for all of which I have never yet received anything'.

Widows of Dutch soldiers killed at the battle applied for money so that they could return home. They were given four or five rix dollars to buy passage to Holland.[193]

It would be a mistake to assume that the pursuing Jacobites were all wholly consumed by bloodlust. Many, some of whom were wounded, were taken prisoner by the Jacobites. Several prisoners were officers: Captain Van Best of Ramsay's, Captain Donaldson and Lieutenant John Nisbet of Kenmure's, Lieutenant Finch of Hastings' and Lieutenant John Hay.[194] Prisoners were initially taken to a lower room in Blair Castle where they were questioned by Dunfermline and Cannon, now the senior Jacobite officer. Those taken were led away, but as Nisbet recorded, Colin Mackenzie 'was very kind to the witness and had twice given him money and some other necessaries' on the march along Loch Rannoch. Their eventual destination was Mull, though many did not reach there until the end of August.[195] As for the rank and file, it was difficult for the Jacobites to hold their 500 prisoners, due to want of provisions, so after having them swear that they would not bear arms against James II, they were dismissed.[196]

All this was in tune with the convention of the time. Rank and file prisoners were expensive to keep in terms of food and shelter, carried the risk of disease and tied troops up as guards and so were usually released. Only officers were kept prisoner and were often exchanged in time.[197]

The loss of baggage was also substantial. This should be unsurprising as one of the motives of some in the Jacobite army as loot. Officers were robbed of gold and clothing 'which was considerable'. Major Simekell lost 200 guineas and was stripped of his clothes.[198] According to Lanier, 500–600 horses

191 Royle, *Civil War*, pp.340–341, 345, 349; Chandler, *Marlborough*, pp.334–335; Barratt, *Battles*, p.118.
192 *RPCS*, 15, pp.123, 151, 181.
193 NRS, GD124/15/808.
194 *Ibid.*, 16, p.76.
195 *Ibid.*, 14, pp.232, 239, 351, 379.
196 Thomson, *APS*, Appendix, XI, pp.56–57.
197 *Ibid.*
198 Clarke, *Life of James the Second*, II, p.353.

were taken as well as a whole month's pay for the whole army.[199] Lieutenant Ferguson lost £400 worth of gold, money, horses and other equipage.[200] Leven lost over £1,000 at the battle.[201] All the army's tents, baggage, provisions and artillery were taken, along with the King's standard carried by MacKay's regiment.[202] The cannon and copious quantities of ammunition was lost.[203] Dunfermline wrote, 'We got their cannon and such a plunder that I never thought a Scots army could have had the like for there was a great deal of silver work and money in abundance'.[204] Horses were also taken; John Grant of Ballindoch rode a bay horse taken from one of the prisoners.[205] Balcarres later wrote of the Jacobites also collecting a great number of cannonballs from the field, a not uncommon practice which had occurred with the besiegers of Edinburgh castle in the previous century.[206]

On the following day, the surviving Jacobites viewed the field of battle. It was a grim sight:

> The dreadfull effects of their fury appeared in many horrible figures. The enemy lay in heaps almost in the order they were posted; but so disfigured with wounds, and so hashed and mangled, that even the victors could not look upon the amazeing proofs of their own agility and strength without surprise and horror. Many had their heads divided into two halves by one blow; others had their sculls cut off above the eares by a backstrock, like a night-cap. Their thick buff-belts were not sufficient to defend their shoulders from such deep gashes as almost disclosed their entrails. Several picks, small swords and the like weapons, were cut quite through, and some that had scull-capes had them so beat into their brains that they died on the spott.[207]

Cannon later wrote that the corpses were all buried on 28 July; this may have been carried out by the prisoners as occurred in Ireland in 1690.[208] The bodies were almost certainly buried on the battlefield, though these mass graves have not yet been located by archaeological digs. However, there have been press reports noting skeletons having been found close to the River Garry.[209]

What is perhaps worth noting is that Killiecrankie, out of the nine battles of the Jacobite campaigns of 1689–1746, was almost certainly the bloodiest. The numbers cited by historians of the fatalities of this battle have always struck me as being exceptionally high that I once doubted them. This doubt cannot be upheld because of the remarks of contemporaries for fatalities. Yet

199 Childs, *The British Army in the Nine Years War*, p.37.
200 EUL, Laing MSS, II/89/338.
201 MacPherson, *Original Papers*, p.370.
202 NLS, MS 3740, 96.
203 NRS, GD77/189.
204 *Ibid.*, GD26/13/98.
205 EUL, Laing MSS, II/89/338.
206 NRS, GD112/39/145/11.
207 Thomson, *APS*, Appendix, IX, p.57.
208 NLS, MLS 3738, f.30r.
209 *The Scotsman*, 14 Oct. 1932.

their significance has never been particularly remarked upon. It is customary for historians to note the severe casualties inflicted at the battle of Culloden on 16 April 1746 when the Jacobites suffered their worst and final military defeat. Contemporaries have been divided, but a consensus figure of about 1,500 (perhaps out of 5,000) has been reached, as well as about 50 British soldiers being slain; making a total of about 1,550 combatants out of about 13,000 men on the field, or about 12 percent. Yet the fatalities at Killiecrankie were about 2,100 at the most conservative estimate, out of a total of about 5,400, or about 40 percent. These were indeed severe. It is possible that this has been overlooked because of the political and emotional significance that Culloden has been invested in. Killiecrankie was the most terrible because of relatively effective musketry on Mackay's part, the bloody hack of the melee and then the terrible revenge inflicted by the Jacobites to avenge their fallen comrades shot during the onslaught. This analysis does not suit the romantic glow that Jacobitism is often covered with; slaughtered Jacobites at Culloden fit this picture, but Jacobites slaughtering their enemies (and more so, mostly fellow Scots) does not.

Aftermath

The first knowledge of the battle came to the government on the day afterwards when a number of junior officers and men engaged in the battle arrived in Edinburgh on the evening of 28 July. One was from a Lieutenant Harrison, 'coming it seems so early away'. His relatives differed as to his behaviour with some believing he left the field too soon 'and has done him no good heer'.[210] Another report was from a lieutenant in Mackay's regiment. Hamilton wrote on 29 July that there were various accounts of the battle, 'but to tell true, they all differ in particulars'. He added that only 'inferior officers and souldiers come' and 'none of ym van give certain accounts of the loss'.[211] Melville wrote that it was feared that Balfour and Lieutenant Colonel Mackay had been killed.[212]

Hamilton, understandably put the blame on Mackay, writing:

> It seems Mackay has been too forward that after a march of 16 miles should engadge the enemie when his men were weary and the nixt day there was 4 troops of Horse and 2 of Dragoons to have joined him and I fear his foot did not stand to it and they should but run after some firing when the Highlanders came to a close fight with ym.[213]

Lady Castlehaven wrote likewise, 'many condemn him for going to that place that was fatal for dragoons to fight in'.[214]

210 Cameron, *Memoirs,* pp.270–271.

211 Fraser, *Melvilles and Leslies*, 3, p.118; Kane, *Campaigns*, p.13.

212 NRS, GD406/1/3647.

213 *Ibid.*, 3595.

214 *Ibid.*, 3644.

On 29 July, Mackay started to put the case for his defence. He assessed what had happened, writing, 'there was no regiment or troop with me, but behaved lyck the vilest cowards in nature, except Hastings and my Lord Levens, whom I praise at such a degree, as I cannot but blame others, of whom I expected more'. His troops and he were now clearly exhausted after having marched 'without halt or rest for two days and two nights' and Mackay himself wrote that he was 'now so overtaken with sleep that I can say no more'.[215] Murray believed that 'how many of Mackay's men deserting him was the true cause of that unfortunate defeat'.[216]

Mackay also promoted his own position to Murray shortly afterwards:

> What men may speak to my disadvantage I doe not much care, for I dessyre them to get a man more zealous and upright for the cause; and if they attack mee in point of conduct, they must know the trade better than I, to condemne me withal. When the King thinks he can be better served of another in Scotland, no man shall be more read to resign the charge in anothers hand then myself, to serve His Majesty's interest elsewhere, if he has occasione for me, so that those men who will charge me with any blame, will lose their aime, for I am prepared for those recontres, having no other interest in this whole matter but that of conscience for my religion and affection to my souveraigne and the country wherein I was born, for whose peace and settlement I shall not only pray, but with God's assistance, willingly fight.[217]

What was needed next, 'is, that men goe quickly to work to stop the consternation of our friends, as well as the hops and pryde of our enemys'. He told Hamilton that Lanier's and Colchester's cavalry should be sent to Stirling and that Bargany's infantry march to Dundee until he could gather the troops he needed to 'chasse those highland barbarians again'.[218]

When news of Killiecrankie arrived in Edinburgh there was anxiety. Balcarres, who was there under arrest, later stated, 'Never were men in such a consternation as Duke Hamilton and the rest of the Parliament at Edinburgh, when they knew from those that fled of the defeat of MacKay'. Some thought of leaving the city to seek safety in England or in the West. There was discussion whether the Jacobite prisoners should be released or guarded more closely, though the latter was what happened. There were visits by those who had supported the Revolution to Jacobite prisoners assuring them of their continued support for James. Despite Lauder telling that all was lost, they decided to await further news.[219] According to Cameron it was not initially known that Dundee was dead and the lack of this knowledge led some to fear that because of 'the rapidity of his motions … were convinced that he would allow them no time to deliberat'.[220]

---

215 *Ibid.*, 3595.
216 NRS, GD26/13/26.
217 Mackay, *Memoirs*, pp.255, 257.
218 Atholl, *Chronicles*, p. 301.
219 *Ibid.*, p.309.
220 Mackay, *Memoirs*, p.255.

Melville wrote that 'I have done all I can to represent the present nakedness of the country as to arms and ammunition and otherwise ... the said party of our forces under the command of Major General Mackay by which the said party did sustaine considerable loss, which perhaps my animate and encourage any who are disaffected to joyne with the rebels against us'.[221]

Hamilton wrote from Edinburgh to tell Melville that 'after a sharp ingadgement Dundie being much stronger, the Major General was quiet defeat'. Lauder had managed to get to Perth and told Lord Ruthven that the army had 'being wholly routed'. Detailed accounts of the battle were lacking, however. It was not known that Dundee was dead and it was believed that Mackay was killed or captured.[222]

Yet there was another account of the battle, 'That Major General Mackay has had an engagement with the Lord Dundee near the Blair of Atholl, and that he has given him and all his forces a total Defeat; the Viscount of Dundee himself being killed, and several of his most considerable officers. A great number of prisoners of all sorts are taken, and brought to the castle of Stirling'. This was found to be in error, 'occasioned by the various and different reports that were then made of the late engagement'.[223]

It was thought that the defeat at Killiecrankie would have far reaching consequences for William's entire campaign against James. Hamilton wrote, 'my humble opinion is, that his Majestie must first beat Dundie and secuir this kingdom [bef]or[e] he attempt any other thing'. He thought that, as Dundee was now master of all Scotland north of the Forth 'great numbers of disaffected' would join him 'so the King must make hast to assist us to reduce him, for I fear wee shall not be able to defend this side of the Forth long'.[224] He feared that Perthshire and Angus would rise for the Jacobites.[225] Hamilton wrote on 1 August, 'by which the said party did sustain considerable loss, which may perhaps animate and encourage any who are disaffected to join the rebels'.[226]

Panic was not the only response in Edinburgh. On hearing of the military defeat, Hamilton called a meeting of the Privy Council. There it was decided that all regular troops should be concentrated at Stirling. Currently these were the infantry regiments of Mar, Blantyre and Bargany, whilst Argyll with his own regiment, Glencairn's and Angus' were summoned. Messages were sent to the west to request all the militia from there. Lanier wrote to call the English forces in Northumberland, specifically instructing Heyford's Horse to Glasgow, but he did not think they could arrive until 6 August. Meanwhile, he went to Stirling to take command there, 'to put the troops yr in as good condition as he can', though there was a shortage of general officers in Scotland. Lanier feared that Leslie's and Berkeley's units in the north would be cut off by the Jacobite army between them and Stirling.[227] Hamilton wrote, 'if we not able to defend Stirling this place we cannot stay in

221 Balcarres, *Memoirs*, p.48; Cameron, *Memoirs*, p.282.

222 Cameron, *Memoirs*, p.282.

223 Fraser, *Melvilles and Leslies*, II, pp.140–1.

224 Mackay, *Memoirs*, p.248.

225 Balfour-Maitland, 'Estates', I, pp.183, 185.

226 Mackay, *Memoirs*, p.249.

227 NRS, GD406/1/3595.

but must returne to England'. Parliament was not, however, adjoined on that day as to do so might discourage the populace.[228]

Two infantry regiments and two troops of Horse were to guard Glasgow whilst two troops were to be stood near Cardross. The Selkirk and Roxburgh militia were summoned into being. The 1,200 muskets received from London were allocated to those survivors of Killiecrankie who had thrown away their arms, whilst Edinburgh resupplied Leven's men with powder, ball and matches.[229] Money had arrived at the capital by ship, which was of use, but the cannon and mortars on board were not thought necessary so were sent back.[230]

As days passed, news of Dundee's death arrived and that there would now be no Jacobite advance. Together, as Balcarres stated, these 'put an end to their fears, for they knew well there was none in his army had abilities, name or reputation enough, to make a just use of the victory'.[231] Or as Cameron put it, 'the news of that great man's death quickly dissipated all their fears, and the short lived loyalty of these politicians shortly thereafter was changed into ane affected bigotry, and ill nature against all who differed from them in opinion'.[232] Their enemies agreed: Lanier writing on 3 August referring to 'the misfortune that happened to Major General Mackay' but he added, 'the certainty of Dundee's being killed hath stopt many that began to rise'.[233]

English commentators seem to have thought that the battle was the most noteworthy of those in Scotland in 1689–90. Henry Prescott, Deputy Registrar of Chester noted in his diary for 3 August, 'The newspapers bring I know not what definite or indefinite news about a battle that has been fought between Mackay and Dundee in Scotland'.[234] Three days later Evelyn noted, 'Dundee slaine in Scotland'.[235]

The government's official newspaper put, predictably, an optimistic spin on matters, though was not unwholly untruthful:

> Dundee's men exceeding ours in number, they being about 6000, part of our Forces were put into disorder; Whereupon Major General Mackay thought fit to retire with the rest … with 1500 men, who retreated in a body, and in good order… [Hastings' and Leven's regiments] behaved themselves with extraordinary Bravery and Resolution, maintaining their Ground to the last; and keeping the field after the rebels were drawn off the field.

More particulars were promised in the next issue but none were ever forthcoming.[236]

---

228 *CSPD*, 1689–1690, p.205.
229 *RPCS*, 14, pp.3, 16, 20.
230 NRS, GD406/1/3595.
231 Balcarres, *Memoirs*, p.48.
232 Cameron, *Memoirs*, p.282.
233 NLS, MS 3740, 96.
234 John Addy (ed.), John Prescott, *Diary*, III (Record Society of Lancashire and Cheshire, 1994), p.727.
235 Evelyn, *Diary*, p.811.
236 *The London Gazette*, 2476, 1–5 Aug. 1689.

This report missed out what was the battle's main result: Dundee's death. Contemporaries on both sides saw this as being decisive. According to Balcarres:

> Your friends who knew him best were in doubt if his civil and military capacities were most eminent. None of this nation so well knew the different intelligences, tempers and inclinations of the men most capable to serve you. None had more the ability to insinuate and persuade; he was extremely affable, and, although a good manager of his private fortune, yet had no reserve when your service and his reputation required him to be liberal, which gained him the hearts of all who followed him, and brought him into such reputation, that had he survived the day, in all probability he had given such a turn to your affairs, that the Prince of Orange could neither have gone nor sent to Ireland , so your Majesty had been extremely master of that kingdom, and in a condition to have landed with what forces you pleased in Scotland, which of all things your friends most desired.[237]

Cameron agreed with him, writing:

> But the true reason why this victory became ineffectuall was the unseasonable death of the great Dundee. He seemed formed by Heaven for great undertakings, and was in ane eminent degree possessed of all those qualitys that accomplish the gentleman, the statesmen and the souldier ... the onely step that he is to be blamed in was his too much eagerness in exposeing his person; but that he did with a view of gaining a reputation among the Highlanders him he humoured in all things.[238]

Enemies concurred with allies. Defoe wrote, 'Dundee being killed by an accidental shot after the fight, the resistance ended soon after; whereas, indeed, had that accident not happened, Dundee, who was a bold enterprising man, had certainly marched southward and give King William a journey to the north.'[239]

Mackay thought so, too, 'he now looked upon his defeat to be of greater consequence, and more beneficial to his master's interest than the most absolute victory could have been'. This was because 'the Highlanders will allow none of their own chiefs to command as General; and they have no other officer that either can conduct them, or that so much as knows how to make proper use of so important a victory'.[240] Melville wrote on 5 August, 'I apprehend Dundee's death will bridle a little his party's joy and retard their progress'.[241] Likewise, Lockhart wrote on 30 July, 'Dundee and Colonel Canon are both killed for sertin and so I hope tho we have lost the field we have wine the day for I know not any who can take it'.[242] Creighton noted that

237 Balcarres, *Memoirs*, p.47.
238 Cameron, *Memoirs*, p.273.
239 Defoe, *Tour*, p.650.
240 Cameron, *Memoirs*, p.299.
241 Fraser, *Melvilles and Leslies*, III, p.142.
242 NRS, GD26/13/23.

William said 'He knew Lord Dundee so well that he must have been either killed or mortally wounded, otherwise before that time, he would have been in Edinburgh.'[243]

If this was a Jacobite victory, it appears not to have felt like one, as Cameron described the victorious army's condition on the 28 July:

> The death of their brave Generall, and the loss of so many of their friends, were inexhaustible fountains of grief and sorrow. They closed the last scene of this mournfull tragedy in obsequys of their lamented General and other Gentlemen who fell with him, and interred them in the church of Blair Atholl with a real funeral solemnity, there not being present one single person who did not participate in the general affliction.[244]

Murray agreed, writing, 'I have heard ye neus of Lord Dundee bean killed, wch is a gretter loss then all their vicktory will gane them. It will hinder people from going to that party.'[245] On the other hand, Dunfermline, writing on 29 July to Breadalbane, wrote, 'My lord, seeing all things I is going soe well with the King … have what men you can at this place on Saturday next for all the countys hear about are rising if Your lordship doe not joyn I am afraid it will make people have a bad opinion of you.'[246] Yet he was encouraging Breadalbane to join the Jacobite cause, so such an optimistic spin is understandable.

If there was any retrospective consolation for the Jacobites, Dundee was celebrated in poem with lines such as 'None noble Roman character/ Fam'd for learning or for war/exceeds our Caledonian Star'. He was said to be the 'last champion of Scots loyalty', 'Thou stoutest leader of old loyall clans', 'Thou last of loyal Scotts' and 'your courage will and loyalties a happy union'.[247]

There was some evidence for Jacobite support in the north of England. Rumours came to the government's attention about armed meetings at the homes of some of the Catholic elite in Northumberland, of men being enlisted for the Jacobite cause in Cumberland, and some verbal support for the Jacobite cause in Lancashire and Newcastle. Financial support from England to the tune of £35,000 was also allegedly forthcoming had it not been for Dundee's death.[248] Had Dundee lived, this nascent Jacobitism might have become a more dangerous force for a shaken government.

Two pieces of Jacobite propaganda were published shortly after the battle, both being allegedly written by Dundee, though neither can have been, as he was not noted as having addressed the army prior to the battle in which he was killed, and could not have penned a letter afterwards. Yet both were

243 Creighton, *Memoirs*, p.269.

244 Cameron, *Memoirs*, p.282.

245 Atholl, *Chronicles*, p.303.

246 NRS, GD112/39/145/11.

247 *Ibid.*, GD26/8/70.

248 Paul Monod, *Jacobitism and the English People, 1689–1788* (Cambridge: Cambridge University Press, 1989), pp.309–310; Leo Gooch, *The Desperate Faction? The Jacobites of North-East England, 1688–1745* (Hull: University of Hull Press, 1995), p.16.

written probably by person/s shortly afterwards in order to encourage support for James.

The first is as follows:

> Gentlemen,
>
> You are come hither this day to fight, and that in the best of causes: for it is the battle of your King, your religion, and your country, against the foulest usurpation and rebellion; and having, therefore, so good a cause in your hands, I doubt not but it will inspire you with an equal courage to maintain it. For there is no proportion betwixt loyalty and treason; nor should be any beytwixt the valour of good subjects and traitors. Remember that today begins the fate of your King, your religion, and your country. Behave yourselves, therefore, like true Scotchmen: and let us, by this action, redeem the credit of this nation, that is laid low by the treacheries and cowardice of some of our countrymen; in which, I ask nothing of you, that you shall not see me do before you; and, if any of us shall fall upon this occasion, we shall have the honour of dying in our duty, and as becomes true men of valour and conscience: and such of us as shall live and win the battle, shall have the reward of a gracious King, and the praise of all good men. In God's name, then, let us go on, and let this be your word: King James and the Church of Scotland, which God long preserve.[249]

It has also been alleged that the wounded Dundee wrote to his King on the evening of the battle:

> Sir,
>
> It has pleased God to give your forces a great victory over the rebels, in which 3-4ths of them are fallen under the weight of our swords. I might say much of the action, if I had not the honour to command it; but of 5000 men, which was the best computation I could make of the rebels, it is certain there cannot have escaped above 1200 men. We have not lost full out 900. This absolute victory made us masters of the field and the enemy's baggage, which I gave to the soldiers, who, to do them all right, both officers and common men, Highlands, Lowlands, and Irish, behaved themselves with equal gallantry to whatever I saw in the hottest battles fought abroad by disciplined armies, and this McKay's old soldiers felt on this occasion. I cannot now, sir, be more particular; but take leave to assure your Majesty the kingdom is generally disposed for your service, and impatiently wait for your coming; and this success will bring in the rest of the nobility and gentry, having had all their assurances of it, except the notorious rebels. Therefore, sir, for God's sake, assist us, though it be with another detachment of your Irish forces as you sent us before, especially of horse and dragoons, and you will crown our beginnings with a complete success, and yourself with an entire possession of your ancient hereditary kingdom of Scotland. My wounds forbid me to enlarge to your Majesty at this time, though they tell me they are not mortal. However, sir, I beseech your Majesty to believe, whether I live or die,
>
> I am sincerely yours,
>
> Dundie'.[250]

249 Dundee, *Letters*, pp.81–2.

250 *Ibid.*, pp.82–85.

Despite Dundee's death, Episcopalian clergymen in the Highlands celebrated the victory. John Blair of Scourie, 'he cryed that it was the best news for him in this world, and when he heard the death of the Viscount of Dundee he said the greatest bulwark for the Protestant religion and against Poperie was gone'. William Murray, the minister at Crieff declared 'This is the day God made, in it well joy triumphantly.' David Drummond of Kilmadoc entertained parishioners with news of the battle 'very cheirfully'. Robert Young at Kipper was 'rejoising at the report of the loss at Gilliecrankie and saying it was good news that Cannon hade won the day'. Finally Thomas Fowler of Kinnoull 'thanked God for Dundie's victory against Major General Mackay at Killiecrankie'.[251]

The other question to ask is how a poorly-armed and poorly-trained outnumbered force could defeat a better-armed and larger army. Professor Pittock stated that the Jacobites triumphed 'because of the lack of good government artillery (they did not face canister and cartridge shot at close range); their charge was better co-ordinated from rising ground; and because the plug bayonet of William's army incapacitated the user's musket'.[252] Lenman cites the advantage of ground, too, the Jacobite aggression and Mackay's thin line.[253] Reid pooh-poohs the bayonet argument, noting that very few were employed, but that Mackay's regiments were diversely spaced apart and crucially some of the regiments in the centre of the line were exposed and isolated, unable to benefit from the defensive fire of their comrades in adjacent battalions. He likens this to the British defeat at Isandlwana in 1879.[254]

There are several reasons which would seem to account for the Jacobite victory. Mackay, in attempting to reach Blair Atholl, put his army into a tactically unsound position, by being in a valley whilst his enemy held the heights. His men, especially the cavalry, were largely inexperienced in warfare. There were no reserves in order to repulse any initially successful attack. He gambled on musketry alone being enough to repel the Jacobites and in this he failed, despite inflicting severe casualties. Finally his troops were unable to successfully fight hand-to-hand against their enemies.

Hopkins does not discuss the reason why the battle ended as it did, but highlights its importance in the campaign. He suggests that had Dundee lived and the support to the Jacobite cause was then significant, then William's whole strategic position would have been threatened. Supporters might have become lukewarm.[255] Linkwater and Hesketh agree, stating that William's hold over the Three Kingdoms was tenuous and that he would have had to divert the forces earmarked for Ireland under Schomberg to deal with Dundee.[256] Reid, on the other hand, thinks not, arguing that Dundee was but a minor figure, socially and militarily and lacked substantive support

---

251 *RPCS*, 14, pp.176, 257, 305, 353, 373, 386.

252 Murray G.H. Pittock, *Jacobitism* (Basingstoke: Macmillan, 1998), p.22.

253 Lenman, *Jacobite Risings*, p.31.

254 Reid, *Killiecrankie*, p.13.

255 Hopkins, *Glencoe*, p.161.

256 Linkwater and Hesketh, *Bonnie Dundee*, p.225.

Memorial to soldiers killed at Killiecrankie. (Author, 2017)

from either the nobility or the masses.[257] In any event, the matter, though interesting, is speculative. Scott wrote, 'with Claverhouse's death, King James' cause disintegrated'.[258] Dundee was as dead as Charles II and it remained to be seen how this would affect his master's cause in Scotland. His death was without a doubt, though, a blow to the Jacobite cause.

Biographers of Dundee end their accounts here, naturally enough as their subject was now dead. Yet the campaign was not over. Battles were still to be fought and hundreds of men were still to die to determine who ruled Scotland.

257 Reid, *Sheriffmuir*, p.5.
258 Scott, *Bonnie Dundee*, p.231.

6

The Battle of Dunkeld

Dundee's death and the battle of Killiecrankie did not bring about a halt in the campaign. Hard on the heels of that battle there was another, though this one is less well known and certainly has not been celebrated in verse or song, unlike its predecessor (and oddly, its successor), perhaps because it was unsuccessful for the Jacobite cause.

Despite Dundee's death, the Jacobites were at their numerical peak in Scotland in the weeks after his demise. This was because he had already set in motion this momentum in the days and weeks prior to his death, though whether his successor could maintain this remained to be seen. Cannon took over the leadership of the Jacobite army, for he was the most senior commissioned officer present. They spent the two days after the battle of Killiecrankie at Dunkeld. Their strength increased. On 30 July, as had been already arranged by Dundee, John Cameron brought a further 500 of the clan along. There were also 200 Stewarts of Appin, a number of MacGregors, 250 MacPhersons, the MacDonalds of Glencoe, men from Lochaber and many of the Atholl men. On 31 July, at Braemar, the Farquarsons, the Frasers and the Gordons of Strathdon and Glenlivet joined them. According to Cameron, the army numbered 5,000 men. More were expected from both Lowlands and Highlands. This was significant and positive because in Montrose's campaigns of 1644–1645, the Highland army had suffered considerable desertions and men went home with plunder gained after the battle: the same was to occur in 1715, too.[1] Yet not all obeyed the summons: Lord Strathallan ordered Colin Campbell and other of Perth's vassals out on 29 July to meet at Glenliharve, but they did not do so.[2]

Their enemy massed at Stirling as planned. We need to bear in mind the strength of the government's position. There had been 10 regiments of infantry raised in March and April, as well as 12 troops and one regiment of cavalry. In addition there were the three Dutch regiments, two regiments of English infantry and two of English cavalry. Of these the three Dutch regiments, two of the Scottish regiments and one of the English regiments had been severely mauled, to varying extents, at Killiecrankie and the two troops of cavalry

1 Cameron, *Memoirs*, p.283.
2 NRS, GD26/8/27.

there had been scattered and so can be left out of the equation. Two of the Scottish regiments and one of the English were at Inverness. That left one English regiment, six Scottish regiments and 10 troops and one regiment of Scottish cavalry and two of English.

On 31 July there were 2,000 infantry and 700 cavalry at Stirling. Another 2,000 infantry and 300 cavalry were expected. Argyll, with 3,000 infantry, were also anticipated. Apart from Colchester's Horse, the cavalry was all 'new levied' and the former was deemed 'very weak', presumably numerically. There were also attempts to offer, again, an indemnity to the Jacobites by suggesting pardons in order to reduce their numbers. Not surprisingly, with the Jacobites recently victorious, none chose to accept.[3]

Mackay ordered Lanier to go to Edinburgh to hasten the arrival at Stirling of Lanier's Horse and Hayford's dragoons. He did not think that the thousands of men who had come from the West to defend the government at Edinburgh were necessary and so had them discharged. Apparently this was because their 'pretensions appeared already exorbitant enough' and he did not want them to feel that they were indispensable to William. Being satisfied that there were enough troops to defend the government, on the afternoon of 31 July, just four days after his defeat at Killiecrankie, Mackay had recovered sufficient confidence to march northward from Stirling to Perth, initially with Colchester's Regiment of Horse, six troops of Scottish Horse and two troops of Cardross' dragoons (totalling 400 men), with Mar's and Bargany's regiments of infantry behind them.[4]

On the evening of that day his little force halted at a village en route to Perth, as he feared that a night march might invite an ambush. One reason for such a bold move was because there was no intelligence to be gained north of Stirling by other means. At daybreak on 1 August he continued his march towards the River Earn, just three miles short of Perth.[5]

More men were expected for the Jacobite cause. According to Cameron:

> The Northern Shires were all in arms, and the greatest part of the Low-Country gentry, through all parts of the kingdome, were ready to joyn them, and expected their advance with impatience; and it was generally computed that, before they arrived at the Borders of England, they would be forty thousand strong at least, so general was the inclination at that time to have restored King James.

Yet the news of Dundee's death dissipated these alleged Jacobite inclinations.[6]

Cannon's leadership began badly. He sent a party of Struan Robertson's men and some from Braemar to Perth to take the meal and other provisions that he had heard were stored in the city, having been left there for Mackay in the previous week, by order of the Privy Council. They arrived at their destination, but 'loytered so long after they had executed their order'.[7]

3 Balfour-Maitland, 'Estates', I, pp.190, 220.
4 Mackay, *Memoirs*, pp.62–63.
5 *Ibid.*, p.63.
6 Cameron, *Memoirs*, p.283.
7 *Ibid.*

Mackay heard of their being there. Four of his scouts riding but a short distance ahead of the main body, met two Jacobite horsemen. The latter shouted 'Qui vive' and attacked. The Scottish government forces fired, killing one and wounding the other. Mackay suspected that a larger force was nearby, though they could not get any information from the wounded Jacobite. His force left the main road and marched onto a heath over a steep slope. Instead of marching directly to Perth, he advanced to its north. There he learnt that of the foe immediately at hand, 30 cavalry had passed the River Tay, but there were 300 infantry half a mile from Perth and so within reach.[8]

According to Mackay, once the Jacobites knew of his approach, they 'came to ane halt as irresolute what to do'. Mackay knew that that part of the river between them was fordable, detached four troops of dragoons to prevent the Jacobites taking that route. The Jacobites then returned to Perth. However Mackay did not then know where the bulk of the Jacobite army was, and having no infantry to force an entry into the town, he had Colchester's three troops of horse charge them whilst his remaining cavalry kept on the heights.[9]

The Jacobites fled, many being drowned in the Tay. Although Mackay claimed that his men killed 120 or 150, 'the most parte of them' and captured 30 (all of whom were Atholl men) for the loss of one man dead, the Jacobites alleged only losing 30 men and the majority being able to retreat to the mountains, despite being pursued by cavalry, its moral impact was not insignificant coming as it did when it did. Cameron stated: 'it not onely exposed their want of conduct, but also showed that they were not invincible, as their late behaviour at the battle of Kilychranky made many people fondly believe they were'. Mackay wrote, 'this little action which nevertheless served to good purpose' and sent Lord Belhaven to inform Hamilton of it. However he wrote on 2 August that had he three regiments of good infantry, he could have scattered them.[10] James Ogilvie informed Seafield, that 'the Highlanders were totally defeat and the toun retakne from them'.[11]

Mackay's self confidence increased. He was also well acquainted with his fellow officers and was eager to take the offensive against the Jacobites to a degree that, with lesser numbers, he would never have done so against Dundee.[12] He also wrote to Cannon to ask about whom he held prisoners and on what conditions they would be released, suggesting that they exchange men of equal rank. Mackay told Cannon that 'the state of their affairs is not a happening advanced by her victory, and how little the expectation wherewith those highlanders are fed of James' landing shall turn to their account'. He recommended that they address the Privy Council so that 'they may expect the King's clemency a gracious indemnity for past faults'. He thought that Dundee's death and the non-arrival of James would lead the Jacobites to consider their position. He recommended to Hamilton that if 'Baleuchan and

8 Mackay, *Memoirs*, p.63.
9 *Ibid*., pp.63–64.
10 *Ibid*., pp.64, 259; Cameron, *Memoirs*, p.284.
11 Grant, 'Seafield Correspondence', p.51.
12 Cameron, *Memoirs*, p.284.

all the other transgressors might be pardoned to procure a speedy settlement of the nation in peace.'[13]

Cannon replied immediately and defiantly, on 5 August. He stated that he had set all the common soldiers taken at Killiecrankie free, observing to Mackay:

> This was not your way of treating those that fell in your hands who by your order [not quite the case, as noted in chapter 2] were hanged in the north. Your way of defending the Protestant revolution is neither soe honourable nor Christian to deserve an answer. As for your threatening to confine us to the hills with your horse, you shall have liberty to boast of it when you have done it. Till then you must think our forces are better than yours ... Those vast armies you threaten us with, we hope will be in a short tyme be confounded ... Wee are in a condition not to fear them.

He suggested that Mackay return to his allegiance to James.[14]

A similar letter of defiance, but with stronger sentiments, was sent by on 17 August by Cameron and other chiefs in response to another overture by Mackay:

> You tell us in both your letters that His Majesty has hot wars in Ireland, and cannot in haste come to us, which though it were as true as wee know it is not, is onely ane argument for safety and intrist. And that you may know the sentiments of men of honour wee declare to you and all the world wee scorne your usurper and the indemnities of his government. And to save you further trouble by your frequent invitations we answer you wee are satisfied our King will take his own time and way to manage his dominions and punish his rebels. And altho' he should send no assistance at all, wee will all dye with our swords in our hands before we fail in our loyaltie and sworn allegiance.[15]

This proximity of the enemy meant that the Jacobites had to make a decision. Although much ink has been spilt by historians of the Jacobite campaigns over whether the Jacobite army in 1745 should have marched from Derby to London, with some suggesting that an advance on the capital would have led to a second Stuart restoration, and some have suggested that Mar's campaign in 1715 would have succeeded for the want of boldness, little attention has been paid to this potentially momentous decision. It should be recalled that the Jacobites were at their strongest numerically and that they had beaten Mackay convincingly at Killiecrankie. However, Mackay had been able to dent their confidence by winning the skirmish near Perth.

A council of war was held in the castle of Auchindoun, near Elgin. The first question was whether the Lowland gentlemen who had acted as volunteers in the army, but without commands, should attend the council with voting rights. The second question was whether they should fight Mackay, whose

13 Mackay, *Memoirs*, p.260.

14 Fraser, *Melvilles and Leslies*, II, p.118.

15 Thomson, *APS*, ix, Appendix, p.60.

command was mainly one of cavalry, or whether they should obey orders from James who wanted them to march to Kintyre in the west, presumably to be in a position to receive troops sent from Ireland.[16]

The Highland chiefs were opposed to the Lowlanders having votes on the grounds that they knew nothing of the Highlanders' methods of making war, accustomed as they were to the ways of conventional warfare, so that their votes would have potentially harmful effects. Because the Lowlanders had brought no men to the army it seemed wrong that they should have equal voting rights to those who had. It was agreed, however, that they could act on the council in an advisory capacity.[17]

The second point was rather more important, with the prospect of battle looming. Cameron spoke first. He announced that because they were fighting by James' authority, they should not dispute his commands. However, he also admitted that 'his Majesty could not att that distance rightly understand the present situation of his affairs here, he declared that they ought immediately to fight MacKay, and then march westwards'. He felt that the army was enthusiastic to avenge Dundee and others, and that to encourage waverers another victory was needed. The enemy might be superior in cavalry but the flight of the cavalry at Killiecrankie had removed the Highlanders' former fear of them. Cameron even offered to fight Mackay's entire force with his own men and the 300 Jacobite cavalry. In conclusion:

> If they lossed this opportunity, when Mackay had no more than equall numbers, and began a cowardly retreat, when it was in their power to serve the King effectually, and gain honour to themselves, they would not onely loose their friends, their reputation, and their army, which would dayly diminish, but they would even become the jest and diversion of the kingdoms.[18]

Although Cameron was supported by the other chiefs, it was decided that the Lowland officers could vote and with a decision against immediate battle, the council decided to march through Aberdeenshire and over the Caramount, without fighting. Cameron was outraged, believing it hard to justify such a plan, except that by marching north they might increase their numbers by others joining them there. Yet an army which shuns combat looks defeated; 'the army became dispirited, and dayly diminished, when they saw every thing goes cross to their inclinations'. Conversely, Mackay's reputation increased.[19]

In retrospect it is tempting to suggest that Cannon should have pressed on. Mackay was at Perth with 400 cavalry and two regiments of infantry, so he would have outnumbered them, but as we shall note, defeating forces defending a town was to prove far from easy. Even if he had been victorious, this might well have led to the numerous units of the English army in the north of England, crossing the border to support the remaining

16 Cameron, *Memoirs*, p.284.
17 *Ibid.*
18 *Ibid.*, p.285.
19 *Ibid.*

English and Scottish forces in Stirling and around Edinburgh. Secondly, the Jacobites may have hoped for more support from Ireland. Thirdly, Cannon was a conventionally trained soldier and thought conventionally and conservatively. To risk all by pushing into the Lowlands where support might well be limited might be to risk catastrophe. Yet a rebellion on the defensive must inevitably fail, however long that day is delayed. The moral effect of the victory at Killiecrankie had now been thrown away; a second major victory on top of that one could have led to triumph. But it was not to be.

Some of the Jacobites left the army. Cameron did so, claiming James' orders were being neglected and that the campaign was being badly conducted. He did not withdraw his men, hedging his bets, but left them there under his son's command. Sir Donald MacDonald also withdrew and so did others, though leaving their commands with Cannon, under the orders of near relations, doubtless for similar reasons to Cameron.[20]

Mackay was now entrenched at Perth, determined to remain there until reinforced. He wrote to Lanier to bring his regiment and Hayford's to Perth and summoned his own regiment of infantry there. Mackay wanted to take to the field as soon as possible and regain the initiative by keeping the Jacobites out of the Lowlands. Livingstone was ordered to maintain the defence of Inverness and if he was threatened, Mackay promised to march to his aid with 1,400–1,500 cavalry. Perth was made more defensible by its being palisaded, for Mackay was outnumbered by the Jacobite army at this time which was only a day's march away, but he believed that 'the Highlanders are not good attackers where they cannot run to with sword in hand'. He also sent out patrols to bring in any notice of any Jacobite advance on Perth, oblivious to Cannon's intentions.[21]

By about 6 August, Mackay learnt Cannon had replaced Dundee as Jacobite commander and that he had marched his men northward, keeping close to hills so as to avoid being caught in the open by cavalry. Leaving two regiments at Perth he marched to Coupar, 10 miles away, and spoke to some of his men who had been taken at Killiecrankie but who had subsequently escaped. They told him that Cannon was still falling back, so Mackay marched to Forfar, when Cannon was at Glenlia and then to Clova. After resting the men two days at Forfar, Mackay found that Cannon had passed into Braemar and there he might aim towards Inverness or Aberdeen. To counter this, knowing that there were Jacobite sympathisers in both places, he requested Lanier come to Forfar and he would feint northwards and then march direct to Aberdeen, where he arrived within two days, to the delight of the majority there.[22]

Two days later he stated his plan was for 'the enemy on all syds hemm'd in, and hinder'd all communication with the Low Countreys, which will make them disperse in a short tyme, as well as to lose their adherents in the Highlands'. He believed that they were on the defensive after his counter-attack of a week ago. Therefore Dundee was to be garrisoned by Berkeley's

20 *Ibid.*, pp.285–286.
21 Mackay, *Memoirs*, pp.64–5.
22 *Ibid.*, pp.65–66.

dragoons and Bargany's infantry. Argyll was to be at Perth with the one regiment of Angus' infantry, Mar's regiment and what was left of Balfour's, with four troops of cavalry. To be centred on Forfar to defend the Lowlands was Lanier with his own regiment of horse and Cornbury's English Horse.[23]

There were also orders for the troops newly arrived from England. Mackay wrote, 'finding no pressing occasion at present I ordered the most part of them to quarter upon the borders' at places such as Berwick, Carlisle, Morpeth and Alnwick. However, Beaumont's infantry and three regiments of dragoons were kept close to Edinburgh. Unless the Jacobites had substantial help from abroad, principally Ireland, which he though unlikely, 'they will give you it cheap' [24]

Mackay wanted to know where the Jacobite army was and feared it might try to enlist others, so sent a message to Livingstone at Inverness. He was to cross the Spey with his regiment of dragoons and arrive at Strathbogie, leaving Inverness to Sir James Leslie. On 17 August Mackay was at Strathbogie and complained to Melville that he lacked money, provisions and tents. He also showed the ruthless side to his nature by regretting that there were no frigates on the Western Isles 'for they could burn and ruine their countreys'.[25]

Mackay was hoping for a battle with his cavalry against the Jacobite army, but if only they would leave the hills and stand on 'attackable ground'. He wrote that he led cavalry 'for dispatch, but should be careful to give them no advantage of the ground'. To this effect he ordered up additional troops, but the Jacobites lay behind difficult terrain and the intelligence from country people for Mackay was poor. Yet when Cannon moved to the River Dee, before marching into Angus and Mearns, Mackay, had only 1,100–1,200 cavalry to oppose about 4,000 Jacobites, for he 'could not without manifest hazard venture that passage'. He therefore returned to Aberdeen and wrote to Lanier, asking him to keep him informed of the Jacobites' progress.[26]

In the meantime, the government's realisation that the defeat at Killiecrankie was not going to lead to a major Jacobite onslaught, the English and Dutch troops in the north of England had their orders to march to Scotland countermanded. Troops at Chester which were to be shipped to Scotland were to be sent to Ireland instead. Another reason why cavalry were not sent to Scotland was due to the logistical difficulties in having to support large numbers of horses there. Other good news, though from Ireland, for William and his governments in Scotland and England in early August, was that the siege of Londonderry had finally been lifted. There were even unconfirmed rumours that James had fled.[27]

Cannon had now to keep on the defensive, as his numbers had fallen from their brief peak after Killiecrankie. He remained in the mountains and Mackay kept to the plains. They were often in sight of each other, but neither wished to fight at a perceived disadvantage.

23 NRS, GD406/1/3617.

24 NLS, MS 3740, 98.

25 Mackay, *Memoirs*, pp.66, 268.

26 *Ibid.*, pp.66–67, 269; NLS, MS 3740, 98.

27 *Ibid.*, pp.261–2.

However a battle was imminent. Overshadowed by that of Killiecrankie, this battle was arguably more decisive a victory for the government. It was an equally heroic encounter and has been described as 'Rorke's Drift in tartan', though such comparison with the Zulu war battle of nearly two centuries later hinders as well as illuminates. There are no songs, poems or ballads concerning the battle as there are about Killiecrankie, probably because this battle was not a Jacobite victory. However in recent years there has been a novel which features the action, following its central protagonist from Drumclog to Dunkeld.

A contemporary publication described Dunkeld thus:

> A Town on the north of the Tay, at the foot of the Grampian Hills being surrounded by pleasant woods ... chief market town of the Highland ... The Ruin of the cathedral church are yet to be seen, but that which chiefly adjoins it, are the stately buildings, lately erected by the Marquis of Athole, father of the present Duke.

Most of the roofless cathedral's walls still stood, as did its tower. It stood just to the west of the town, overlooking it, whilst Athole's mansion, Dunkeld House lay to the church's immediate north and the town spread itself out in a line from the church, beginning with the Dean's House and the street leading to the market square with its cross at the centre of the little town's windy roads and streets. The town lay on the banks of the River Tay, with a bridge over the river near the road to Perth.[28]

Meanwhile, Lanier was currently at Forfar with two regiments. Colonel Ramsay was at Perth with three regiments of Anglo-Dutch infantry who had not been at Killiecrankie. On 19 August an order was issued to Lanier to take Blair Castle by force. He was supplied with four six-pounder guns and Monsieur Drury, having survived the debacle at Killiecrankie, with 15 men to handle them. There was also 38 of Blantyre's men to assist. Lanier marched with his men to Brechin and there was a skirmish on 15 August near there with the advance party of the Jacobite army. A few men on both sides were killed, but then the Jacobites returned. This may have been because Cannon received news that there was an isolated Scottish regiment at Dunkeld and so there was an opportunity to cut it off. Lanier knew nothing about this. He retired to Forfar, where he received orders from the council to march to Atholl in order to garrison Blair House and Finlarig House. Next day he marched to Coupar, within 10 miles of both Dunkeld and Perth.[29] Similar behaviour occurred next year, when he was serving in Ireland: Lanier made many unnecessary delays on his march to Cullen to guard the artillery camp and in doing so allowed Sarsfield's cavalry to destroy it.[30]

The Privy Council, 'without the consideratiuoin of the insuffiicencie of the place for defence, ordered the Earle of Angus' regiment to Dunkeld, ten miles above Perth, separate from all speedy succour, and exposed to be

---

28 *Theatrum Scotiae*, (London, 1693), p.8.

29 Mackay, *Memoirs*, pp.68–69; *RPCS*, 14, pp.62, 84.

30 Kane, *The Campaigns*, p.6.

Dunkeld Cathedral. (Author, 2017)

carried by insult, without the least prospect of advancement to the service by their being posted there'.[31]

Following instructions from the privy council, Ramsay ordered the regiment from Perth to Dunkeld at the beginning of August, in order to observe the enemy and to secure the town from them.[32] They had been paid on 6 August and had been at Doune and Dunblane until 12 August when the momentous decision was made, though when they arrived there, Cleland was told to contact Lanier and the commanding officer at Perth of this and then to obey their orders from that point on.[33] On Saturday, 17 August, Angus' regiment arrived at Dunkeld.[34] Concerned that the Jacobites might be close at hand, they stood to their arms that night, being within the walls near to the cathedral and at the mansion belonging to the Marquis of Atholl. Their night was undisturbed.[35]

31 Mackay, *Memoirs*, pp.68–69.

32 Balfour-Maitland, 'Estates', I, p.220.

33 *RPCS*, 14, pp.34, 20.

34 Mackay, *Memoirs*, p.68.

35 *Exact Narrative of the conflict at Dunkeld* (Edinburgh, 1689), p.1; Balfour-Maitland, 'Estates', I, p.223.

A trooper in Eglington's Horse later wrote, 'The toun heiring of yr coming all the men went out of it ... marching into Cannon's army.' The townsmen told Cannon that there would only be one regiment at Dunkeld.[36] Cannon learnt that Angus' regiment were stationed in Dunkeld, apparently with 'a designe to destroy the country of Atholl'.[37] The Jacobites 'had not such prejudice at any of the forces at this regiment, whom they called the Cameronian Regiment, whose oppression against all such as were not of their own sentiment made them generally hated and feared in the northern counties'.[38] Apparently, 'the noise wheirof immediately alarmed the whole country, who heard that they were Cameronians and Argyll's men, names most odious to them ... they were come with a peremptory commission to burn and kill all before them without disturbance, which was firmly believed'. The Cameronians had been virulent enemies of the Episcopalians following their persecution in the 1670s and 1680s, though Cleland denied that this was their aim, 'he came to exude King William's commands, that he was not to plunder but to impress ane indemnity, and treat all as enemies, who would refuse it'.[39]

Next day, Sunday 18th, the Jacobites began to appear on the hills around the town. As yet they were only in relatively small numbers. Lieutenant John Blackadder of Angus' regiment, stated that there were only groups of 20–30 men in sight. Angus' men were busy that day in defending the town by constructing entrenchments in Atholl's property. Where there were breaches in the walls, loose stones were placed there. Dykes were scaffolded. In all this they were undisturbed.[40]

The Jacobites who were sighted were probably scouting parties who noted the presence of the regiment in the town and reported this news back to Cannon. Cameron later wrote that the latter 'had intelligence that the Cameronian Regiment, so called from their following one Cameron, ane extravagant Fanatick Preacher ... commanded by Lieutenant Colonel Cleland, had taken possession of Dunkeld ... To prevent this, he resolved to dislodge them, and might have easily affected it'.[41]

That afternoon, the Jacobites had been building up their strength near to Dunkeld. According to Blackadder, 60 or 80 men were now visible at a distance on the hill, but another account puts their numbers at 300 and they were on the hills to the north of Dunkeld. It was customary in siege warfare for the besiegers to offer parley to the defenders as a prelude to any armed confrontation and this convention was followed here. A Jacobite fixed a white cloth to the top of a halberd (he may have been a sergeant and this weapon may have been taken from the field of Killiecrankie), and also brought a letter for the commanding officer with him.[42]

36 G. Neil (ed.), 'Journal of a Soldier in the Earl of Eglington's Troop of Horse', *Transactions of the Glasgow Archaeological Society*, I (1868), p.44.

37 Cameron, *Memoirs*, p.286.

38 Mackay, *Memoirs*, p.69.

39 *HMC Athole*, p.43.

40 *Exact Narrative*, p.1; Balfour-Maitland, 'Estates', I, p.223.

41 Cameron, *Memoirs*, p.286.

42 Balfour-Maitland, 'Estates', I, p.223; *Exact Narrative*, p.1.

Cleland, the commander, received the man and read the letter. It claimed that the Jacobites asked 'Whether ye come for Peace or War, and do certifie you, that if ye burn anyone's house there, will we destroy you'. Blackadder stated that the letter was 'full of great threatening and boastings' and that his commander answered it 'briskly'. In detail, Cleland stated, 'We are faithfull subjects to King William and Queen Mary … if you who send these threats, shall make any hostile appearance, we will burn all that belongs to you and otherwise chastise you as you deserve.' Cleland also had the government's Act of Indemnity, offering pardon to anyone submitting to their authority, read out at the market cross, though the intended audience for this is unclear unless the message bearer was still there and it was for his benefit and those to whom he might later relay it.[43]

More practically, Cleland must have realised that by his act of defiance, an attack on the town would probably not be long delayed. Without knowing what numbers would be opposed to his men, he may have feared the worst. At some point in that day he sent a messenger, almost certainly on horseback, to Perth, about 10 miles to the south-east, to ask Ramsay for reinforcements, stating that the Jacobites were 'coming down upon him'.[44]

On the next morning, that is to say, Monday 19 August, there was good news for Cleland and his men. Ramsay, in charge of the troops at Perth, had sent cavalry (for speed) to Cleland's aid. Or had he? According to a trooper in the force, they 'marched without orders of the comidant' and did so at night time. Once they were within two miles of Dunkeld, they halted to refresh the horses and set sentries to watch until daylight. The force was led by Lord Cardross and consisted of the troop of Grubbit's Horse, a troop of Eglington's Horse (on 3-4 June Grubbit's had apparently 50 men and Eglington's 41) and three troops of Cardross' dragoons; a total of five troops of cavalrymen, possibly numbering 500 men in all, but more likely was only about 200. One estimate of the government's complete strength at Dunkeld was between 1,400–1,500, though this is almost certainly an exaggeration. The cavalry marched that morning to the town and drew up at its rear in a barley field. Cleland and his officers showed the newly arrived officers where the Jacobites were, on the hills above the town. Apparently there were 400 Jacobites within a quarter of a mile of the town and more in the hills; some of the former were allegedly 'so neare as they wer heard to call us traitors and rebells'. Meanwhile the troopers entered the town and took refreshment, though were told to be ready for action at the sound of a trumpet.[45]

The trumpet call came and two troops of Cardross' cavalry; Bennet's and Agnew's troops, marched out of town towards the Jacobites. They reconnoitred the fields near to the town and marched towards the hills. According to a trooper of Agnew's, 'So soon as they noticing us advancing towards ym retired, all in throw a wood, we persewing ym'. They seized four or six Jacobites. Seven or eight horses were also taken, but they could see

43 *Ibid.*; *Exact Narrative*, pp.1–2.

44 Balfour-Maitland, 'Estates', I, p.223; NRS, GD26/9/229.

45 Balfour-Maitland, 'Estates', I, p.223; *Exact Narrative*, p.2; *RPCS*, 13, p.lviii, and 14, p.82; Neil, 'Journal of a Soldier', p.44; NRS, GD26/9/229.

no one else, so returned to the town that night. At that time, Cleland learnt that the fiery cross (the traditional device of summoning the Highlanders to gather) was being used to summon Jacobite supporters to their cause. Combat could not be long delayed.[46]

That afternoon, Ramsay wrote from Perth the following letter to Cardross:

> My Lord,
> I was uneasie till I heard from yow, but knowing of yow being there and of your good conducke, it quieted me much. I think these dragoons and Horse can be of little use in these grounds, so I thincke yow lordship may come back here with them. Lieutenant Colonel Cleland says he wold be able to maintain his poste if he got provisions and ammunition. He will be able, I hope, to do it, for I have sent him part of bothe this day with yowr captain-lieutenant, and shall send him more the morrow.
>
> I am, your lordship …
>
> My lord, stay not on that side of the water the toune is on, but stay a mile on the other side of the water till day and then come to this toune tomorrow.[47]

It is not certain when this letter arrived, perhaps on the morning of the 20th. There is no suggestion as to how Cardross responded to it. Nor is there any evidence that the ammunition promised by Ramsay ever arrived, but it suggests that Cleland's men had little.

Ramsay also wrote to Lanier, who was now at Coupar, letting him know of the Jacobite advance towards Dunkeld and where they could defeat Angus' regiment there.[48] Ramsay believed that Angus would be defeated and asked Lanier what his orders were. Lanier did not know the country and delayed acting until he had reached Perth.[49]

Jacobite strength near Dunkeld had been building up. Apparently on Tuesday morning 'many people appeared upon the tops of the hills' and in the woods; variously estimated at between 500–600 to 1,000. On 20 August one Alexander Stewart was in charge of the Jacobites there and he sent posts to hasten the remaining forces there. These were 600 Athollmen, two companies of Strathsay's infantry and some horse. Jacobite campfires were visible. The Jacobites began firing on their enemies. At eight in the morning, Cleland's force marched out of the town to engage them, and Jacobite numbers were thought to number about the same as his own. A small number of Eglington's Horse under a lieutenant acted as scouts. They had some infantry with them to cover their retreat if needed. Captain George Monroe, with 40 fusiliers, 15 halberdiers and 30 Horse spearheaded the force. Then there was Sir James Agnew with 20 dragoons. Then more of Angus' regiment; Ensign Lockhart with yet another 30 halberdiers. Apparently 'the halberds were excellent weapons against Highlanders' swords and targets in case they should rush

46 Balfour-Maitland, 'Estates', I, p.223, *Exact Narrative*, p.2; *RPCS*, 14, p.82; Neil, 'Journal of a Soldier', p.44.
47 Fraser, *Melvilles and Leslies*, II, p.119.
48 Mackay, *Memoirs*, p.69.
49 *Ibid.*, p.69.

upon the shot, with their accustomed fury'. Captains John Campbell and Robert Hume, 'two brave young gentlemen' then led 100 fusiliers. Captains Borthwick and Harries with 200 musketeers followed them. An unspecified number of pikemen made up the rear. Left in the town, manning the dykes, were 150 men. These may have included Lieutenant Blackadder for he only stated about the ensuing action that there was some skirmishing between small parties of each side. Either he had no experience or knowledge of these encounters or deemed them to be insubstantial.[50]

It must have been a leisurely march because the same account which cited eight o'clock as the time of their marching out claimed that it was not until six hours later that the Jacobites were found. According to the trooper in Agnew's troop, the advance force was 14 men from that troop and 14 from Livingstone's. Two or three hundred Jacobites were concealed in a glen in ambush. They opened fire at long range. Cornet Livingstone of Grubbit's Horse was unfortunate to be wounded in the knee, and between two and four of his troopers were shot, but none fatally. The cavalry then may have retired or held their ground, accounts differing, and Monroe advanced with his company of 40 fusiliers and sent a volley of musket balls towards the Jacobites, several of whom fell; perhaps as many as 21 being killed (a large number if true), which led to the latter retreating to join their main party of about 600 men. They rallied on the next hill, however. The wounded cavalrymen returned to Dunkeld to have their injuries dressed.[51]

These were not the only Jacobites in view. They also included cavalry as well as infantry. The main body of Cleland's troops advanced against the Jacobites and the anonymous trooper, whose wound had been seen to and returned for more, wrote, 'We lying clos ower against other, skirmishing and fyring all yt day with little loss'. Cleland ordered Monroe to send a sergeant and six men to a house near the wood to dislodge the 20 Jacobites who he had seen there. This feat accomplished, albeit with three men wounded, one of whom later died, the little army then retired in good order to Dunkeld. This was probably because night was falling. The cavalry had apparently been eager for a fight but could not do so as the enemy had withdrawn. Retreat was also imperative because the cavalry left first, followed by the infantry though Blackadder claimed the horsemen came away after only one or two hours in the field and 'our lieutenant colonel did the like'. Losing so many men made their continuance in the open dangerous. Young William Sandilands, an ensign, had been particularly active, firing his gun 11 times. Apparently 30 Jacobites had become casualties claimed a Jacobite prisoner on the following day.[52] A few prisoners were taken, 'who denyed their being concerned with them, though I doubt not but they were'. They also informed Cardross that the Athollmen and Strathspey men would arrive on the next today and then on that day after Cannon and others.[53]

50 *Exact Narrative*, p.2.

51 *Ibid.*, pp.2–3; Neil, 'Journal of a Soldier', p.45.

52 *Exact Narrative*, p.3; Balfour-Maitland, 'Estates', I, p.223; *RPCS*, 14, p.82; Neil, 'Journal of a soldier', p.45.

53 NRS, GD26/9/229.

Cleland received the second of two messages sent by Ramsay for Cardross. These were that the cavalry led by Cardross were to return to Perth as soon as possible.

Ramsay wrote, that afternoon:

> My Lord,
> I desir'd yowr lordship last night to retire the Horse and Dragoons under your Command. Except yow have orders from some generall person to the Contrarie yow must do soe yet or be answerable for what shal fall out. Major General Lanier knows of Angus Regiment being there. I had a letter from him last night which acquaints me of the bodie of the enemy moving towards Atholl, one letts me know he intends to move this way, yet I thincke it fits yow yet retire, this is from my lord, yow lordships most humble servant …
>
> My lord, take such measures that the enemy come not betwixt us and yow and so stop your passadge.[54]

Mackay thought that Ramsay did not think that the cavalry he had sent would be of use in defending the town. Yet Mackay later wrote that Ramsay should either have marched all his forces from Perth to Dunkeld 'to maintain the post if he thought it of consequence'. Or he should have given Cleland orders 'if he found not the place tenable against such numbers as he could expect against him' to retreat up the river.[55]

On receipt of the first letter, Cleland had informed Ramsay that he had been 'engaged with the Enemy, and it was necessary he should stay'. The second message could not be resisted, however, and so by the day's end the five troops of cavalry departed for Perth. Cardross wrote, 'I came unwillingly away but behaved to obey my reiterated orders'. The trooper wrote, 'he would not allow of yt, but ordrd us in all haist to return wt the king's standart'. Blackadder stated, 'Our men were mightily discourag'd to hear this'. Cleland considered that the cavalry were too few against the numerous enemy. Once the cavalry had gone, some of the officers and men of the remaining battalion suggested that they should follow suit, on the basis that they were in an 'open, useless, place, ill provided of all things and in the midst of Enemies growing still to greater numbers'. This latter they knew because the vanguard of Cannon's main force had been sighted that afternoon, just before light faded.[56]

Initially, Cleland 'charged those retreating dragoons with the loss of his regiment'. To combat the wish for departure, Cleland 'compelled them and told them, that tho every man went away, he resolved to stay himself alone'. Apart from this moral blackmail, some of his officers used 'Arguments of Honour' that every soldier, but especially the officers, were expected to hold. The officers then assembled their horses and shot them in order that their men not doubt their staying and that 'they would run all hazards with them'.

54 Fraser, *Melvilles and Leslies*, II, p.120.

55 Mackay, *Memoirs*, p.71.

56 NRS, GD26/9/251; Balfour-Maitland, 'Estates', I, pp.221–223.

These actions and words were effective. The troops stood at their arms that night in Atholl's house and gardens.[57]

The battle was to be soon at hand, so we shall now examine those forces participating in it.

Lord Angus' Regiment

Officer commanding (Captain unless otherwise stated)	Lieutenant	Ensign	NCOs and drummers	Privates
Colonel the Earl of Angus (absentee)	__ Walsh	Robert Crichton	7	57
Lieutenant Colonel William Cleland	Andrew Gilchrist	John Pringle	7	54
Major James Henderson	Henry Stuart	John Boyd	7	61
Ker of Kersland	William Oliphant	Hugh Ferguson	7	61
George Monroe	Charles Dalzell	William Campbell	6	57
Roy Campbell	__ Hutchinson	James Campbell	7	59
William Hay	John Forester	Francis Nasmith	6	57
Dhu Campbell	William Cathcart		7	57
William Borthwick	Nathaniel Johnston		7	47
Robert Hume	William Campbell		6	57
__ Ballantine	James Cranston	John Lang	6	57
John Haldane	__ Veitch	John Cleghorn	7	57
William Herries	Robert Tait	Andrew Derriston	4	61
James Lindsay	James Ballantyne	John Wilson	4	60
Ninian Steel	John Blackadder	John Kirkland	6	57
James Gilchrist	__ Calder	Archibald Wilson	7	57
John Mathison	William Clarke	Francis Hislop	7	60
John Caldwell	Adam Hackness	__ McCulloch	7	57
John Stephenson	John Stewart	John Hay	6	62
William Grieve	James Aikeman	__ Stephenson	7	59

Gideon Elliott was the surgeon and Alexander Shields the chaplain.[58]

Total strength at muster on 10 July 1689 was 61 officers and 1,281 men, the latter including 39 sergeants, 51 corporals and 37 drummers with 1,154 privates.[59]

Unusually, the regiment had 20 companies rather than the standard 12. Its strength at Dunkeld has been variously estimated. Cameron states it was 1,200 men strong.[60] The contemporary history, written by the victors, states there were between 700 and 800 men who arrived at Dunkeld on 17 August

57 Balfour-Maitland, 'Estates', I, pp.223–224; *Exact Narrative*, pp.3–4; *RPCS*, 14, p.82; Mackay, *Memoirs*, p.71.

58 Dalton, *Army Lists*, III, pp.87; *NRS*, E100/13.

59 NRS, E100/13.

60 Cameron, *Memoirs*, p.286.

1689.[61] On 6 July the Privy Council noted that they had 1,140 men, but this may well have been reduced in the subsequent seven weeks due to illness and desertion.[62] A victorious army often downplays its strength to inflate its victory whilst a defeated one inflates it to mitigate its own defeat. However there is another possibility: as we have seen, reinforcements had arrived – and then departed after briefly seeing action – and it may well be that the higher number as stated by Cameron refers to his enemies' strength when at their temporary numerical height.

The other point is whether all of the regiment was present at Dunkeld. On 8 August Mackay wrote that it had been divided into two battalions, one stationed at Perth and another at Stirling. It is possible that only one battalion was present at Dunkeld, which would suggest that numbers might only have been in the region of 600 men. We know from officer casualties that the following companies were present: Cleland's, Henderson's, Kerr's, Campbell's (not stated which), Hay's, Steel's, Caldwell's, Borthwick's and Monroe's. So it is possible that only the battalion from Perth was present at the battle, but there can be no certainty as to this and therefore no clear estimate of how strong Cleland was. There was no artillery and no cavalry.

Allegations were made against Cleland's running of the regiment. He was alleged to have had the men train with insufficient ammunition, march on the Sabbath day, sleep in fields rather than in proper quarters. He was accused of pocketing the money he should have used to pay for the men's hats and stockings and kept them short of food and ammunition, all of which 'are very discouraging to many of ye officers and soldiers and my Lord Angus'.[63] How true these are is another question, for Cleland was never in a position to counter them.

Jacobite Strength

Blackadder believed the Jacobites were between 3,000–4,000, and claimed a prisoner stated it was the latter number.[64] Another estimate was 4,000.[65] The anonymous account stated the Jacobites were 'repute in all above 5,000'.[66] Cameron has the lowest number, 'now declined to about three thousand men'.[67] The units in the Jacobite army at this point in the campaign were as follows, but the numbers cited below had declined prior to the battle.

61 *Exact Narrative*, p.1
62 *RPCS*, 13, p.lviii.
63 NLS, MS 542, f10–12.
64 Balfour-Maitland, 'Estates', I, p.223.
65 *RPCS*, 13, p.82.
66 *Exact Narrative*, p.4.
67 Cameron, *Memoirs*, p.286.

Unit	Strength
Stewarts of Appin	200
MacGregors	Not given
Camerons	620
MacPhersons	250
MacDonalds of Glencoe	Not given
Athollmen	600
Fergusons	Not given
Frasers	120
Gordons of Strathdown and Glenlivet	Not given
MacLeans	200–500
Irish regiment	300
MacDonalds of Glengarry	400
MacDonalds of Clanranalds	400
Sir Donald MacDonald	500
Four Cavalry Troops	300

Strengths given are the numbers stated just after Killiecrankie; that of the Irish regiment is the number given at the previous battle and are probably not those they enjoyed at Dunkeld; that for the Irish perhaps lower as the cavalry is not known to have taken any casualties at Killiecrankie whereas the infantry may well have done.[68]

The Jacobites, unlike their enemies, also had artillery. Cameron refers to their having 'several cannons and field pieces which had been taken from the enemy'. These were presumably the three guns taken from Mackay's army at Killiecrankie. However, as Cameron quickly added, 'he had not so many balls as he had guns'. It is not known whether he had any men who knew how to fire these guns, either.[69]

Cleland's men were outnumbered by at least four to one and quite possibly more. It may have looked hopeless and in the open field would have been. Yet small numbers could prevail against larger in defensive positions; the defence of Glasgow in 1679 and Bristol in 1685 had shown that. At least they had adequate time to make what defensive preparations they could. According to Blackadder, he was not dismayed. He posted his men behind the ditches and dykes that he had had erected previously. Others were posted in the cathedral and Atholl's house. Some soldiers were posted in forward positions which had escape routes. Captain Hay and Ensign Lockhart went to a little hill. An officer and 28 men advanced to a stone dyke at the foot of a hill.[70] Another contemporary noted that the defenders had 'advantages of walls, hedges, ditches, houses'.[71] Yet the defences were far from adequate, Mackay writing, 'all their defence was but low gardens, in most places not above four feet high'.[72]

68 Cameron, *Memoirs*, pp.266, 283, *RPCS*, 13 p.82.
69 *Ibid.*, p.286.
70 *Exact Narrative*, p.4; Balfour-Maitland, 'Estates', I, p.224.
71 *Memoir of Lord Dundee*, p.35.
72 Mackay, *Memoirs*, p.69.

Cannon's plan was to launch a frontal attack on the town. This was criticised in retrospect by Sir Ewan Cameron, admittedly a critic of his, writing:

> He resolved to dislodge them, and might have easily effected it, had he used a little policy, and sent a small party of five or six hundred men to have trained them out of the town, where they were strongly fortified, and kept the army att a short distance, as he could easily have done, without the enemy's getting any intelligence, the people thereabouts being all his friends.[73]

At dawn on that day, Wednesday 21 August, the Jacobite army appeared on the hills above the town. Their baggage was in the hills to the west, en route to Atholl. Apparently they had a train of 1,000 horses, taken from Mackay's army at Killiecrankie. Before seven in the morning, the Jacobite artillery was moved down the hills and towards the town. It was accompanied by 100 armoured soldiers, and a regiment of infantry. Two troops of horse marched around the town and took up a position to the south-west, between the ford and the cathedral. Another two troops of horse stood to the north-east of the town, apparently they 'shewed much eagerness to encourage and push on the Foot' into action; possibly there may have been a reluctance among some of the infantry for the fight.[74] Blackadder believed that the Jacobite cavalry was also posted so as to cut off any retreat that the battalion might make, 'which they nothing doubted of'.[75] According to one source two guns employed by the Jacobites made a breach on one of the town's defences. Afterwards they fell silent.[76]

The attack, when it came, was unsubtle. Blackadder wrote 'the enemy approached very fast, the Highlanders came running on like desperate Villains, firing only once, and then came on with Sword and Target'. Cameron wrote, 'he … marched his army … in a full body towards their trenches'.[77] John Cameron., the chief's son, later recalled, 'I had the honour to attack at the head of my ffather's men'.[78] Such a charge had been made successfully at Killiecrankie, but against resolute troops under cover, behind defensive works, these tactics were inappropriate. Fighting in a built-up area was unusual.

As the Jacobites approached, there were exchanges of musketry. Hay's men, who had been defending part of the town, fired on the attackers but were driven back, 'not being able to sustain their great number and fierceness'. Hay was the only casualty, among his company, however. At another point, the Jacobites in armour and another regiment, were attacking elsewhere, but 'after they had entertain'd them briskly with their fire, from a pretty space, the Rebels forc'd the Dyke and obliging them to retire, firing from one little dyke

73 Cameron, *Memoirs*, p.286.

74 *Exact Narrative*, p.4.

75 Balfour-Maitland, 'Estates', I, p.224.

76 *Ibid.*, p.221.

77 Balfour-Maitland, 'Estates', I, p.224; Cameron, *Memoirs*, p.286.

78 <www.lochiel.net/archgives/arch173.html>

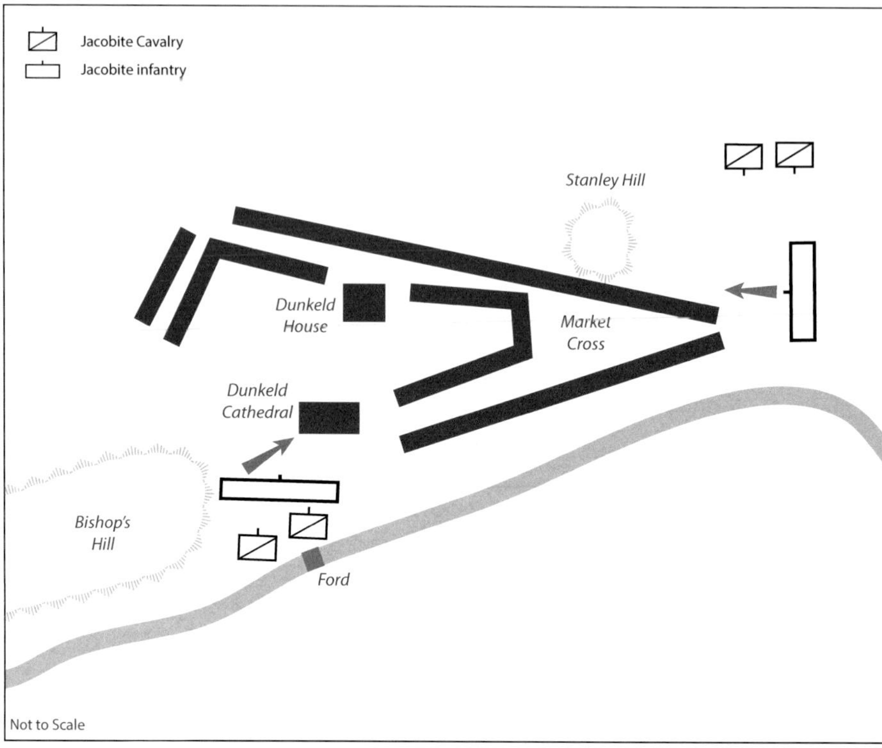

Map 3 Dunkeld and the approximate positions of two of the major Jacobite attacks on 21 August 1689.

N.B. No contemporary map exists so this is an estimate based on contemporary written accounts.

to another, and at length to betake themselves to the House and Yard dykes'.[79] MacLean's men had been the first Jacobite unit to attack, and once they had beaten the defenders from the walls, helped each other over them.[80]

Elsewhere, a lieutenant and his 18 men at the eastern end of the town, advanced three men to fire on the Jacobites and then retreated. The lieutenant burnt some houses and then joined his men as they withdrew. Lieutenant Stewart was defending a barricade near to the market cross and saw some of his comrades retreating. He had his men follow suit. In doing so, he was killed as 'a multitude of the Rebels [came] upon them'. Blackadder wrote they were 'pressing in upon us to the very cross in the middle of the town, where another party of our men fired on them, and then retired in order'.[81] The defenders were being pushed back, but were able to do so in good order whilst inflicting casualties on their enemies, but they could not retreat forever. A stand would have to be made.

Cameron described the battle rather differently and, from the Jacobite viewpoint, more positively as they: 'beat the enemy's out-guards, and entering the town in the very face of their fire, without ant thing to cover them, brock through all opposition, and rushed in upon such of them as were posted in the lesser houses, where they putt all thy found to the sword without any mercy'.[82]

79 *Exact Narrative*, p.4.
80 MacPherson, *Original Papers*, p.371.
81 *Exact Narrative*, pp.4–5; Balfour-Maitland, 'Estates', I, p.224.
82 Cameron, *Memoirs*, p.286.

At the west end of the town, Lieutenant Forrester and ensign Campbell's 24 men fired sharply on the Jacobites who had by then taken possession of a house. Large numbers of Jacobites attacked them and forced them back. All the outer posts had now fallen. Cameron later wrote: 'Never was there, on any occasion, more resolution and less conduct shown than in this; and so surprizeing was their boldness, that they stood naked in the open streets exposed to the enemy's fire, and killed them in the windows, till they cleared the town of them.'[83] There was desperate fighting in several places in the town. One was at Atholl's house. Cameron recalled, we 'drove them into the Marquess of Athol's house, which being a strong place, they were not to be beaten from that post so easily.'[84] Blackadder also described a successful stand of his men as the Jacobites: 'came swarming in on all heads, and gave a desperate assault in four places all at once, first firing their Guns, and then running in on us with their swords and targets; but it pleased God they were also bravely repulsed, our men still firing on them, where they came on thickest.'[85]

There was also fighting close to the river. It seems probable that the cathedral was garrisoned. Although the cathedral had become a parish church after the reformation, part of the cathedral, adjoining the west end of the church, remained in ruins and its windows were at ideal heights for musketeers to fire from in relative safety. Furthermore, there is open ground all round this strongpoint, making it ideal as a defensive position for troops with firearms. Muskets were fired at point blank range, 'the shot liberally pour'd in their Faces'. It was chaos, 'confusion grew so great, which was augmented by the smoke of the Town set on fire in many places, that they [the Jacobites] fell foule upon one another'. Melee took place as well, with the Jacobites attacking sword in hand and their enemies resisting with pikes and halberds and so 'returned their Blows with interest'.[86] Blackadder commended the men's courage, stating that veteran soldiers there claimed 'They never saw men fight better; for there was not the least sign of fear to be seen on any of them; everyone performing his part gallantly'. He ascribed this to 'the Lord wonderfully assisting our men with courage'.[87]

One of the defenders' greatest losses, as had been the case with the Jacobites at Killiecrankie, was that of their leader. At the beginning of the battle, Cleland had been 'going up and down encouraging his men'. The Jacobites were using their muskets as well as swords as some fired from houses as well as from the hills. According to one account, 'And by two shots at once, through the head and another through the liver, the brave lieutenant colonel was kill'd; while he was visiting and exhorting the officers and souldiers at their several posts. He attempted to get into the house that the soldiers might not be discouraged at the sight of his dead body: but fell by the way'.[88] Blackadder stated that this

83 *Exact Narrative*, p.5; Cameron, *Memoirs*, p.286.
84 Cameron, *Memoirs*, p.286.
85 Balfour-Maitland, 'Estates', I, p.224.
86 *Exact Narrative*, p.5; Clarke, *James II*, II, p.354.
87 Balfour-Maitland, 'Estates', I, p.223.
88 *Exact Narrative*, p.5.

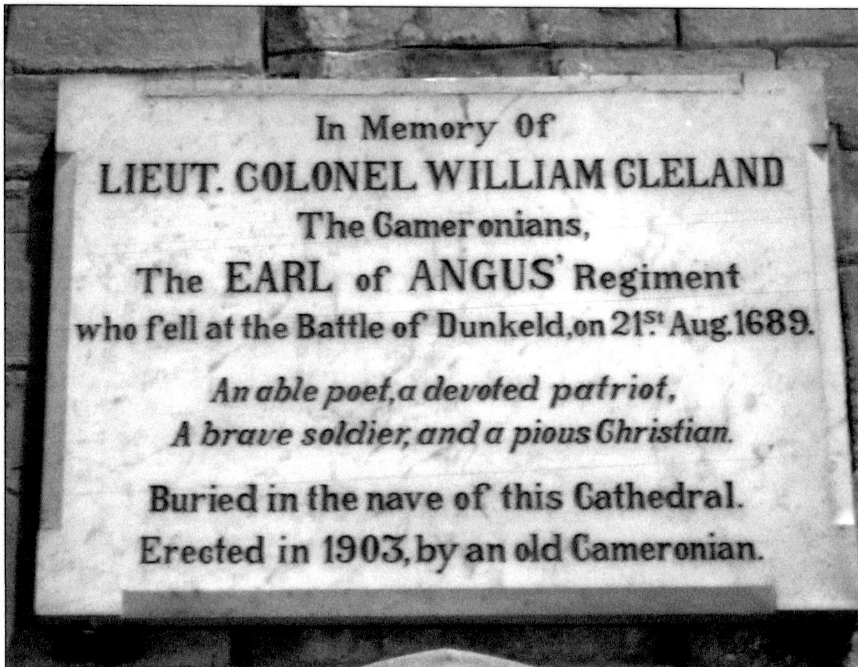

Memorial to Lieutenant Colonel Cleland. (Author, 2017)

death 'which is never enough to be lamented'.[89] Cameron referred to him as being a brave man.[90]

This took place only an hour into the battle. The second in command, Major Henderson, was also struck down by Jacobite gunfire. Wounded by several musket balls, he was incapacitated and died four days later. Other officers also became casualties. Captain Caldwell was shot in the breast and was unlikely to recover. Captain Borthwick was shot in the arm, and whilst his fellow captain, Steel, was wounded, he was patched up and returned to his post. Captain Monroe, in the meantime, took over the command.[91] Possibly he was the senior captain, and was ranked second on the list of the regiment's captains.

Monroe left his own post to the care of Lieutenant Stewart. Finding his men being galled by musketry from Jacobites located in houses, he had his pikemen assemble in small parties with burning faggots 'on pike ends to fire their houses, and where found keys locked and burnt all within: which raised a hideous noise from these wretches and the fire'. Sixteen Jacobites perished thus. The inhabitants had long since fled, either to the surrounding fields or sheltered in the cathedral.[92]

Yet it is possible that the Jacobites may have been on the point of victory, despite the undoubted strength of Atholl's house. According to Cameron, 'their ammunition was all spent to a shott, and they upon the very point of surrendering att discretion, when the General commanded his men, even

89 Balfour-Maitland, 'Estates', I, p.224.
90 Cameron, *Memoirs*, p.287.
91 *Exact Narrative*, p.5.
92 *Ibid.*, p.6.

against their own inclinations, to retire'.[93] Another account noted that the powder was almost exhausted and bullets were long gone, too. But instead of contemplating surrender, to deal with this crisis, men cut lead off the house roofs, melted it down in furrows on the ground and cut it into bullets for instant use.[94] This is possible, for this account states that the battle continued until 11 o'clock. There had been 'continual thundering of shot from both sides and flames and smoak, and hideous cryes filling the air'.[95]

The wind was clearly blowing through the town because apparently all but three houses there were damaged by fire.[96] MacPherson's account has the Jacobites retreating due to their ammunition being exhausted.[97] Another account suggests an alternative, or at least an equal possibility for the battle's ending with the attackers withdrawing: 'At length the Rebels, wearied with so many fruitless and expensive Assaults; and finding no abatement of the Courage or Diligence of their Adversaries who treated them with continual shot from all their posts, they gave over and fell back and ran to the hills in great confusion.'[98]

Blackadder stated that the attackers 'found themselves necessitate to flee back on all hands, leaving a number of dead carcasses behind'. He also recorded that some fled into houses 'to fire upon us, our Men went to set fire to the houses and burnt many of them'.[99]

There appear to have been attempts by some of the Jacobite officers to have recommenced the attack, according to prisoners taken afterwards. The men refused because of the ferocity of their opponents, 'they could fight against men, but it was not fit to fight against devils' or as Blackadder wrote, 'they said we were mad and desperate men'.[100]

It was not absolutely certain that there would not be another attack. The defences were repaired and seats from the church were used to plug any gaps that could be found. Trees from a small hill, which in the battle had provided some Jacobites with cover, were cut down and pressed into service, too. It was only after these precautions had been taken that there was the luxury of celebration. News of the fighting was despatched to Perth.[101]

The defenders rejoiced. They beat their drums, flourished their flags and shouted their contempt for their enemies. God was praised for their deliverance, too, as Blackadder stated, 'Our men gave a great shout and threw their caps in the air, and then all joined in offering up praises to God for a considerable time for so miraculous a victory'. Psalms were sung. He added 'It was not by might, or Power, nor by Conduct, (our best officers being killed) …' The men's courage was also stressed by Blackadder.[102]

93 Cameron, *Memoirs*, pp.287.
94 *Exact Narrative*, p.7.
95 *Ibid.*, p.6.
96 *Dunkeld its Straths and Glens* (Dunkeld: A. MacLean and Son, 1865).
97 MacPherson, *Original Papers*, p.371.
98 *Exact Narrative*, p.6.
99 Balfour-Maitland, 'Estates', I, p.224.
100 *Exact Narrative*, p.6; Balfour-Maitland, 'Estates', I, p.224.
101 *Exact Narrative*, p.7; Balfour-Maitland, 'Estates', I, p.224.
102 *Exact Narrative*, pp.6–7; Balfour-Maitland, 'Estates', I, p.224.

Houses in Dunkeld which survived the battle. (Author, 2017)

William's Force's Casualties

Several officers were killed: Cleland, Henderson and Captain Wall. Captains Hay, Caldwick, Steel and Borthwick were wounded. About 8–10 privates were killed.[103] A newspaper reported furthermore that 14 men had been wounded.[104] Cameron thought that the government forces had been severely mauled: 'There were above three hundred of them killed, and a great many more wounded ... the greatest part of the slaughter was of those who were slain att first in the little and less tenable houses of the toun'.[105] Another Jacobite account claimed 120–200 dead.[106]

The regimental muster roll noted that one man from Ker's company had been killed in the battle and that one man from Campbell's company had been killed and another wounded.[107] Clearly more were slain than these two, but it would seem that numbers were remarkably low.

Jacobite casualties

There is a great deal of variance with the losses suffered by the Jacobite army. The government's newspaper stated that 150 had been killed and several wounded.[108] Higher estimates were also given; about 300 slain claimed a contemporary account of the battle.[109] Cameron dismissed such high figures and claimed, 'Many of the Highlanders were wounded, but not above eighteen or twenty of them killed, which looked like a miracle'. According to him, the reason was their enemies' faulty marksmanship, 'the enemy's shott somewhat resembled thunder, in this, that it had more noise than effect; for, observing that the Highlanders put their guns to their eye, and that they seldome missed their mark, they had not courage to expose themselves, but shott at random, whereby they did little execution'.[110] MacPherson states that two captains, a captain lieutenant and other officers of MacLean's regiment were dead and their colonel had had his leg broken by a musket ball.[111] Scottish horse and dragoons from Perth scoured the countryside after the battle and found more Jacobite corpses: presumably men who died from their wounds.[112]

There had also been significant damage to the town itself. Apparently the Jacobites 'kindled some houses in other quarters' and Cleland's men had done likewise elsewhere. Thomas Young had lost his brewery in the town and

---

103 *RPCS*, 14, p.82.

104 *The London Gazette*, 2484, 29 Aug.–2 Sept. 1689.

105 Cameron, *Memoirs*, p.287.

106 MacPherson, *Original Papers*, p.371.

107 NRS, E100/13.

108 *The London Gazette*, 2484, 29 Aug.–2 Sept. 1689.

109 *Exact Narrative*, p.7.

110 Cameron, *Memoirs*, p.287.

111 MacPherson, *Original Papers*, p.371.

112 Balfour-Maitland, 'Estates', I, p.226.

Memorial to soldiers killed at Dunkeld. (Author, 2017)

so could not pay his tack duty normally payable. In all only Atholl's house and those belonging to Mr Bennermane and Mr Barter were unburnt.[113]

The Jacobites had been defeated but their forces had not been routed. The battle served to blunt their offensive yet again, following Cannon's previous refusal to engage Mackay and further weakened his leadership. Admittedly a frontal, unimaginative assault on a defended place against resolute defenders was never going to be easy. Cannon took that chance, though and in doing so failed. Yet it was not wholly successful for the government either. More could have been made of this battle had Lanier and Ramsay marched towards Dunkeld in order to turn a Jacobite setback into a rout. Neither had Mackay's confidence and so missed a chance to end the campaign there and then. Mackay later wrote tersely 'they behaved well against the rebels at Dunkeld'.[114]

Cardross and his cavalry returned to Dunkeld on the day after the battle, arriving in the afternoon. He saw that the Jacobites had retired a little to the north of the town. When Jacobite scouts noted his arrival, they left and the main body retreated to Atholl thereafter. On the Thursday morning, 100 infantrymen from Perth arrived to reinforce the Dunkeld garrison.[115]

---

113 *HMC Athole*, p.43; *RPCS*, 16, p.477.

114 Thomas Carter, *Historical Record of the 26th or Cameronian Regiment* (London: Byfield, Stanford & Co., 1867), p.15.

115 NRS, GD26/9/251.

they laid down their arms to Mackay's men at Blair Castle.[129] Even Cameron contacted the government, offering his clansmen fight for William and Mary.[130] The campaign was not over, but it was running out of steam and the brief momentum it had enjoyed in the summer was now a thing of the past.

In discussion on 14 September over the need for new garrisons in Scotland, it was noted that: 'any new insurrection of the Highlands which is not much fared since most of the leading men of the clans have accepted the benefit if the Indemnity as have also many of the common people and have delivered up their arms to General Mackay and taken the oaths'.[131]

In the meantime Mackay marched to join Lanier at Brechin, keeping Livingstone and his cavalry (his own regiment of Horse, six troops of Horse and three of Cardross' dragoons) in the north to overawe any potential Jacobites there. Mackay was in Perth on 26 August with Hayford's and Colchester's Horse and three troops of Scottish horse. Joining with the forces at Perth, after leaving an infantry regiment and five troops of cavalry there, they marched into Atholl on 27 August, 'threatning to leave not a standing house in Athole, and to burn and destroy all the corn if the House of Blair, where he designed a garrison, should be burned by the enemy'. He made this well known: 'I have sent them word that if they should offer to burn the castle of Blair, I shall not leave a hous standing betwixt it and Dunkell.' Mackay had a great distrust of the Athollmen in their allegiances.[132] At least he had the co-operation of the sheriff of Forfar in supplying 400 horses to transport his force's baggage.[133]

Destruction of Jacobite property by the soldiery was not uncommon. At Perth in September, it was reported by Sir Patrick Murray:

> The souldiers did great abuses their and in the neighbourhood during their abode, pillaging houses, seizing cattell and carrying in vast quantities of shorn cornes, notwithstanding their was abundance of forage and provisions layd into their commissary … in his [Mackay's] march to Dunkeld and Blair, he had burned numerous places, and his soldiers everywhere broke and pillaged all within doors, destroyed the cornes and all they could reach without they stript clothes of such as mett them.

Mackay took 200 cows and 200 sheep near Atholl for the army and even those who were not Jacobites 'were treated with equal severity with the others. The soldiers seize everything at their pleasure'.[134]

In October there was a report that Major George Wishart of Stathnaver's regiment with three companies of this unit had caused considerable damage to Tarbat's castle. Doors had been broken, furniture damaged, the interior

129 *Exact Narrative*, p.8; Balfour-Maitland, 'Estates', II, pp.1–2; *Calendar of State Papers Domestic of the Reign of William III, Preserved in the Public Record Office, 1689–1690* (London: HMSO, 1913), p.213. Henceforth *CSPD*.

130 Balfour-Maitland, 'Estates', II, p.4.

131 *CSPD, 1689–90*, p.255.

132 Mackay, *Memoirs*, pp.71–72, 269–270.

133 *RPCS*, 14, p.160.

134 Fraser, *Melvilles and Leslies*, III, pp.197–198.

set alight, windows had been smashed. In the parish of Kilmure soldiers had quartered themselves in private houses at entirely the householders' expense.[135] In part this could have been in response to the lack of pay; Glencairn informed Hamilton on 5 August that half of his regiment had not been available for duty as their pay had not arrived and he surmised that this was not unique, 'I believe you will find others heir in the same conditione'.[136] Likewise, on 24 September, Alexander Munro was critical of Angus' regiment, 'They are the worst payed of any of the forces and they are naked, and their heads are blown up with such notions as renders them intolerable … They refuse all subjection to discipline, they run away and return as they please, their own officer complies with them in all their disorders'.[137]

By 30 August Mackay was at Blair Castle, marching via Perth and Dunkeld. He found the castle empty and undamaged. He thought that this was because of the impact of his threatening messages. Whilst there a number of country people arrived, seeking the benefit of the royal pardon, and he told them that they must surrender their arms if they wished to benefit by the indemnity. He was convinced that not all would do so, so he was assured that he would 'be obliged to deale rigorously with such as shalle refuse to cum in upon these termes, for they have shown such enmity to the government already'. Most did so, taking the oath of allegiance and handing in their weapons. As to the Highlanders who had returned home, 'if they let passé the limited time prescrybed by his Majestie for their submission, that it ought not to be given them anymore, but to rouse them out of the nation as the bane thereof'. He regretted that his advice about having frigates and a garrison at Inverlochy to harass the Highlanders in their Western heartlands had been ignored.[138] He assured Atholl that 'I order'd the commander to treat your people civilly, which I am persuaded he shall punctually obey, for I am for no violence but towards the incorrigible'.[139]

Blair Castle was garrisoned by 500–600 regular infantry. It was also strengthened with palisades and a breastwork. The officer in command was ordered to search nearby properties where arms were suspected to be concealed. Mackay thought that the garrisoned castle 'shall secure a great parte of the Highlands' for he thought that Atholl had provided 'a large third part of the rebels strength'.[140] He learnt that there were a number of Jacobites at Struan's house. He sent Colonel Lauder to seize them there. On approaching the house they were fired upon by Captain Patrick Auchmouty's men. Resistance was short, however, and a number of Jacobite leaders were taken: Struan, David Graham, one of Dundee's brothers, and Sir George Barclay, though a few others escaped [141] At Blair, Dundee's death could be confirmed: witnesses told of having seen his body, which included an eye wound.[142]

135 *HMC Athole*, p.43.
136 *HMC Hamilton*, Supplement, p.114.
137 *HMC Roxborough*, p.119.
138 Mackay, *Memoirs*, pp.271–273.
139 NRS, GD112/39/146/10.
140 Mackay, *Memoirs*, pp.276.
141 NRS, GD112/39/146/19, pp.4, 7.
142 *Ibid.*, pp.5, 10.

Due to bad weather, coupled with the lack of baggage horses, tents and provisions, the army did not stay for long at Blair nor send, as intended, a garrison for Finlarig. Lord Cardross at Perth also had great difficulties in procuring horses to carry ammunition and provisions. Such prevented a march to Loch Tay and garrisoning Finlarig, Breadalbane's house, which Mackay thought was 'one of the chiefest and cunningest formentors of the trouble'. In fact bad weather continued for weeks, preventing any further offensive action that year. Mackay intended to return to Perth.[143]

Mackay was in Edinburgh by 10 September. Having placed three regiments and some Scottish horse at Perth and, once the weather was better, hoped to send troops to garrison other towns 'to shut up the Highlanders in their hills, and cover the low countreys'. He was feeling confident that the campaign was over, telling Melville, 'I am of opinion that the neck of this rebellion is broke, if all succour from Ireland be hinder'd, as I am hopefull it shall'. As evidence of this he noted that 'Very many cum in dayly to take the benefit of His Majesty's gracious indemnity, and I believe many more would cum in if they had tyme'. However, 11 September was the deadline. It was not only the common men who took the oaths of allegiance, but so did Breadalbane, Southesk and Strathmore on 10 September, and on the last day, the Earl of Callendar and the Lords Levingston and Duffus, along with some of Cannon's Irish officers. It was noted, 'There is such a confluence of the Highland lairds and heads of the clans, that come in daily to take the benefit of an Act of Indemnity, the oath of allegiance, and give security for their peaceable behaviour in time to come, that such a scene has not been seen, in our streets in many years'.[144] However, none of the leading Jacobites had done so, but this did not worry him unduly for, assuming the Jacobites were defeated in Ireland, he believed he would be able to subdue them with the help of his garrisons. As to Cannon, Mackay believed that he 'is in no reputation or esteeme by them, for he and Dunfermling doe nothing but drink acquavity as I am informed'. Meanwhile 'The whole north is very peaceable at present'.[145]

Mackay wanted an exchange of prisoners. Several officers from his army taken at Killiecrankie were held at Mull.[146] Conditions for the prisoners of Mull were variable. At one extreme, Captain Balfour was robbed of his clothes, gold and silver and was also stabbed. Two lieutenants were in poor health. The Macleans robbed some of them and officers were obliged to exchange their buttons for bread. Accommodation as well as food was poor. The Privy Council agreed to treat with Cannon and called on Sir Hugh Campbell of Caddell to negotiate on their behalf. Mackay's nephew was one of those released in October.[147]

143 Mackay, *Memoirs*, p.72.

144 Balfour-Maitland, 'Estates', II, p.12.

145 Mackay, *Memoirs*, pp.277–278.

146 Balfour-Maitland, 'Estates', II, p.2.

147 *Ibid.*, pp.19, 25, 38, 42.

On 19 September Balfour and Captain Ferguson had been exchanged for George Barclay and David Graham.[148] Some Jacobite officers in captivity were often treated well. Alexander Strachan, taken prisoner by Mackay in September 1689, wrote that Mackay 'shewed him unusual civilitys', often dining with him. Struan stated that all were dealt with in this way. Struan spent time in Perth and Edinburgh for a few months before being exchanged for Robert Pollock.[149]

The temporary cessation of major hostilities now that the campaigning season was being de-escalated meant that Mackay had an opportunity to improve his forces. Once assigned to winter quarters he planned to make good his losses by recruiting. He also planned to have them drilled and exercised. An officer who had disappointed him was Captain John Slezar, an artillery officer, who had refused to serve under him and he desired his dismissal.[150]

He also lobbied Melville on behalf of dependants of officers killed at Killiecrankie. He requested that the widow of Captain Lammy, 'a gentlewoman', should be given an allowance. The widow of Lieutenant Chambers, who was with child, was another 'whom I recommend also to your lordships charitable offices by their Majesties'. Apparently she was 'not able to goe by land' and 'shee is a stranger and expects charity'.[151]

Other troop movements took place that autumn. By 28 September, Mackay was eager to have his men find winter quarters. Angus' regiment had been billeted in Montrose by 11 October. Captain John Fullerton of Leven's regiment became Angus' new lieutenant colonel in November. Ramsay's regiment were sent to quarters in Aberdeen in November.[152]

In fact, the Highlands was so relatively secure that on 16 September, Mackay could leave to go to London to see William and Mary to discuss matters in Scotland face to face.[153] Four regiments were to be sent to Ireland including the newly formed Cunningham's, as well as the English regiments of Lanier, Hastings and Hayford.[154] Lanier was ordered to sail with his regiment, too.[155] Colchester's and Berkeley's were marched into England in early September.[156] This was probably because the horses had greatly suffered from the weather and the terrain, Mackay writing, 'This country not being fit for English horses'.[157] Mackay considered that Hastings' regiment was 'very waike and losste the most part of their cloathes and arms'.[158]

In early October, Mackay spent his time in Perthshire, re-ordering his garrisons. There were the 500 men in Blair Castle and finally 200 men were placed in Finlarig, despite a comment in the previous month about

148 NRS, GD26/8/41.
149 NLS, ADV 13.1.8.
150 Mackay, *Memoirs*, pp.278–9.
151 *Ibid.*, pp.281–2.
152 Balfour-Maitland, 'Estates', II, pp.19, 33, 52, 61.
153 *Ibid.*, p.16.
154 *Ibid.*, p.80.
155 NLS, MS 3740, 110.
156 Mackay, *Memoirs*, p.72.
157 NLS, MS 3740, 106.
158 NLS, MS 3740, 102.

bad weather ruling this out of court. It is not know how strongly Weemys was garrisoned; one source states 200 men, but Mackay wrote of 50 men of Bargany's there, 'without picks' on 7 October. It was later palisaded. The 600 men of Angus' were stationed in Camsmore, Cardross and Drumkill. Meanwhile, two regiments and Blantyres', Eglington's and Ross' cavalry were at Stirling; Balfour's, with Argyll's, Newbottle's and Grubbit's Horse at Perth, Ramsay's two regiments and Annandale's and Belhaven's Horse at Dundee. The other regiment of Angus' and Cardross' cavalry were divided between Munro, Brechin, Arbroath and Forfar. At Inverness were Livingstone's regiment of dragoons, six troops of Horse, Leslie's, Strathnaver's and Grant's infantry. The weak regiments of Mar, Bargany and Glencairn were stationed at Coupar, Inverkeithing and Dunfermline. Leven's and Beveridge's were at Leith and Canongate. This would, wrote Mackay, 'by this disposition the low country over all is guarded, and the forces so lodged, that in a short time a good body of them may be drawn together whether in the south or north: but if this winter they interprise anything, it will be in the north, because it doth lyne near them'.[159]

A major difficulty was the lack of money to pay all the troops. According to Mackay, the Scottish government had raised less than £40,000 in revenue in 1689. Ramsay's and Leven's men were in particular want of money and Mackay wanted the cash to be brought from London by ship. One solution was to reduce the state's commitments. Disbanding of troops was thus on the cards. Mackay was asked to advise on this matter. He was insistent that 'none of the hors or dragoons be disbanded this winter' unless other cavalry were to be sent to replace them. Of the 10 newly raised Scottish regiments, at least five or six should be maintained including Leven's. Disbanding too many would be dangerous, for 'if a competent number of forces in the kingdom be wanting, ther shall appear more enemeys then doth appeare as yet'. Expenditure on troops in Scotland was thus essential 'then to hazard a longer continuation of the troubles in this kingdom, which is not yet so very setled as could be wished'. One reason why troops were needed was because the Jacobites still had hopes of assistance from Ireland and until this possibility remained, that hope would persist, and by the end of 1689 there were still significant Jacobite forces in Ireland.[160] Mackay suggested that money should be obtained, not from Parliament but as loans from individuals.[161]

Those regiments which could be dispensed with, were, according to Mackay, Mar's, Blantyre's, Kenmure's and Glencairn's, 'for certainly they are the worst'. Angus' two battalion regiment could be reduced to one, but needed a better commander, 'though the men are good' and 'because they behaved well against the rebels at Dunkeld'. According to him, Strathnaver's and Grant's were the best and had their numbers up to strength. He also thought that the troops of horse should be formed into regiments 'for they shall not otherwise be capable of serving so well nor be so well cared for'.[162] Yet he also

159 Mackay, *Memoirs*, pp.283–4; NLS, MS 3741, 8, 17.
160 *Ibid.*, pp.284–5, 296.
161 *Ibid.*, p.292.
162 *Ibid.*, pp.286–288, 290.

advised caution, 'we ought not to retrench considerably the number of the forces here till things be brought to a greater settlement, and their Majesties' authority better fixed over all the kingdom'.[163]

There were still some security concerns, especially over the north of Scotland. Melville evidently had reports about such for Mackay referred to them in a letter dated 15 October. The latter had no definite news. He seemed certain that Livingstone's strong cavalry force would be sufficient to hold Inverness and to deter any active Jacobites in the north of Scotland, 'neither do I believe they will come to any considerable body abroad this winter … they shall not doe much harme, for they cannot lodge in the hills, nor safely descend into the low countrey for our hors and dragouns'. Mackay added that he had sources of information from the places where the Jacobites might gather; in the hills, woods and bogs.[164]

Mackay waited several weeks before a decision could be reached as to the King's 'final resolution as to the forces (which shall be kept on foot for this winter)'. This was so that he could order a final arrangement of them in garrisons in case of any Jacobite attempts and to keep others from rising. Melville replied at the end of October to assure Mackay that whilst the King had read all his letters, he 'was so weary that he gave no orders thereanent, therefor yow get not a full answere'.[165]

In order to finish the campaign, in Mackay's opinion, what were needed were sufficient garrisons in and near to the Highlands. This could not be accomplished until the following year, but 'which will make them as peaceable as any other country of the kingdom whereof Cromwell's government left as an example'. To vanquish all the Jacobite clans in battle was deemed impossible, 'none shall stand out but such as dwell in the remotest Highlands, render'd for us inaccessible by the raining season and cold water'. Yet these could be held in check from encroaching in the Lowlands by judicious garrisoning.[166]

Money worries were another major concern as the months progressed. Mackay suggested that Cromwell's methods of financing troops in Scotland be used. This was that the men were paid out of English revenues, which were far higher than those of Scotland and were from a country in which armies were not fighting over. He wrote to both Melville and Portland on this, again suggesting a loan.[167]

On 29 October, Livingstone's dragoons were sent northwards to prevent any Jacobite depredations by the Glengarrys and were stationed at Inverness in early December. There was some fighting at Castle Brahan involving the Seaforths. There was an alleged Jacobite plot to attack Glasgow and Lord Belnagown's cows were plundered. Abergeldie Castle in Craithie was garrisoned by Major John McDougall's men from Mackay's regiment.[168]

163 NLS, MS 3740 102.
164 Mackay, *Memoirs*, p.289.
165 *Ibid.*, pp.294–5.
166 NLS, MS 3740, 102.
167 Mackay, *Memoirs*, pp.297–8.
168 Balfour-Maitland, 'Estates, II', pp.43, 51, 69–70, 80.

By early December, Sir James Leslie, in Inverness, was stating that 'the enemie is drawing together in a verry considerable body', preventing him from sending men to garrison Eclass. Apparently 400–500 Jacobites under Glengarry had arrived at Urquhart but Leslie did not feel the castle there was in danger as the garrison of three companies had two to three weeks' provisions. He acknowledged that one weakness was that he had absentee officers, a not uncommon dilemma in early modern warfare, especially in winter, when there was less militarily to occupy them. Many more Jacobites were expected there; the Mackenzies, the Frasers and additional men under Cannon. The artillery Leslie had been promised had not arrived and so he suggested Melville had it sent by sea. Meanwhile he was ordering in men from his outposts; three companies of Grant's and 120 men from two castles. Strathnaver's and Grant's men were lacking in uniforms, 'and are very ill arm'd … they are very good bodyes of men but have neither swords nor bagganettes'. Furthermore, Strathnaver's men had 'but bad armes, most of them being match locks'. It was not certain whether the Jacobites had designs on Inverness, Ross or Murray, as he had heard that they were in two bodies and that if they could not attack Inverness they would burn corn, straw and mills nearby and Leslie felt himself too weak to march from Inverness and attack them in the open. His troops were scattered in their quarters due to being ill paid.[169]

Three days later, Leslie had had converse with Lord Lovat who assured him that the Frasers were not among the Jacobites, but Leslie was not confident that this was so. Supplies of corn and straw were difficult to procure, for though there were dragoons gathering them in, the Jacobites threatened to destroy them. To counter this he ordered three troops to come from Elgin to be stationed at Castle Stuart, Culloden and Bodlum. Three companies of Grants were also pulled out of Elgin. Yet there were fears that Seaforth was planning to join the Jacobites and could threaten Inverness.[170]

Mackay tended to play down Sir James' fears, for there were three regiments of infantry, four troops of horse, three of dragons and he had Livingstone's four troops to march there, as well as there being another troop of Horse in Aberdeenshire. Therefore he concluded, 'There is no hazard for the town of Inverness'. Mackay, however, did suggest that Leslie call out the county militia, though he was unsure how far these could be relied upon.[171]

It was only at the year's end that William sent down his instructions to Mackay for the reorganisation of the Scottish army. He wanted there to be seven infantry regiments to consist of 13 companies, including a grenadier company, of 60 privates each. The cavalry were to be three troops of horse and three of dragoons, were to be of 50 men to a troop, each led by a lieutenant. Mackay was to select all the officers himself. The existing regiments to be maintained were those of Angus, Argyll, Glencairn, Kenmure, Strathmore and Grant. A seventh was to be commanded by the laird of Cunningham. Mar's, Blantyre's and Bargany's were to be disbanded. Men in these regiments

169 Mackay, *Memoirs*, pp.299–300; NLS, MS 3740, 104.
170 *Ibid.*, pp.302–4.
171 *Ibid.*, p.305.

could be assigned to the others. However of the seven regiments, only three were to remain in Scotland and the other four shipped to Ireland. The cavalry were to be reorganised into three regiments; Lord Cardross, Robert Jackson and Patrick Home to be their colonels. Horse troops were to be led by Eglington, Sir George Gordon and the Master of Forbes.[172]

Mackay, Leven and Munro had a number of comments about this scheme. As matters stood, the total number of Scottish infantry amounted to about 4,000 men in 10 understrength regiments, but to make up seven regiments each of 780, an additional 1,500 men would be needed. Mackay wrote 'which is feared will be ill to be got, ther being no levie money, and the people haveing gotten ill impression of the service, because of ther late ill payment'. Without arrears of pay being paid, Mackay feared mutiny and in the case of the cavalry, horses would be lost, too. In all, this would lead to the rebellion being rejuvenated. They decided to delay the implementation of the King's instructions by eight days so that he might have further time to consider their objections. It seems that their hopes were not met, for on the last day of the year, Mackay wrote despondently, 'litle regarde is had to what I have reiteratively wryt upon that subject'.[173]

Mackay was very unhappy about his advice being ignored, based as it was on the opinion of someone who had less knowledge than he as commander in chief. He reminded Melville that peace had been kept in the north only because he had sent additional cavalry there and if the King had those forces disbanded, 'I am apprehensive he shall not be long master of the north, and will cost him more than the keeping of them for a feu months more can stand him to recover it'. He was also dismayed by the 'slow and irregular methods of the government' and 'the scarcity of money'. He was frustrated by the Jacobites being able to levy war by committing 'all sorts of violence and disorder' and by having to command new recruits 'who have not proved generally very good, especially the foot regements'. He even talked of resignation, 'I have many raisons to be weary of this command, and to wish with all my heart, som other might be pitched upon to supply it'. He wondered whether a younger and ambitious man might replace him writing 'I am extreamly weary of this sort of war, and is certainly more fit for a man of fewer years and more accustomed with this manner of the country, then for mee'. He became increasingly disillusioned, 'I had long since given over to wryt, because I seldom or never get the satisfaction to know whether any thing I propose be had in any regard or the contrarie'.[174] On 1 November he had written, 'I have my fill of Scotland and wish their Majesties' service may never require my return hither againe if it please God'.[175] Furthermore, his family resided in Holland and he wanted to be with them in the forthcoming winter. It was only his 'zeale for their Majesties' service and the interest of the Protestant religion' that kept him in harness.[176]

172 *Ibid.*, pp.307–309.
173 *Ibid.*, pp.310–311, 314.
174 *Ibid.*, pp.314–317.
175 NLS, MS 3741, 15–16.
176 Mackay, *Memoirs*, pp.272–3.

Meanwhile, James took the time to contact his followers in Scotland. He acknowledged their bravery and devotion to his cause, thanked them for it and expected the like behaviour in the following year. He urged them not to despair at the costs they had incurred, for when he was restored he would bestow his royal favour on the loyal men. He promised he would send the Earl of Seaforth over to them, as well as the Duke of Berwick 'with considerable forces to their assistance as soon as the season would permit'. Victory would result in their religion and liberty being safeguarded. Finally James recommended that they keep together and obey their superior officers.[177]

Alexander Strachan was sent from Ireland with additional news: that, when the right moment came, James would 'sett on foot a considerable army in Scotland; and on arrival of the French fleet, which he dayly expected, to send over the Duke of Berwick with 8000 Irish troops'. Strachan was seized at Glasgow, however, and sent to Edinburgh, where he confessed everything and delivered all his information, leading to the arrests of Jacobite sympathisers.[178]

By 10 September, Cannon was at Mull.[179] It was reported that he had little powder or ammunition and that the people of Lochaber and Mull were unfriendly towards Cannon's remnant. However, despite Cameron's overtures to the government in September, by late October he was consorting with Cannon at Inverkely. Despairing of Scotland, Cannon returned to Ireland by the end of November, as did Purcell.[180]

The campaign of 1689 was over and as Cameron reported, 'This winter all was pretty quiet in the Highlands' as one would expect it would have been, as it was outside the conventional campaigning season. Yet there were attempts made on behalf of William III that hostilities there would come to a permanent end. He needed to focus his military resources on the campaign in Ireland where his principal enemy remained with an army. Londonderry had held; this was a setback to the Jacobite cause but not a conclusive defeat.[181]

Diplomacy and the power of monetary reward was offered to his erstwhile Scottish enemies. Lord Tarbat was entrusted with this mission, but he persuaded the council to give the role to Breadalbane as he knew the Highland chiefs personally. A sum of £5,000 as well as other rewards, were on offer. Yet this nobleman was concerned about acting in this was without the permission of James, but it was suggested that a cessation in hostilities might assist the Jacobite cause in giving time for their allies in Ireland to arrive. The Privy Council wanted fresh orders from William about Breadalbane, as the latter had formerly not supported him, but William had left for Ireland and so negotiations died stillborn.[182] Mackay's knowledge of Jacobite intentions was clearly minimal, for on 18 December he wrote to Weemys thus, 'if you

177 Cameron, *Memoirs*, p.288.
178 *Ibid*.
179 Balfour-Maitland, 'Estates', II, p.9.
180 *Ibid*., pp.19, 43, 58.
181 Cameron, *Memoirs*, p.289.
182 *Ibid*.

can get a person among the enemys whom you can make sure … to fournish tymly intelligence of what shall be resolved'.[183]

The Jacobite offensive in the Highlands had been contained, in spite of the spectacular, if costly, victory at Killiecrankie. The battle of Dunkeld had blunted their onslaught and support was being sapped. However James' forces in Ireland remained a dangerous threat to the new regime, though they had not triumphed throughout Ireland. The Jacobite cause in Scotland as elsewhere was far from being defeated as 1689 drew to a close.

183 NLS, MS 3741 18.

7

The Battle of Cromdale, 1690

The Haughs of Cromdale
'As I came in by Auchindoun,
A little wee bit frae the toun,
When to the Highlands I was bound,
To view the haughs of Cromdale,
I met a man in tartan trews,
I speir'd at him what was the news,
Quo' he the Highland army rues,
That e'er we came to Cromdale.

'We were in bed Sir, every man,
When the English host upon us came,
A bloody battle then began
Upon the haughs of Cromdale.
The English horse they were so rude
They bath'd their hooves in Highland blood
But our brave clans, they boldly stood
Upon the haughs of Cromdale'.

But alas! We could no longer stay
For o'er the hills we came away,
And sore we do lament the day,
That e'er we came to Cromdale ...'

The second year of the campaign began with dissension in the Jacobite camp; a not uncommon state of affairs for any force without a clear leader and command hierarchy, especially one that has suffered military defeat and has not received the promised support in terms of men and money.

To exacerbate matters, there were some minor losses at the year's onset. Lieutenant Colonel Mackrigour, 'one of the greatest Robber and Plunderers' was taken by Kilmarnock's Horse. Cannon wrote to Mackay to tell him that this man must be treated well or he would cause 10 of his own prisoners to die. Meanwhile, Laird Macknel of Colloughie submitted with 30 men.[1] There were two reported minor attempts to take government-held towns in January. One hundred Jacobites attacked Aberdeen, but in the fighting they lost 20 men dead and 15 taken, the government losing eight men killed.[2] A planned Jacobite attack on Inverness at the end of January by Colin Mackenzie with 200–300 men was discovered and so was repulsed, with some of the attackers being killed or captured.[3]

Hopes for – and promised – support from Ireland and France were largely disappointed. On 8 February three ships arrived from the former, bringing a number of officers: Colonels Buchan, Maxwell, Wauchop and others.[4] The Earl of Seaforth, a Catholic Highland nobleman, came in the spring, but 'brought nothing with him butt Letters and Commissions to the Chiefs'. Cameron had written to James in a letter of 14 February to ask for supplies, and the reply, dated from Dublin on 31 March, was as ever optimistic. James, after explaining that the delay was due to the difficulty in transporting horses, stated that the French fleet was there and so 'Now, we shall take all necessary measures, and loose as little time as we can in executing them.' As always, though, no immediate help, was forthcoming, and so James urged his followers in Scotland to keep the faith, as he knew from experience that they had in the past, stressed how they had risked much for him and that he was convinced that Providence would be with them.[5] Yet there were some crumbs from their master's table. On 18 January, James sent £900 to Buchan, of which £300 was earmarked for Cannon, £100 to Purcell and the remainder for the Irish troops in Scotland.[6]

The chiefs held a council of war after receiving such letters. Present were Seaforth, Generals Buchan and Cannon, Colonel Brown and others, as to how to conduct the year's campaign. Apparently 'they were generally so enraged att finding themselves disappointed of the relief they expected of men, arms and other provisions of war, that many proposed to offer their submissions to King William, upon terms which they were then very sure to obtain'. They recalled their losses which had reduced some to poverty, they cited the imminent garrisons planned for subduing the Highlands and expected nothing but ruin by Scotland being 'the seat of a bloody war' and that it was therefore best to come to terms in order to save what they could from the wreckage.[7]

Others went further and accused James of leaving them to their mutual enemy and that it was madness to continue supporting him. They thought that it must be easy to 'waft over some thousands of the Irish'. James was blamed for neglecting his own affairs and for ignoring his ministers. Therefore, 'it was now high time for them to look to themselves, and to observe the first principles of nature, which was self-preservation'. Many present subscribed

1 Balfour-Maitland, 'Estates', II, pp.86-87, 102–3.
2 Luttrell, *Brief Relation*, II, p.3.
3 *Ibid.*, p.95.
4 *Ibid.*, p.104.
5 Cameron, *Memoirs*, p.290.
6 HMCR IV, p.529.
7 Cameron, *Memoirs*, p.291.

to such sentiments.[8] The laird of Glenmoriston told Livingstone he wished to come to terms.[9]

These sentiments were not universally held. Sir Donald MacDonald, Sir John MacLean and the Captain of Clanranald all declared their continued adherence to James. Cameron then delivered a major speech. He said that what he had already heard from many was shocking. That they had 'renounced their duty and alledgiance, as well as the respect they owed to the majesty of their Sovereign' was disgraceful. He wondered whether they had been deceived by their enemies. He claimed that he would support their legitimate sovereign as long as he was able to as he was their lawfully anointed. He reminded them of James' pledges of support and future rewards. He spoke at length and 'After this discourse, which was delivered with great warmth and zeale, none present had the assurance to speake any more of peace'. Buchan was appointed as commander-in-chief until that year's general rendezvous. He encouraged waverers with promises of French aid in the way of supplies to look forward to.[10]

Glengarry received a letter of encouragement from James, written on 1 April: 'Wee need not therefore exhort you to the continuance of your Endeavours for us, since wee have it from all hands that none is more earnest and zealous … how intent we are upon helping you out of your present difficulties'.[11]

Yet all was not well with their enemies, either. Mackay was also despondent and had lobbied to be sent to Holland at the year's beginning, but William wanted him to remain in Scotland 'till the things were further settled'. Meanwhile in January 1690, Mackay had further orders to reduce the number of units in the Scottish establishment from 10 to seven regiments of infantry, losing Mar's, Bargany's and Blantyre's, and to disband 12 troops of horse and dragoons. Mackay thought that the reduction in cavalry was folly for there was 'the necessity of a considerable body of horse and dragoons, without which it was impossible to secure the authority of the government in the north'. Instructions came from the court dated 4 January to disband others, too. If there were insufficient funds to maintain regiments, then the number of companies in each should be reduced. The troopers in Annandale's and Ross' cavalry were to be distributed among the remaining cavalry troops to make their numbers up to the establishment strength; any remaining were to be discharged. Mackay also noted the instructions from the court to put Leven, 'tho' but a colonel and a youth without service' on an equal footing with him and deemed that this was 'a token of His Majesty's mistrust of him', but avoided showing his displeasure.[12]

The extent of the suggested troop reduction was ameliorated. Mackay, Leven and Major General Munro wrote to the King that the retention of the cavalry was essential for the security of Scotland. The infantry loss was also

8 *Ibid.*

9 *RPCS*, 15, p.92.

10 *Ibid.*, pp.293–4; Balfour-Maitland, 'Estates', II, p.126.

11 RA, CP1/24.

12 Mackay, *Memoirs*, pp.103, 82–3, 319–320.

softened for the men of the disbanded regiments formed a new regiment, Cunningham's, and the remainder made up a company in each of the other seven regiments.[13]

Mackay wanted Captain John Hill of Leven's regiment to be appointed as adjutant general. Mackay had no one in this role and he stated that it was necessary in order to distribute orders, muster troops and have the cavalry made useful for service. Such work would greatly assist Mackay in bringing the war to a swift resolution.[14]

Arms, ammunition and uniforms were also insufficient at the beginning of the year. The Privy Council requested 3,000 muskets with ammunition on 10 January. On 1 April they asked for new uniforms for Mackay's, Ramsay's and Lauder's regiments.[15] Beveridge's regiment was poorly armed because the men had muskets of different calibre; perhaps a mix of matchlocks and flintlocks. Yet in other ways, the condition of the troops at the year's onset was good. They were being paid out of English resources and were mostly up to strength 'and in good order'.[16] Mackay also ordered six three-pounders for use in the field, but there is no evidence they ever fired a shot in anger.[17]

Mackay's policy was to have towns, cities and other places garrisoned to deny them to the Jacobites and to restrict supplies available to the Jacobites. The Castle of Erchless, to the south-west of Inverness, belonging to Chisholm of Strathglass, was garrisoned by Lieutenant Colonel Lumstone with seven companies of Strathmore's regiment, for example. Expeditions were sent to attack and capture Jacobites. On 1 March Captain John Hay of Livingstone's Horse, at Banff took suspected Jacobites at Lord Oliphant's house at Bachlen. At the end of the month, Livingstone sent horse and dragoons to Strathglass, killing and capturing Jacobites there, and taking some cattle to Inverness.[18]

The first prong of Mackay's strategy was to have a garrisoned fort in the West Highlands, an issue which he had raised in the previous year. He later wrote 'the only formidable rebels then in the kingdom might be subdued by placing a garrison in Innerlochy'. This meant ships, boats, spades, shovels and pickaxes and frigates to convoy them there. Yet delays occurred, due to the overriding precedence claimed by William's expedition to Ireland and the Scottish government lacking money. It was not until March that such necessaries could be supplied. Mackay met members of the Privy Council and gave them an account of what he had requested to the court.[19]

Feeling that the Privy Council would be unreceptive to his plan, he suggested to them that troops be transported along the coast to prevent any of the Islanders from reinforcing the Jacobites on the mainland. Paying for war was difficult: the Lords of the Treasury supplying £600, but this was

13 *Ibid.*, pp.83–4.
14 *Ibid.*, pp.320–321.
15 *RPCS*, 15, pp.20, 175.
16 NLS, MS 3740, 135.
17 NRS, E96/35/1.
18 Balfour-Maitland, 'Estates', II, pp.112, 115, 130.
19 Mackay, Memoirs, pp.103–4.

inadequate given 'so great was the disorder and poverty of the government'. Glasgow was zealous for the cause and made up the shortfall in funding.[20]

Fort William was thus established. It had three six-pounders, six three-pounders with 130 balls, and a dozen culverins, with 20 balls each. There were also 800 grenades.[21] However, instead of 1,200 men in the garrison as planned, there were only 900 allocated, which was further reduced by desertions. The palisade was weak. On 21 July, Hill wrote of the Jacobites, 'they stir not yet but come not in'.[22]

Secondly, part of Mackay's strategy to defeat the Jacobites was to send the newly promoted Major Jacob Ferguson of Lauder's regiment, with 600 men to be shipped at Greenock and for Captain Edward Pottinger of HMS *Dartmouth* with other ships, to work together against the Jacobites of the Western Islands. They were to 'resolve and do every thing unanimously and with one accord'. Pottinger was to have the final word on seaborne matters, Ferguson to have the lead as to landing troops and in land-based operations.[23]

The aim was stated by Mackay in his instructions to Ferguson:

> The main desseyn of this detachment being to make a diversion, allarme the rebel coasts, cut their communication with the Islanders now in rebellion against their Majesties authoritie, and to take away or burn all their boats and berlins whether on the Isles or along the coasts of the rebelles upon firme land: the Major is to undertake nothing as to landing but upon visible and apparent advantages and humane assurance of success.

Mackay added that although this was to be done 'with all the rigour of military executions, such as shall continue obstinate in their rebellion, with this proviso, that women and children be not touched or wronged in their persons.[24]

There were difficulties and delays. Ferguson had to wait five weeks for the provisions for his expedition. Meanwhile, Mackay broadcast his plans for Ferguson, though stating that he had far more men than was the case in reality, in order that numbers accruing to Cannon and Buchan would be reduced. According to Mackay, the Jacobites, instead of supplying 4,000–5,000 men, only 700–800 were sent out with Buchan. Thus 'the gross of the rebels, particularly such as dwelt near the sea with the inhabitants of the isles stayed at home to guard their country against the frigates, with Ferguson's detachment, at the every noise whereof they were very much terrified.[25]

Ferguson's raiding, assisted with help from the Campbells, resulted in property belonging to Jacobites in Mull being destroyed. Castle Duart, stronghold of the MacLeans, was left alone. However, inhabitants of Kintyre and Mull yielded by early June.[26]

20 *Ibid.*, p.104.
21 NRS, E96/33/7.
22 NRS, GD26/9/274/2.
23 Mackay, *Memoirs*, p.322–3.
24 *Ibid.*, pp.92–93.
25 Balfour-Maitland, 'Estates', II, pp.193, 202.
26 Mackay, *Memoirs*, pp.323–324.

If Ferguson thought that with 300–400 men he might master the Isle of Mull, he was to contact the laird of Ardkinglas, sheriff depute of Argyllshire, who was then to assist him with 'the most resolute and best armed men of the shire' (later that year 600 Argyllshire militia aided his troops). Generally, boats held by the Jacobites were the main target for without them they would be unable to assist their allies on the mainland with men or provisions. Men swearing allegiance to their Majesties and delivering their weapons were to be protected but their chiefs had to surrender themselves to Ferguson in person. The major also had to keep his men under control or else punish them. MacLeod, though he had not declared his open allegiance to their Majesties, was to be assured of protection once Ferguson was on the coast.[27]

From May to October there were three ships cruising off the north-west of Scotland. These were HMS *Dartmouth*, a 32 gun frigate with a crew of 135 men under Pottinger. Then there was the smaller *Larke*, a sixth rate frigate of 18 guns and 85 men under Captain Andrew Douglass. Finally there was the *Fanfan*, of two guns and 30 men under Richard Finch.[28] There were at least 500–600 Jacobites on Mull near the castle Duart to oppose them.[29]

Initially the two larger ships focussed their attention on Islay. On 19 May they landed troops there, on different sides of the islands. Pottinger's and Captain James Hackett's detachments had orders to 'burne and destroy those rebels, and [the latter] did accordingly land 30 men'. The *Lark* sent another 19 soldiers ashore. Four prisoners were taken. On the next day they were at Mull. Captain Robert Mackay took 200 sailors and soldiers ashore to march to Castle Boy, 'they having sett severall towns afire' by nightfall. On the following day, further towns were burnt and boats were destroyed. In the remainder of the month and in June, the ships landed men to destroy further boats and houses and to make prisoners, destroying 'such as fall in their way'.[30]

Pottinger wrote 'glowing' reports on Ferguson's effectiveness. On 19 June, whilst cruising off Mull, he wrote:

> Major Ferguson, his men, ships and boats, done the best service wee were capable of, by burning & destroying the severall islands & houses, boats, cattle &c. of such as are in actuall Rebellion. To be particular would be too tedious to yo. Hon., tho' on some islands the souldiers have scarce a beast, nor a hutt to shelter in.

Pottinger noted, following Mackay's orders, that he had given instructions that the men had been 'strictly charged not to molest' women and children'. Yet his initial incursions had been resisted. The MacLeans, Glengarrys and Camerons 'continue as obstinate as Jews' but 'which in good time I hope shall be reduc't'. Ferguson lost a dozen men in his expeditions, mostly by straggling. One man had been caught by the Jacobites and hanged 'most barbarously'.[31]

27 *Ibid.*
28 TNA, ADM2/8.
29 *RPCS*, 15, p.249.
30 TNA, ADM51/389/4.
31 *Ibid.*, ADM106/399/355.

The *Fanfan*, on 20 June, landed a Captain Piercy Kirk of the Queen Consort's Foot and 50 soldiers on an unnamed island, after firing from the ship at Jacobites on the shore. The raiding party killed three Jacobites and the rest fled to the mountains. No losses were incurred by the soldiers. On the following day the ship fired at people on the shore of the Isle of Mull.[32]

Sir Donald MacDonald's son sought terms with Ferguson by early July, but his father objected to such a surrender. This led to his house 'the prettiest house in the Highlands of Scotland' being reduced to 'flames and ashes'. The *Dartmouth*, a half mile away, fired 'betwixt 3 and 400 shott' at it before men landed to finish the job, 'what my guns could not batter down'. Pottinger, writing on 31 July, considered that his expedition had been a success, for it had 'kept ye clans of these islands from joining: who could have brought in a body above 3,000 men to have joined Buchan and Cannon. The apprehension they concerned of our landing, kept each of them to preserve their own self interest'.[33]

Yet for Pottinger, this success would come, ultimately, at a very high price. The expedition was not without loss, apart from those men already referred to. On 18 September *Fanfan*'s captain learnt that the *Dartmouth* had been lost at sea in Collander Bay. Only five men and one boy had been saved. Pottinger was dead.[34] Colonel Hill wrote, 'tis a very great loss'.[35]

Thirdly, Mackay ordered Livingstone, who had been at Aberdeen and Inverness since August 1689, to march north with his dragoon regiment for he knew the country, the people and the latter's intention better than any other. Mackay gave him varying instructions dependent on the intelligence he received from Livingstone.[36]

On 6 February, Mackay wrote an upbeat letter to Melville, assuring him that 'no man serves his interest with lesse regard to his owne than I doe'. He added, 'I question not but with Gods assistance, to be able to give a good account of the Highland rebellion before the end of Appril'. His difficulties, though were a lack of experienced officers as subordinates who could hold independent commands and advance notice of supplies sent northwards.[37]

Fighting was occurring on a low level. At the end of March, two troops of horse and two of dragoons, along with a few infantry, were besieging Castle Glendaleth. There was firing on both sides, but the besiegers could not enter. Captain Charles Dundas of the Royal Regiment of Foot was killed, 'being over forward with two or three mor of ye dragoons, and a few wounded of ye Foot'. They then retreated on hearing that 500 Highlanders were on their way.[38]

Meanwhile in the north of Scotland on 22 April, Livingstone, having recovered from the illness that had afflicted him in February, heard that there were Jacobites at Mackintosh's house at Aberarder, Strathearn, which was 15

32 *Ibid.*, ADM51/345.
33 *Ibid.*, ADM106/399, 357, 361.
34 TNA, ADM51/345.
35 NRS, GD26/9/274/3.
36 Mackay, *Memoirs*, p.86.
37 *Ibid.*, pp.324–5.
38 NLS, MS 7012, f45.

miles from Inverness. With 1,000 infantry, four troops of horse and some dragoons, with artillery, moved to attack them. The Jacobites retreated when they were within six miles of them. Ramsay's and Angus' regiments were to march to join Livingstone, but on hearing there was a Jacobite threat to Montrose, returned there.[39]

Mackay's plans were known about by the Jacobites and apparently, 'the very noise of it occasioned such alarm among the rebels'. Buchan, as the senior major general to Cannon, took over command of the Jacobite army. According to Balcarres, the plan was for him 'to go down to the borders of the low country, to amuse the enemy and fatigue their troops by allaruming them in severall of their quarters'.[40]

He asked the clans to supply him with 100 men each (on 18 March Cluny of MacPherson was asked for 200 men) and had 1,200–1,500 men with him; the low numbers due to the attacks on the West as already noted. He hoped to collect more supporters before marching to the Lowlands. At the end of March they marched from Keppoch to Kilwinny at the end of Loch Ness. By the middle of April, they were in Strathspey and remained on the north bank for 10 days; Balcarres writing that instead of taking action as discussed, he 'continued there without doing anything'. He was advised to quarter his men in the woods of Glenlochy 'where they could not be attacked but under great disadvantage, yet he would not hearken to this advice'. Instead he put his men in the villages near Cromdale, 'though all the clans positively protested against that march'. Two hundred men led by Grant and Brody were sent to guard the fords over the Spey, and apparently they 'were so well posted that they might have stopt the enemy from crossing that great river'.[41] They would have known that their enemies were at Inverness and so the danger was from the north.

Mackay learnt that Buchan was 'taking the field' and ordered Livingstone to monitor his progress. His command, based in Inverness, consisted of three regiments of infantry, his own regiment of horse and an unquantifiable number of dragoons. He was also instructed to 'labour, by a detachment of the best of his men, to get a catch of them, or at least to hinder the grouth of their number'. However, although Livingstone was able to learn of their whereabouts (apparently by threatening to torture a captured Jacobite agent, which then in Scotland was a lawful tactic) and to march to that vicinity, his problem being that of supplies. It was only with 'great difficulty' that the cavalry could find forage and the infantry their victuals. As soon as Buchan retired to the hills, he was obliged to return to Inverness. Livingstone gave Mackay 'nothing but Ill News'.[42] Upon hearing this news, Mackay gathered 3,000 troops from Stirling, Dundee and Glasgow, to march to Perth. This was so that they could then march to counter any further Jacobite support that might accrue to Cannon and Buchan.[43]

39 NLS, MS 3740, 135; Mackay, *Memoirs*, pp.142, 145, 146.

40 NLS, MS 3738, 32r.

41 *Ibid.*; Cameron, *Memoirs*, p.294; Mackay, *Memoirs*, p.104; *Memoir of Lord Dundee*, pp.35–36; 'Gleanings from the Cluny Charter Chest', TGSI, XX, (1894–1896), p.237.

42 Mackay, *Memoirs*, p.93; *A True and Real Account of the Defeat of General Buchan and Brigadier Cannon* (London, 1690.); *HMC Le Fleming*, p.270.

43 Mackay, *Memoirs*, p.94.

Livingstone discovered that despite the difficulties of coming to blows, he must act as soon as possible. Many of those who appeared to be supportive of the government were now intimating that they intended to join the Jacobites. Livingstone wrote that the Jacobite march 'increased as a snow ball daily ... affrighted and discouraged the country'.[44] He wrote to Mackay to tell him what his plan was and that many in the north were planning to join the Jacobites.[45]

Livingstone's field forces consisted of the following:

Leslie's Infantry regiment, 400 men

Captain	Lieutenant	Ensign
John Fowke		John Meres
Tankard	George Villars Carleton	
Sir James Leslie		Edward Juckes
John Price		William Kerr
Major Tankred		George Morris
William Rugeley	Clifford Lowther	
	James Baker	
John Price		

Six companies of Grant's infantry regiment, perhaps 300 –350 men.[46]

Rank	Names
Field officers	Colonel Laird of Grant, Lieutenant Colonel Patrick Grant, Major Hugh Mackay
Captains	Alexander Grant, John Grant, John Forbes, Laird John Burgiss, George Gordon, Robert Grant, Robert Ross

One company of Mackay's Highlanders, 100 men
Three troops of Livingstone's Dragoons, 300 men

Colonel Thomas Livingstone		Cornet Williams
Sir William Douglas	Lieutenant Robert Preston	Cornet Patrick Gray
Major Aeneas Mackay	Lieutenant Lewis Lawder	Cornet John McDuigall
Captain Henry Balfour	Lieutenant William Murray	Cornet David Crichton
Captain John Islay	Lieutenant Andrew Agnew	Cornet George Boswall
Captain Sir William Douglas	Lieutenant David Beaton	Cornet Cavillie

Minister, Alexander Sutherland, ADC James Afleth.[47]
One or two Troops of Lord Tester's Horse, perhaps 50-100 men
Total: c.1,200 men.[48]

44 *A True and Real Account.*
45 Mackay, *Memoirs*, p.93.
46 Dalton, *Army Lists*, III, p.92.
47 NRS, GD26/9/302.
48 Mackay, *Memoirs*, p.93; *A True and Real Account.*

Jacobite forces

Jacobite officers claimed their force numbered between 1,400–1,500 men; Mackay that they had 'much the same' as Livingstone. Mackay also wrote that they had '800 of their worst men' and had been reinforced by 'some Badenoch men'.[49] The force included several companies of MacLeans, judging by later lists of prisoners.[50] It also numbered many Camerons, too.[51] The two forces were roughly the same number. Neither possessed any artillery to slow them down.

Livingstone marched his men eight miles from Inverness on 27 April in search of the Jacobites. They reached Brodie and remained there for two days, waiting for the slow moving baggage trains carrying crucial supplies. They also waited for an additional three troops of dragoons and Captain Burnet's Troop of Horse. Patience was also necessary to gain additional intelligence. Mackay ordered further troops and supplies to march towards Livingstone; Ramsay's regiment of infantry, Angus' battalion and five troops of cavalry.[52]

The Jacobite forces were in Strathspey, 'threatening to slay and Burn all that would not joyn', according to Livingstone. On 30 April he learnt where they were: eight miles from Strathspey. This was in the land of the laird of Grant, a supporter of William III and a Scottish privy councillor. A captain of a company of Grant's regiment which held a castle in Strathspey had reported that the Jacobite force had left Badenoch to march for Strathspey and had marched to within two miles of the castle.[53]

On 30 April Livingstone marched his forces through the night, and given that his men were tiring and were negotiating a difficult pass he considered halting to stop for the night, but an officer who knew the lie of the land convinced him to proceed. The Jacobite encampments became visible by its campfires. This was probably just to the west of the hills known as the Haughs of Cromdale and about a mile to the south-east of the Spey. Some men were above Dellachaple and some near the castle of Lethendry. Scouts discovered the lie of the land, how deep the river was and that 'the Ground was somewhat boggish'. Livingstone's force was two miles from his enemy and had been marching through the evening and night. Livingstone wrote, 'I form'd a Design to attack them by surprise, for they did not know of our being arrived, but my Men and Horse being so extremely wearied, I gave them about half an hour to refresh themselves'. Furthermore, the land was boggy and the nature and depth of the River Tay was unknown.[54]

Captain Grant at Balla Castle knew of Livingstone's advance and kept the castle gates locked in order to prevent any of those who had taken shelter there from leaving it and letting the Jacobites know of their peril. Livingstone's forces were ready at two in the morning on the first day of May.

---

49 Mackay, *Memoirs*, pp.97, 104.

50 *RPCS*, 15, p.304.

51 <www.lochiel.net/archgives/arch173.html>

52 *A True and Real Account*; Mackay, *Memoirs*, pp.93–94.

53 *Ibid.*; Mackay, *Memoirs*, p.94.

54 *Ibid.*; James Rennie, *In the Steps of the Clansmen* (London: Rich and Gowan, 1951), p.107; Fraser, *Melvilles and Leslies*, II, p.151.

Captain Grant met Livingstone and showed him where the Jacobites were. He offered to guide him there himself.[55]

A council of war was held for Livingstone to brief his officers prior to the attack. He was still not certain whether an attack should take place. He asked his subordinates to see to the condition of their men to ascertain 'if they were able to do it'. The officers declared 'they would stand by me to the last man and desired earnestly to go on'. Fortunately for them, the Jacobite camp was on the plain, a mile and a half from any strong ground, for they did not know that their enemies were so close. Mackay later wrote, it was 'just as if they had been led thither by the hand, as an ox to the slaughter'.[56]

A night attack is extremely risky, as would have been well known to soldiers in 1690. Only five years previously, Monmouth's forces had marched through the night to surprise James II's army at Sedgemoor. It was a bold plan and a necessary one in order that irregular troops had a chance of defeating regulars. The attack failed because the attackers were unable to achieve the crucial surprise necessary for success. Monmouth's army was decisively defeated the following morning.

Livingstone's force marched by a covered way, the glen of Auchnarrow, to conceal their approach until the last moment and arrived by the river. It is presumed that no man pulled a trigger by accident as one of Monmouth's had in 1685, and so surprise was achieved. There was a ford on the river Spey, near to the church, guarded by two companies of 200 Jacobites led by Captains Grant and Brody. It was now three in the morning. Livingstone had some infantry and dragoons skirmish with them, to distract their attention from the main assault, whilst the bulk of his forces marched a quarter of a mile towards another ford, guided by the knowledgeable Captain Grant. This thrust was spearheaded by two or three troops of Livingstone's Dragoons, a troop of Tester's Horse and Captain Mackay's Highlanders. None of Grant and Brody's men seem to have been assigned to give their comrades in the main camp warning and none defended the other ford, below Kyle-na-fhithich (Raven's wood) as all rushed to the scene of action, leaving the other ford undefended.[57]

Two troops of dragoons and Mackay's company crossed the river without being noticed and they were able to advance unnoticed further by riding along a road concealed by birchwood. The rest of the infantry '[ran] up to us, yet they marched after us with all diligence possible'. Security must have been slack, with officers reliant on the men near the church being able to give ample warning in case on an attack. The Jacobites were asleep in tents and houses. Livingstone later wrote, 'and then we do see them run in parties up and down, not knowing which way to turn themselves, being surprised'. The Jacobites 'take the alarm as moving confusedly as irresolute men'. He then 'commanded all the Horse and Dragoons to joyn, and pursued them, which affrighted them so'.[58] Apparently 100 Jacobites were killed 'in the first hurry'.[59]

55 Mackay, *Memoirs*, p.95.

56 *A True and Real Account*; Mackay, *Memoirs*, p.95.

57 *Ibid.*; Rennie, *In the Steps of the Clansmen*, p.107.

58 *Ibid.*; Fraser, *Melvilles and Leslies*, II, p.152.

59 Cameron, *Memoirs*, p.294.

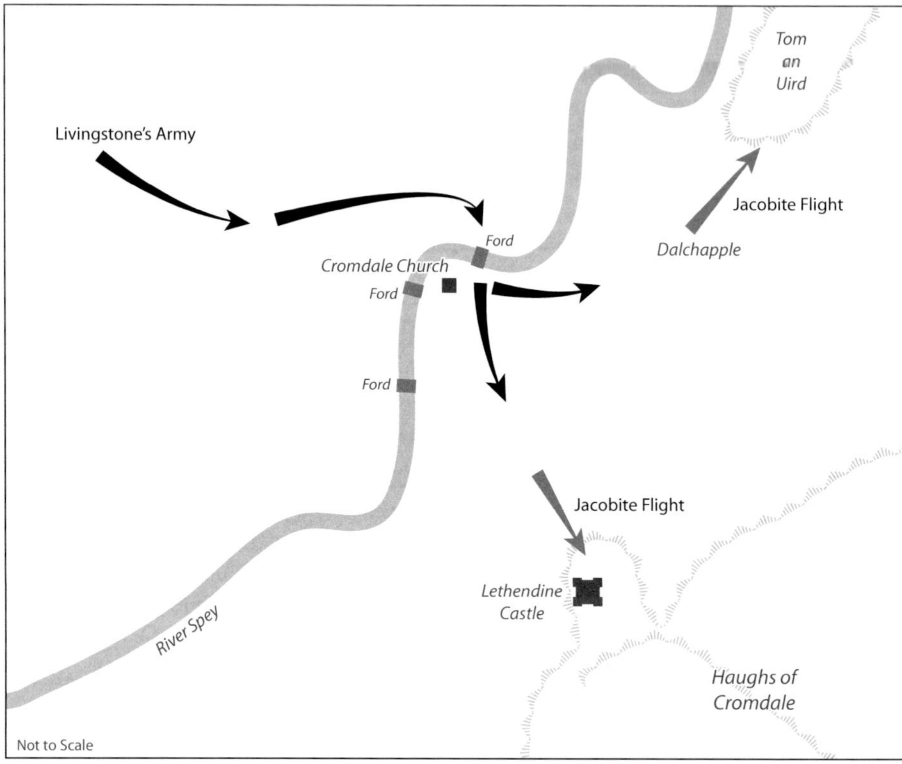

Map 4 Troop movements at Cromdale on 1 May 1690.

N.B. No contemporary map exists so this is an estimate based on contemporary written accounts.

The Jacobite account of the battle has it that, 'as soon as they recovered themselves, they formed into partys, made head against the enemy, and fought with that desperate resolution in their shirts' with their swords and shields. These were the Camerons and the MacLeans. This stand may have occurred because they saw the Highlanders arrive at the hills before the cavalry, and so 'seeing him so weak, resolved to stand, but upon the sight of the rest of the party, which was following with all speed they could make, they began to run for it'. Some ran to Tom Lethendie and some to the hills; the MacDonalds had camped near Dellachaple and Garulin, escaping up the slopes of Tom Uird. Luckily for him, Dunfermline had left the Jacobite camp on the previous day.[60]

However, Livingstone wrote that 'they took themselves to the hills, at the foot of Combrel we overtook them, attacked them, killing betwixt three and four hundred upon the place and took about one hundred prisoners, the greater part of them officers'. Killing confused and virtually defenceless men would have been easy for the cavalrymen, just as the slaughter of fleeing redcoats had been to the Highlanders at Killiecrankie. Livingstone stated that the Jacobites only escaped because mist descended 'so we could scarcely see one another, otherways the slaughter should have been greater'. Apparently 'few would have escaped them, had not a sudden fog favoured the enemy's flight'. The retreat was successful for the pursuers' horses were

60 *Ibid.*; Mackay, *Memoirs*, p.95; Rennie, *In the Steps of the Clansmen*, p.107.

ready to collapse and the force was drawn up on low ground. Yet according to a Jacobite, 'Sir Thomas was glade to allow them to retreat without attempting to pursue them.'[61]

The Jacobite leaders had been caught napping. On the first alarm Buchan sent away his nephew and some officers and men, though they later surrendered. Buchan escaped, though, he 'got of, without hat, coat or sword'. He was later seen, in a state of exhaustion, at Glenlivet, at a cousin's house. Cannon also escaped; in a nightgown Dunfermline had, providentially, left the day before the fighting. Buchan and Cannon fled in different directions, the former looking for Cannon's men. Livingstone had nothing but praise for his men, 'The resolution and forwardness of the Troops was admirable' and though most of the fighting had been by the cavalry, the infantry, unable to get to the front line, yet they 'marched after us with as great Diligence as possible'.[62]

About 50 of the Jacobites, mostly gentlemen, went to the nearby Lethendy Castle with the intention of holding it to the last. Livingstone sent a messenger to them to offer them mercy if they surrendered. The Jacobites opened fire during this attempt at parley. Two grenadiers were shot dead and another was wounded. Lieutenant George Carleton of Leslie's Foot had experience of using grenades from campaigning abroad, or so he claimed. Putting four into a bag he crept towards the castle by using an old ditch to reach an old house near to the castle. He intended to be close enough in order to throw his missiles into the castle.[63]

He threw the first, which 'put the enemy immediately into confusion'. The second grenade fell short. The third one exploded just after it had been thrown and so likewise was ineffectual. The fourth went through a window in the castle 'so it increased the confusion, which the first had put them into; that they immediately called out to me, upon their parole of safety, to come to them'. Carleton went to the barricaded main door, which had been reinforced by great stones. The Jacobites inside were ready to surrender if mercy would be granted.[64]

Carleton returned to Livingstone to relate his account and pass him the news of the wish for a conditional surrender. Livingstone told Carleton to return to inform them that 'He would cut them all to pieces, for their murder of two of his grenadiers, after his proffer of quarter'. Carleton left, full of these melancholy tidings', but as he did, his commander came towards him. He said, 'Hark ye sir, I believe there may be among them some of our old acquaintances (from the Dutch service). Therefore, tell them, they shall have good quarter'. Carleton 'very willingly' took this news back and delivered it. The Jacobites immediately threw down their barricade and one Brody, who had earlier fought at the ford, came out from the main door. Apparently he had been wounded by having part of his nose blown off by one of the grenades Carleton had thrown. The two men went to Livingstone,

61 *A True and Real Account*; Cameron, *Memoirs*, p.294.

62 *Ibid*.

63 *Memoirs of Captain Carleton* (London, 1808), p.56.

64 *Ibid*., pp.56–7.

who confirmed Carleton's message and then all the Jacobites surrendered. Carleton wrote, 'the Highlanders never held up their heads so high after this'.[65] Lady Roxburgh's brother Alexander, an officer in the government army, was sorry that he was not there.[66]

Losses

Cameron stated that 'the loss on both sides was pretty equall'.[67] However, Livingstone stated that between 300 and 400 Jacobites had been killed; 20 officers and 400 others.[68] A government report claimed that 900 were dead and 100 captured; surely an exaggeration.[69] Another account states there were 400 Jacobite dead and 200 prisoners.[70] John Cameron wrote that 'Our Clan had a considerable loss at that unhappy business of Crombdale'.[71] The prisoners were sent to Inverness by 17 May, with the rank and file being accommodated in the castle and the officers allowed their liberty in the town but under guard. Yet there was not accommodation for them there. Most of the latter were soon sent to Edinburgh, guarded by 90 dragoons. By 26 May, 54 prisoners were there; including Sir David Ogilby and Archibald Kennedy.[72] Their lot was not a happy one, as one Francis Beatton, in Edinburgh's Tolbooth, complained to Argyll, 'being taken at Crombdaill and ever since kept upon a very small allowance (2d per diem) which we could not subsist upon had it not been supplied by the charity of some tender hearted Christians'.[73]

The Jacobites also lost all their baggage, provisions, 1,000 arms and ammunition. The standards of King James and Queen Mary were captured. There was plunder for the victors, too, as Livingstone noted. Healths were drunk with wines taken from the Jacobite camp. Livingstone believed that he had had three men wounded, but none seriously, as well as having had a dozen horses killed and a greater number disabled.[74] This ignores the two grenadiers killed at the castle.

A government report was that this was the 'Entire Defeat of the most considerable Force of the Highland Rebels'.[75] Mackay wrote, 'the news whereof did very much good to the King's affairs both in Scotland and England, by abating the confidence of their Majesties' enemies in both Parliaments'.[76] Carleton wrote that 'The Highlanders never held up their heads so high after this defeat.[77]

65 *Ibid.*, pp.57–58.
66 NLS, MS 7012, f65.
67 Cameron, *Memoirs*, p.295.
68 *A True and Real Account*; Mackay, *Memoirs*, p.97.
69 Balfour-Maitland, 'Estates', II, p.157.
70 *The Manuscripts of S.H. Le Fleming, Esq. of Rydal Hall* (London: HMSO, 1890), p.270.
71 <www.lochiel.net/archgives/arch173.html>
72 Balfour-Maitland, 'Estates', II, pp.171, 174, 181–2.
73 NLS, MS975, f63.
74 *A True and Real Account*.
75 Balfour-Maitland, 'Estates', II, p.153.
76 Mackay, *Memoirs*, p.96.
77 Carleton, *Memoirs*, p.58.

Mackay concluded that the victory had been due to numerous reasons. Firstly, Livingstone had procured intelligence that the Jacobites were in close proximity to him. Secondly that his troops were led in silence towards the enemy, thirdly that the inexperienced captain of the troops in the castle concealed his march. That Buchan camped his men in a vulnerable position contrary to usual Jacobite procedure. Mackay lastly wrote 'tho' Sir Thomas Livingstone did all that could be expected of a carefull diligent officer, the captain of the castle, altogether a novice, seemed to have had the greatest share in this favourable success'.[78]

The Jacobites dispersed: they had been on campaign for six weeks, had been defeated, scattered and had lost their supplies. They also wanted to see their families again.[79] A government newssheet from Edinburgh, published a week later told that the Jacobites had told James that they could not hold out any longer, that they were in a starving condition and how 'the rebels are in a great consternation, faring they shall have no relief from Ireland and doubts not but the common people will yield at the first approach of any of the King's forces'.[80]

As with the fighting at Dunkeld, the results were as much moral than physical. Cameron wrote, 'the ill conduct of General Buchan so discouraged the Lowland gentlemen, that not a man of them thought fit to joyn with him'. Some Highland chiefs began to submit to the government; MacDonald of Largo and McAlastair of Loup did so on 16 June.[81] The fighting was not at an end, however.

Encounters between the two sides continued but on a smaller scale. On 20 May the house of the laird of Clova was raided and several Jacobite gentlemen were seized.[82] On 18 June Mackay marched with 3,000 infantry and cavalry from Perth, feinting as if to march to Badenoch, but actually marching northwards to join Livingstone. The difficult nature of the terrain in Badenoch also led him to postpone movement there. Eight days on from leaving Perth, the two forces met at Strathspey. On 1 July, with four troops of cavalry, Mackay appeared to advance towards a Jacobite held pass in Badenoch and news of this advance led Jacobites to believe that. Meanwhile his cavalry joined the rearguard of his main force which was by then marching into Lochaber by Glenspean in the night time when wholly unexpected.[83]

On 5 July Mackay was at Inverlochy, which was his goal. Work had begun on the fort and its first stage was completed by 16 July. The height of the ramparts topped with wooden palisades was 20 feet, with a couvert and a glacis, 'a perfect defence against all attempts of such an enemy'. Although Mackay had hoped to send an expedition to the Isle of Mull, and had already shipped their provisions ahead, he had a letter from the Privy Council. It was bad news; the Anglo-Dutch fleet had been defeated in a naval battle at Beachy

78 Mackay, *Memoirs*, pp.96–97.

79 *Memoir of Lord Dundee*, p.36.

80 *Great News from Scotland and Ireland*, 1690.

81 Cameron, *Memoirs*, p.295.

82 Balfour-Maitland, 'Estates', II, p.174.

83 Mackay, *Memoirs*, p.98.

Head in the Channel with the French. Apprehensions of a possible French invasion in England or Scotland led him to march his forces southwards on 18 July. He left 1,000 men at the fort, with 2,000 bolls of meal, 30 hogshead of drink, £500 in cash and 60 fat cows.[84]

Concerns about the implications of French victories were longstanding; and the French had been successful on land as well as on sea, winning the battle of Fleurus. As late as 2 November, Hill wrote, 'I find the Highlander very confident of assistance from France, which if they get it, wee may expect, and prepare for, new troubles in the spring, and if they fail nae doubt the Highlanders might submit'.[85]

Earlier that year, naval matters had been going the government's way. In March there were three frigates patrolling between Scotland and Ireland. On 6 May came news that a ship had been taken travelling from Dublin to Galloway. On it had been artillery and supplies for the Jacobite cause, as well as eight Irish agents who were to concert action between the Irish and Scottish Jacobites.[86]

The laird of Glenmoristoun and 150 men from the Grants also sought terms. This was partly because they had lost confidence in their generals. But it was also because their enemies 'burnt his own seat to the ground, plundered his people, and made such horrible devastations' that submission seemed essential. The Privy Council told Livingstone, at Inverness, to grant him and the laird of Strathglass safe conduct in order to sign a treaty.[87]

On 20 July, Mackay was back in Badenoch. Letting the men rest for a day, he went with 140 cavalry to Ruthven, which had been taken and damaged by the Jacobites in the previous year. He left Reay's Highland company there with instructions to fortify the place. On the 22nd his main force marched to Atholl, arriving at Perth on 26 July. There he heard that Cannon and Buchan had 200 cavalry (one account states 600–800 and 100–120 infantry) close to Stirling, possibly on a recruiting mission. He ordered forces from Stirling to intercept them whilst he waited for supplies of biscuit from Dundee, before leading a detachment from his main force against the Jacobites. However, both the forces from Stirling and Mackay's own expedition, were unable to prevent the Jacobites from arriving at Braemar and escaping their pursuers and Mackay returned to Stirling to write letters to the Earl of Marlborough about how matters stood in England in relation to the naval defeat.[88] Mackay sent three troops of Cardross' dragoons and a troop of horse to join the Master of Forbes in Aberdeenshire, who had four troops of cavalry already. He personally led four regiments of infantry (Glencairn's, Kenmure's, Cunningham's and Beveridge's) and a troop of both dragoons and horse. As ever the bulk of his forces were in garrisons: in Drummond Castle, Perth, Coupar, Doune, Dunkeld, and Glasgow. Yet even at the height of the campaigning season,

84 *Ibid.*, pp.98–99.

85 NRS, GD26/9/274/10.

86 Balfour-Maitland, 'Estates', II, pp.116, 158.

87 Cameron, *Memoirs*, p.295.

88 Mackay, *Memoirs*, pp.99–100; *RPCS*, 15, p.332.

orders had to be sent out to summon all absent officers to return to their commands.[89]

Despite Buchan's defeat, the Jacobite campaign was not over. Cannon, despite his failure at Dunkeld, was still in a responsible position of command. With 600 infantry under Innerrey and 100–200 cavalry, he advanced southwards which put the government into a state of concern. They used 160 men to blockade a garrison of 70 at Abergeldie and the remainder were joined by Jacobites of Aberdeen, Banff and Mearns. Cannon spent time on the braes of Perthshire, surprising Cardross' men and killing some, forced the others to flee to Stirling.[90] Some of Cluny's men were involved in Jacobite raids, though their leader would not fully commit himself, despite his Jacobitism being affirmed to James by Sir Donald MacDonald. James expected him to raise his clan on his behalf and to send him a commission to do so, alleging, too, 'our affairs are now, we thank God, in so good a disposition'.[91]

Likewise, Buchan was still in command of a force of clansmen in Aberdeenshire. There was a body of three troops of horse and dragoons under Colonel Robert Jackson of Cardross' Horse and the Master of Forbes opposing them. Despite his defeat by cavalry at Cromdale, Buchan was impressed how his infantry had fought back against the cavalry and therefore believed that they could win against horsemen. On 8 August, the Jacobites claimed that the two sides met and their enemies avoided conflict, being outnumbered and 'wheeled about and gallopt away as fast as whip and spur could drive their horses'. According to Mackay, the Jacobites deceived their enemy by mixing baggage beasts with other horses and so made their force look numerically stronger than was the case. Yet the government claimed that there was some skirmishing which left two Jacobites dead. Ensconced in Aberdeen, they were safe for Buchan lacked the means to attack the city, though Jacobite numbers rose, perhaps to 15,00, due to this small triumph and the city magistrates were unsympathetic to the government forces.[92] Forbes and Jackson had breast works erected and cannon planted there in case of an attack. They also were reinforced here by further troops and militia.[93]

Mackay sent Colonel Richard Cunningham with his own infantry regiment, six companies of Beveridge's infantry and 10 companies of Kenmure's to Aberdeen. These only amounted to 300 men. There was also an additional two or three troops of cavalry arrived from Montrose, three less than the anticipated six. Having heard nothing more from Marlborough about a possible invasion from France to England, Mackay took Livingstone's dragoons and the three Dutch battalions, these three latter numbering 1,400 men in total. However Buchan and Cannon heard of their arrival and so left Aberdeen and marched southward on 21 August.[94]

89 *RPCS*, 15, pp.363–364. 394–395.

90 Cameron, *Memoirs*, pp. 295–6; Mackay, *Memoirs*, p.100.

91 NLS, MS 3194, 114–115.

92 Cameron, *Memoirs*, p.296; Balfour-Maitland, 'Estates', II, p.257; Mackay, *Memoirs*, p.100.

93 Balfour-Maitland, 'Estates', II, p.258.

94 Balfour-Maitland, 'Estates' II', p.258, 262; Mackay, *Memoirs*, pp.100–101.

There were two skirmishes centred around castles. On 22 August the MacGregors attempted to take the castle of Cardross. The officer commanding did not surrender because he believed there were very few Jacobites there; only 15 men. Therefore he sent 24 men out of comparative safety behind the walls to attack them. In the open they were ambushed by 115 MacGregors. Fourteen were killed and five captured, including their officer. The survivors told the governor what had happened and he sent a message to Colonel Fullerton at Dunblane. Fullerton, with two companies of Angus' infantry and a troop of Rollo's Horse, marched to the castle on the next morning and overtook the hitherto victorious Jacobite infantry, killing 40 and taking another 40 prisoner. Their captives were released. Those cattle and cows taken were also recaptured.[95]

Another similar encounter occurred at Abergeldie castle, held by a Lieutenant Gordon 'having been so long among that country people', Mackay adding 'this country is now full of malicious censurers than any I ever served in'.[96] It was besieged by 200–300 Jacobites led by the laird of Innerey. Mackay sent two troops of Livingstone's dragoons led by Major Aeneas Mackay, perhaps 60 men. On 21 August, the relieving force inflicted a severe blow to the Jacobites at the Pass of Ballater; killing 100 and taking prisoners, without any fatalities of their own. Targets, blunderbusses and headpieces were left behind. Yet Mackay's men were unable to pursue the remaining Jacobites who fled to the hills.[97]

The Jacobite cause was not wholly vanquished, therefore, and Cannon gained additional strength in the way of 300–400 gentlemen from Lennox. After spending some time in Menteith and the adjacent country, he marched northwards to join Buchan. However, news arrived of the battle of the Boyne on 1 July, where William's army had defeated James', resulting in the latter fleeing to France and the Irish capital falling to William. Cameron wrote 'This action in a manner determined the fate of the war'. One consequence of the battle was that Mackay returned to Scotland. He had a substantial army with him and put two battalions at the newly established Fort William at Inverlochy.[98]

Seaforth encouraged support for the Jacobite cause by promising that James would provide aid from Ireland. This would not be in terms of manpower, but in arms and ammunition, money and provisions. He argued that the English fleet would not interfere with such supplies, but not all were convinced by these assurances. He also gave Cluny a colonel's commission from James.[99] Yet by May, some had submitted to Livingstone and in the following month Hill heard from Seaforth that he wanted to live in peace. The Chisholms and MacDonalds of Sleat laid down their arms, and by July Seaforth advocated doing the opposite of what he had only two months previously.[100]

95 Balfour-Maitland, 'Estates', II, pp.262–263.
96 NRS, RH1/2/936.
97 Balfour-Maitland, 'Estates', II, pp.263–265; Mackay, *Memoirs*, p.101.
98 Cameron, *Memoirs*, p.296, 299.
99 Balfour-Maitland, 'Estates', II, pp.184–185, 193.
100 *Ibid.*, pp.215, 216, 219, 223.

Yet by late August he had gathered his Highlanders together with the purpose of joining the Jacobite cause. On Buchan's departure and Mackay's advance, he sent two envoys to the latter to stress his peaceable intentions. Mackay threatened his property with destruction unless he surrendered in person. Seaforth agreed, on the condition he be taken at night time. Although Mackay was positive, Seaforth changed his mind. Mackay then ordered Major Wishart with 200 chosen infantry, and 900 Highlanders of Sutherland's, Reay's and Balnagown's to lay waste to the property of Seaforth's vassals. Theft of possessions and burning houses was not something Mackay relished, as these tenants were Protestants and he would have preferred to take Seaforth prisoner. Meanwhile he had more troops, three battalions of infantry and cavalry from Aberdeen, in case Buchan's forces returned.[101]

Mackay was able to put large garrisons in Glasgow and Stirlingshire. Attempts to bring the Jacobites to battle were frustrated. When it was learnt that Buchan was within 15 miles of Dumbarton, Mackay went in pursuit and although he was at Perth a week later and saw Buchan and his cavalry, the latter escaped. Marching men to the hills proved fruitless. Jacobite raiding parties in Aberdeenshire made attacks, and detachments of dragoons were sent after them; without success. Livingstone went with three regiments of infantry, and 10 troops of cavalry.[102] In late August a feared attack on Inverness was frustrated by Mackay's marching northwards and apparently four hours separated them from a battle.[103] Mackay also laid waste to his enemies' property, writing, without any obvious remorse, 'I burnt 12 miles of a very fertile Highland country, at least 12 or 1400 houses, but had no tyme to go up to the length of Braemar'. Such behaviour probably did not help with learning were the Jacobites were, 'it being impossible for me, in these rebellious countreys, to get any sure intelligence of him'.[104] But nor could the Jacobites prevail.

Throughout the autumn, the same inconclusive pattern was repeated. In September, Cannon and Buchan journeyed through Murray towards Neis, taking horses and other property from government supporters. Mackay went in pursuit, but to no effect. Jacobite forces near Stirling likewise retreated before enemy advances and others lay in the hills near Dunkeld. One reason why the Jacobites were safe was that Mackay lacked the provisions, tents and necessary baggage to follow them.[105] There were still fears, as late as 5 September, that Dunblane might be in danger, so part of Angus' regiment and Rollo's troop of horse was sent there. In the following week, Argyll's, Leslies' and Ramsay's regiments were sent to nearby Stirling. Ruthven Fort had been repaired.[106]

Leslie reported from Stirling on 18 September on the Jacobite weakness as well as on his troops' limitations, as noted when he had sent men against

101 Mackay, *Memoirs*, p.102.
102 Balfour-Maitland, 'Estates', II, pp.245–246, 248, 255.
103 Mackay, *Memoirs*, p.346.
104 *Ibid*., p.101.
105 Balfour-Maitland, 'Estates', II, pp.266, 273.
106 *RPCS*, 15, pp.423, 483.

them. He wrote that 'We have had twice notices of the enemy, and have marched against them, but they have still avoided us and retired to the mountains so that it was not thought fit that we should pursue them'. This was due to a lack of tents and supplies of only bread and water. One regiment had come within five or six miles of the Jacobites, but had been forced to camp out in the open and the season was soon making such impracticable. He reasoned that 'I believe they are not of that strength they are reported to be, for otherwise I persuade myself they would have attacked me either in the night or in my march'.[107] Because Buchan's force was largely cavalry, it was 'no hard task to beat them if he can meet with them'.[108]

These forces were insufficient to bring about a military victory, but the government were wanting peace to be established as soon as possible. They were concerned about sporadic Highland warfare and that the French might invade. Calls for a treaty to be hammered out were made once again. The Highland chiefs were not averse to this, to alleviate the sufferings of their people, but felt that they could not do so without authorisation from James. On 8 September, Breadalbane and the Earl of Menteath were ordered to meet with the Privy Council.[109]

By the end of the year, the Jacobite forces dispersed once more. More had submitted; including the Stuarts of Appin in September. Cannon attempted to engage the MacPhersons and MacIntoshes in Badenoch, but they refused to comply. The Camerons and MacDonalds cold shouldered him, for they had come to an accommodation with Hill. Their leaders had departed; Cannon to MacDonald's of Glencoe's house and then to Ireland, Buchan to the Isle of Mull and then to France, Dunfermline to the Isle of Skye.[110]

Hill had hopes that some would submit but only if the conditions were right, that otherwise they would resort to banditry. Apparently 'they all start out upon the point of full indemnity for what is past'. Hill had done what he could; treating Lochiel, Glengarry and Clanranald, dealing with them civilly and laying before them the reasons for coming to terms, 'I believe they will, if the King's pardon may be granted' and some cash be forthcoming.[111]

Externally, though, matters were not going well for the Jacobite cause. The Jacobite army in Ireland had been defeated at the Boyne, and though not destroyed, had led to the ignominious flight of James II. Celebrations in Edinburgh for this momentous news included the castle guns firing, as they did in Stirling and Dumbarton. Bells rung and bonfires were lit in the capital.[112]

The Jacobite army there was very definitely on the defensive and had no obvious long term prospects for eventual success. Even that event in 1690 which had looked promising for the cause, namely the defeat of the Anglo-

107 NLS, MS 3740, 151.
108 *Ibid.*, MS 1031, 102.
109 Balfour-Maitland, 'Estates', II, p.299–300.
110 *Ibid.*, pp.285, 288. 289.
111 NRS, GD26/9/274/2, 3, 13.
112 *RPCS*, 15, p.311.

Dutch fleet at the battle of Beachy Head and the subsequent fears of French invasion in the summer had led to naught.

Mackay's command in Scotland came to an end in November and he was sent to Ireland. On 10 November Livingstone was formally made commander-in-chief. He had the disagreeable news of being told that there would be further troop disbandment; Glencairn's, Grant's and Kenmure's were to be reduced except for those men with Hill at Fort William. A number of men deserted and this was particularly problematic as some of the cavalrymen (all the single troops of Scottish cavalry were also to be disbanded) were selling their weapons. Proclamations were issued against such behaviour.[113] Although the government's forces had the upper hand, they were unable to bring about a military solution and bring about the Jacobites' submission.

113 *Ibid.*, pp.540, 575, 615–616.

8

The End of the Campaign, 1691–1692

It was not uncommon in the seventeenth and eighteenth centuries for warfare to conclude, not by a knock out victory or unconditional surrender, which is more familiar in the nineteenth and twentieth centuries, but by negotiation, often quite protracted. Neither side feels strong enough to defeat the other and the campaign's purpose was not to aim to destroy the other militarily. Conventionally wars were about seizing towns, cities and fortresses which could be the subject of negotiation. Yet what was deemed by the state to be rebellion, such as in 1679 and 1685, as well as in the cases of those of 1715 and 1745, did end in utter victory for one side and there was no negotiation in any of these instances as the state did not deemed the rebels to be legitimate enemies. In this case it was different. By the end of 1690 it was clear that the Jacobites were not going to achieve an outright victory over their foes, but neither could they be vanquished in the field. But they could act as a major nuisance to a government which needed to conclude hostilities in order to avoid the drain on their financial resources, to say nothing of manpower, and to concentrate on the war on the Continent. So a cessation of hostilities was in the interest of both sides. The question of terms remained, however.

As in the winter of 1689/1690 there were reductions in the strength of the forces in Scotland in the subsequent winter. On 30 December 1690 William III had decreed that all the forces required in Scotland were two regiments of dragoons (Cunningham's and Newbottle's), three of infantry (Hill's, Argyll's and Buchan's), five independent companies and garrisons for the castles of Edinburgh, Stirling, Dumbarton, Blackness and Bass.[1]

Unsurprisingly, morale was low. Men from a regiment of horse on being told that they were to be downgraded to dragoons with loss of status and pay, mutinied.[2] Livingstone wrote on 5 February, 'There are many of the troops who have taken their officers prisoners with the standards and trumpets, entered into a bond of Association and will not submit to any that would convince them to reason'. This was even worse because 'this may

1 *RPCS*, 16, pp.8–13.
2 *Ibid.*, p.78.

be of bad consequence when … the heads of our contrair partie is making Great offers to them'. Money was received a few days later, but it was not enough, 'The Troops are in worse humour as they were befor'. It was only on 17 February after a month's pay had been found and presumably distributed, that Livingstone could report, 'I hope by that means the soldiers may be brought to the conformitie it was reported'.[3] Yet when Leven decided to pay his men for only 28 days per month, his regiment, stationed at Montrose, understandably mutinied and one man was killed in the process.[4]

Military stores were limited, 'Wee are extreamly scarce of powder and ball in all our magazines', wrote Livingstone on 13 February and a month later matters were no better: 'We are reduced to such a small quantitie that we can scarcely provide our Garrisons'. Many captains and lieutenants were absent from their posts. Livingstone's protestations had not gone answered, and on 2 April he wrote, 'We are so il circumstanced, that we schal not be in a condition to draw together; for no provisions, no commissarie for provisions, scars of ammunition, no baggage horses.' There was a lack of gunpowder and it would take two months before an order for it from Holland could be completed. There was 'great sickness' among the soldiers and so few recruits. Colonel Hill wrote of the cavalry at Fort William, 'The troop … are in a very mutinous humour, haveing got no pay as troopers', seized their officers as prisoners and entered into a bond of association to negotiate.[5]

All this was particularly alarming because of their perceived dangers as well as their own weaknesses. Livingstone heard that the Jacobites were 'listing of men up and down the country' and that his woes meant that 'our enemies are encouraged so much'. His former officers who had been involved in a Jacobite plot two years who had now been released and with fears of a French invasion, 'it makes such as we call Jacobins here very insolent'. His dismay was even more so because 'The well affected part in this kingdom are under some fear'. Livingstone writing 'The raport we have had so long tyme heer of a French invasion, is now generally by il and wel inclined believed. If it coms, we schal fynd our selfs in great straits'. Hill thought that the Jacobites expected aid from France and Ireland.[6]

The government's response was that the army in Scotland cost £48,000 per year. Cess and excise taxes had not been paid fully in Scotland in the previous two years, due to 'the troubles and vastations has bene in severall shirs these two years past'. There was not the money to pay officers or soldiers, but there was £10,000 plus 1,000 muskets, 300 barrels of powder and 300 pairs of pistols, to be provided by Captain Slezar from the stores at Edinburgh.[7]

Although there was not even a semblance of a Jacobite army in existence in 1691, there were several reports of Highland raids early that year. Cardross and the lands adjacent were plundered by 'Highland rebels' and there were

3 J. MacConechy (ed.), *Papers illustrative of the Political Conditions of the Highlands of Scotland from the years 1689 to 1696* (Glasgow, 1845), pp.3, 5, 8, 9.

4 NRS, GD26/9/375.

5 NLS, MS 7013, 33; NRS, GD26/9/375.

6 *Ibid.*

7 Maconechy, *Papers Illustrative*, p.7.

calls for military protection. Stirlingshire and Dumbartonshire were 'dayly harassed and oppressed by the incursions of thieves and broken men from the Highlands'.[8] Alexander Bruce, on 24 February, wrote, 'Our Highlanders are now and then falling down upon their neighbours and robbing what comes best to hand, but no force of any sort appears'.[9]

Dalrymple, the new Secretary of State for Scotland, urged Livingstone to be pacific, writing on 28 April, 'not to medle with them at present, so long as they stay quiet, for you know how little the treasury can spare for any utrick or incident charges, in caice they should draw to a considerable body and oblige our army to com together to observe them or reduce them'.[10] Yet on the other hand, the government was determined on a policy that Jacobites should surrender or be attacked. On 12 May Hill received orders from the Privy Council to use his troops to 'fall upon those Highlanders within my reach that do not presently come in and take the oath of allegiance, deliever up their arms'. Although Hill wrote 'I shall endeavour to put in execution', he reported that 'at present they are quiet'. However, he was not confident that orders to deliver weapons and take loyal oaths would be effectual, 'they will rather part with their lives'. Only old weapons had been surrendered by the men of Mull and Atholl.[11]

The naval presence was maintained on the western coast. The *Pembroke* and the *Conception*, under Captains John Every and Robert Fairfax, each of 135 men and 32 guns, were cruising off the Isle of Mull in June and July. They convoyed a ship to Londonderry and helped move Argyll and 100 of his Highlanders. There was some conflict on 2 July as the guns manned by the MacDonalds and MacLeans from Castle Duart fired on the two ships, killing one man from the *Pembroke*, and wounding some of Argyll's. Though the two ships gave it a broadside, they could do little effectively against the castle and so weighed anchor and sailed westwards. In the following month they were joined by the 10-gun ketch, *The Eagle*, under Lieutenant William Martin with 50 men.[12]

Meanwhile there was a minor Jacobite coup when in June the Jacobite prisoners held at the little fortress on the Bass Rock, an island on the Firth of Forth, seized it from their gaolers and declared against the government.[13]

William III was anxious to end the conflict in Scotland as soon as possible. Ever since 1689 he had had proclamations for amnesties issued and had tried to broker peace, as he had done in Ireland in 1689–1690.[14] The Jacobite leaders in Scotland were now willing to be conciliatory, attesting on 20 June:

> We, Major General Buchan and Sir George Barclay, Generall Officers of King James the Seventh, his forces within the kingdom of Scotland, to testifie our aversion of shedding Christian blood, and yt wee design to appear good Scotsmen, and do wish that this Nation be restored to its wounded and happie peace, doe agree and

8 *RPCS* 16, pp.70, 124.
9 NLS, MS 7013, f14r.
10 *HMC 46, Johnstone*, p.55.
11 MacConechy, *Papers Illustrative*, pp.9, 14–15.
12 TNA, ADM8/2; 51/3796, 4285/1.
13 Luttrell, *Brief Relation*, II, p.251.
14 Childs, *Williamite War*, p.229.

> consent to a forebearance of all accounts of hostilitie and depredations committed upon any of the King's subjects, who have been, or are, engaged in his service under our command, either by sea or land, wee haveing given all necessary orders to such as are under command to forebear all acts of hostilities by sea or land until the aforesaid time. Subscribed at Achallader, ye 30th of June 1691.[15]

At the same time, there were doubts that the talks would be effective. Should this be the case, Dalrymple wrote 'the King I believe will order his army to fall upon the Highlanders he hath commanded them to be campt and in readiness on the borders of the highlands … the affair will come to some conclusion'.[16] Meanwhile, Livingstone was ordered to station his troops on the borders of the Highlands only and not march northwards unless the Jacobite clans began to draw together again. There seemed little likelihood of that as 'The Highland rebels have been of late very peaceable … disposed to ly qwyet'. When a soldier of the Fort William garrison was captured by the Stewarts of Appin, and Hill had the clan chief and others arrested, Appin was soon ordered to be freed. In the meantime, some tendered oaths to Hill that they would not rise in arms again.[17]

Breadalbane was selected, as before, by William to act as his plenipotentiary. He had several meetings with the chiefs at Achallader and they drew up a list of five main demands for laying down their arms. Firstly, they demanded that they send a representative to James to explain the state of affairs in Scotland 'and to obtain his permission and warrand to enter into that treaty'. After all, some Jacobites recognised him as their monarch *de jure*. If this article was granted, the next was that they wanted £20,000 to reimburse the losses they had sustained in the fighting, as they were allegedly so impoverished that without it they would be unable to resist 'makeing depredations on their low country neighbours'. Thirdly, William must free them from any vassalage or dependence on neighbouring magnates, as James was to have done and be solely under the Crown. Fourth, that James' officers be allowed to stay at home or leave, without being molested, and in the latter case, transport to France be paid for by the government. Finally, the bearing of arms had to be still permissible, that no oath had to be made save allegiance to the dual monarchy, and that there be a full indemnity for any crimes committed during the campaigns. In return for all this, the chiefs promised to cease warfare.[18]

Yet there was also a stick as well as carrots. The King's declaration also included the ominous phrase, 'And that such as shall continue obstinate and incorrigible after this gracious offer of mercy, shall be punished as traitors and rebels, and otherwayes to the outmust severity of the law.'[19]

The chiefs agreed to these terms, and Breadalbane took their answer to William, who was then on the Continent. On 27 August he wrote a long letter, signalling his agreement with the terms, providing that the chiefs took the oath

---

15 MacConechy, *Papers Illustrative*, p.21.

16 *HMC Hamilton*, 21, p.117.

17 *RPCS*, 16, pp.452, 489, 452.

18 Cameron, *Memoirs*, p.301.

19 MaConechy, *Papers Illustrative*, p.37.

of allegiance to a designated civil officer prior to 1 January 1692. According to him, 'We are graciously pleased, not only to pardon, indemnifie, and restore all that have been in armes, who shall take the oath of alledgiance before the first day of Januarie next'. These had to be taken either before the Privy Council or to the sheriff or his deputy of the county where they lived. The Privy Council then issued proclamations to this effect at the end of the said month, adding, 'if any remain obstinate, they may be prosecute by the severity of the law'.[20]

The strategic position of the Jacobites in Scotland was becoming bleak. Their allies had been decisively defeated in Ireland at Aughrim on 12 July. Following this they made peace with William at the Treaty of Limerick in October and many left for France. The Irish war was thus over. No help could be expected from that quarter. Practically and morally, the end of the Jacobite cause in Scotland could not be long postponed.

Meanwhile there were concerns that the cease fire might not be permanent. Apparently in September, Atholl was persuading Glengarry to have his clan rise again. In the following month it was noted that 'Highlanders are all insolent as ever' which made 'a mock of the proclamation of indemnitie'. Disputes arose over the share of the money allotted to them.[21]

At the end of September 1691 the government took action. It sent Argyll with his regiment to Stirling. He had provisional orders to march to Argyllshire with Glencairn, to reduce the Isles to subservience. Major Ferguson was already there, along with 600 of Argyll's Highlanders under Sir James Campbell of Ardkinglas. The only reported action of these troops was to take Stalker Castle, on an inlet off Loch Laich off the west coast, kept by Stewart of Ardsheall for James, which surrendered on 9 October.[22] Supplies were ordered to be stored at Inverness and at Inverlochy for troops should they need to recommence hostilities.[23]

Sir George Barclay was the man selected to visit James in France to convince James that his followers needed to be released from their oaths of allegiance. Unfortunately, the exiled monarch took his time in coming to a decision and did not do so until the end of the year, which was to prove fatal for some. James' response read as follows:

> Right trusty and well beloved, we greet you well.
>
> We are informed of the state of our subjects in the Highlands, and of the condition that you and our other officers there are in, as well by our trusty and well-beloved Sir George Barclay, brigadier of our forces, as by our trusty and well-beloved Major Duncan Menzies: And therefore we have thought fit hereby to authorise you to give leave to our aid subjects and officers, who have hitherto behaved themselves so loyally in our cause, to doe what may be most for their own and your safety. For doeing whereof, this shall be your warrant: And so we bid you farewell.
>
> St. Germains, this 12th day of December 1691'.[24]

20 Cameron, *Memoirs*, p.304; MacConechy, *Papers Illustrative*, pp. 33–34.
21 NLS, MS 7013, 82, 108.
22 Cameron, *Memoirs*, p.302.
23 NLS MS 7013, 154.
24 Cameron, *Memoirs*, p.311–2.

It was directed to Buchan and Barclay returned to London with it in his possession. Major Menzies took it to Buchan in Scotland, arriving at Dunkeld just 11 days after having set out from Paris. Menzies was by now so exhausted that the letter had to be forwarded on to Buchan who was then at Glengarry. Cameron was not shown it until 30 December and only just took the oath as required at Inverrary in time.[25]

Meanwhile, on 3 December Dalrymple told Colonel Hamilton, of the MacDonalds of Glencoe, 'That's the only popish clan in the kingdom and it will be popular to take severe course with them … what force will be necessary to your garrison … all must be in readinesss by the 1st of 1anuary.'[26]

Menzies noticed, on his arrival in Scotland, that 'the whole forces of the kingdom ready to invade the Highlands'. Melville had written to Hamilton on 19 December 'the discourse is of a Highland campaign to be presently made if the Highlanders come not in'.[27] In order to avert calamity he wrote to both Buchan and Livingstone; the former to urge him to send expresses to all chiefs urging them to submit as soon as possible, and to the latter to have him request that the council give a few days grace for the submissions to occur. Because of the brevity of time, the expresses to remote places could not reach there in time. Likewise, Livingstone was unable to put the request to the Privy Council before 5 January and they refused to give an answer, ordering him to remit his message to the court in London.[28]

Many chiefs did report to the sheriffs to submit. Lochiel, Keppoch, Appin, MacGregor, Farquharson and Macnaughton did so. Glengarry missed the deadline, however.[29] Livingstone wrote on 28 January, 'so that we are neare ane end of that troublesome tho' in itself ane insignificant business'.[30] Dalrymple wrote on 16 January, 'I am extremely glad that the murderer MacIean of Glencoe did not accept the benefit of the indemnity. I hope care will be taken to rout out that …'[31] MacIean had arrived at Fort William on 31 December, but as Hill was a military, not civil officer, the oath could not be tendered to him and it was another six days until he could do so and then returned home, believing that all was well.

It is not the aim of this narrative to examine the massacre of Glencoe in any depth; sufficient books exist to allow the interested reader to do so already and none is better than Hopkins' magisterial study. What follows is a very brief summary based on the said work.

There were a number of chiefs who had not submitted before the deadline. As noted, William was prepared to see violent action against any who did not do so. After all, the penalty for failure had been laid out in no uncertain terms, so none were ignorant. Possibly some may have believed William lacked the means to take strong action in the hills in winter; Mackay had never done so. He was eager to shift as much of Britain's military resources

25 *Ibid.*, p.312.
26 MaConechy, *Papers Illustrative*, p.53.
27 *HMC 21, Hamilton*, pp.123–124.
28 *Ibid.*, p.313.
29 *The London Gazette*, 2731, 11–14 Jan. 1692; 2732, 14–18 Jan. 1692.
30 NRS, GD26/9/335.
31 NLS, MS 7014, f8.

to the Continent as soon as possible as so wished to end the commitments in the British Isles rapidly. Armed with this, Dalrymple had already mooted action, in order to encourage the others to obedience to his royal master. Initially Glengarry's clan was to be the subject of such, but he had a strongly defensible position which would be difficult and time consuming to take with the relatively few troops available in such a short time. An easier target was then chosen: the relatively minor Jacobite clan of the MacDonalds of Glencoe. Dalrymple and Livingstone, as commander-in-chief in Scotland, worked together to organise the troops necessary. This was not an act of clan warfare nor of Anglo-Scottish antagonism but by the political and military agents of the Scottish government at the behest of a Dutch king in London with a European agenda.[32]

William, then at Whitehall, gave a prompt, but blunt answer on 11 January 1692, with an order to march troops against the 'rebels' and with fire and sword, to kill the men, burn property and destroy houses.[33] Such instruments of terror against civilians by soldiers were not novel in contemporary warfare. Far worse had happened in 1688 when Louis XIV unleashed his troops against the Palatinate. Two companies of Argyll's regiment were sent to Glencoe from Fort William and were billeted on the clan on 1 February.

The final act was the order by Major Robert Duncanson to Captain Robert Campbell of Argyll's regiment:

> You are hereby ordered to fall upon the rebels, the MacDonalds of Glencoe, and put all to the sword under 70. You are to have a special care that the old fox and his sons do upon no account escape your hands. You are to secure all the avenues, that no man escapes. This you are to put into execution at five of the clock precisely, and by that time, or very soon after it, I will strive to be at you with a stronger party. If I do not come to you at five, you are not to tarry for me, but to fall on. This is by the King's special command, for the good and safety of the country, that these miscreants be cut off root and branch. See that this be put in execution.[34]

The order was received on 12 February. In spite of two officers refusing to obey orders (later court martialled but cleared) and some soldiers being unenthusiastic or even warning their hosts, the killing commenced early in the following morning. When it did, 38 of the clan, including its chief, were killed; his wife died in the snow as did others, killed by cold and starvation. Most were able to escape as Duncanson's troops had not arrived in time to cut off the escape routes; furthermore the sound of gunshots led many to flee. There was looting as well as murder, arson and theft. As an attempt to wipe out the clan it failed. It was bloody but was mercifully inefficient.[35]

Hill wrote: 'I hope this example of justice and severity upon Glencoe will be enough' and referred to the 'destruction of Glencoe (according to orders from his Majesty)'. It certainly led to other clans, such as Clanranalds,

32 Hopkins, *Glencoe*, p.488.
33 MacConechy, *Papers Illustrative*, p.60.
34 Browning, *English Historical Documents*, p.652.
35 Hopkins, *Glencoe*, pp.335–337.

submitting.[36] Dalrymple wrote in early March, 'All I regrete is, that any of the sect gote away, and there is the necessity to prosecute them to the utmost.'[37] The result was commented upon a few weeks later thus, 'Wrote from Edinburgh, the Earl of Argyll's regiment in their march hither from the Highlands, killed about 60 of them who refused to submit to their Majesties' government.'[38] The killings, however, had the intended results as the remainder of the Jacobite clan chiefs hastened to take the oath of allegiance as demanded in the previous year. The subsequent enquiry exonerated those responsible, though Dalrymple resigned in 1695, but led to bitterness among the Highlands. It was in no way the worst massacre committed in the Highland's bloody history, but what made it infamous was the fact that it had been carried out by guests whilst enjoying their hosts' hospitality.

Occasional attempts were made by the French to reinforce James' supporters in Scotland in January 1692. A French ship with meat, wine and brandy for the Highlanders was intercepted and another was taken off Aberdeen.[39] However, as planned the military forces in Scotland were reduced; in February the regiments of Leven, Ramsay, Lowther and Beveridge boarded ships to Flanders. By the summer there were only three regiments of dragoons and a regiment of infantry left in Scotland.[40]

However, the Jacobite leaders had now left Scotland. In early March, Cannon, Buchan and Colonel Graham spent time in Edinburgh, before leaving with other Jacobite officers by 2 April. There were, though, still concerns about Jacobite activity; a plot to take Edinburgh castle involving Ensign Creton and Major Hume was nipped in the bud. Colonel Hill saw French ships off the coast and feared Gordon and Buchan might be on board. The Jacobites on Bass were supplied by French ships, but by June invasion fears declined.[41]

What also served more to put a temporary stop to Jacobite support in Scotland were external events. Firstly, the Irish Jacobites were defeated at the battle of Aughrim on 12 July 1691, followed by the Treaty of Limerick in October 1691, allowing those who had fought for James to emigrate if they so chose. Meanwhile, in the following year, the French Navy was decisively beaten by an Anglo-Dutch fleet at the battle of La Hogue on 23–24 May 1692. Combined, these battles meant that there would be no help from France nor Ireland to assist the already beleaguered Scottish Jacobites. In any case, French military successes on land obviated against anything as risky as an invasion attempt.

Concerns about Jacobite activity in Scotland continued for some years. Jacobite cries were heard in an anti-recruiting riot in Edinburgh in early 1693. Lords Arran and Hume were arrested for involvement in an alleged Jacobite plot; there was communication with Melfort and one Neville Payne was condemned to death for conspiracy. In part this was because Britain and

36 NLS, MS 7014, 13, 15.

37 MaConechy, *Papers Illustrative*, p.75.

38 Luttrell, *Brief Relation*, II, p.384.

39 *Ibid.*, pp.327, 329.

40 *Ibid.*, pp.361, 442.

41 *Ibid.*, pp.444, 466, 485, 476.

France were still at war until 1697, because there were few troops in Scotland (needed to fight the French in the Low Countries) and because the Jacobite outpost on the Bass remained until 1694. Four new cavalry regiments were raised.[42]

The garrison on the Bass offered to surrender in February 1693, but refused the terms offered and negotiations in May came to nothing. After a French supply ship there was intercepted in January 1694, attempts at a parley resumed. It came to nothing. The Privy Council considered an attack with two ships and regular troops, but this came to naught. Despite the French supplying men and supplies, the garrison of 24 men surrendered on 26 April 1694, and were given £200 and the liberty to go where they wished.[43]

As to the principal soldiers on either side, both Lanier and Mackay served in Ireland and then in the Low Countries (Mackay now being a lieutenant general), both being killed at the battle of Steinkirk in 1692. Livingstone survived longer, becoming Viscount Teviot and attaining the rank of lieutenant general before dying peaceably. Buchan left Scotland in 1692 but adhered to his Jacobite creed, whether at the exiled court in France or conspiring in Scotland in 1708 and 1715 for the return of the dynasty. He eventually died in Scotland. William retained the throne, though after Mary's death in 1694, ruled alone, surviving assassination plots and having fought Louis XIV to a standstill by the war's end in 1697. James died in exile at St. Germain in 1701, though his son and eldest grandson were to make subsequent attempts to regain the throne; albeit always unsuccessfully.

Some of the others who fought also took part in the attempt to put James' son on the throne in 1715. Struan, John Cameron and Clanranald all fought at the battle of Sheriffmuir; the latter was shot dead before his clan could charge. On the other side, Donald McBane, having served in Flanders, was an elderly junior officer at the battle of Preston on 12–14 November 1715, where Angus' battalion took part in an assault on that town. Blackadder was put in charge of the Glasgow militia in 1715 and became deputy governor of Stirling Castle.

The Jacobite cause in Scotland failed for a number of reasons. After the death of Killiecrankie there was a lack of an outstanding leader. Secondly, only a minority of Scots, even among the Highlands, supported the cause. There was very little aid from Ireland and none from France. Thirdly, their opponents were able to defeat them in battle, held the major centres of supply and constructed a strongpoint in the western Highlands, as well as possessing effective naval support. For Jacobite success to have been achieved, all or some of these conditions would have had to have been overcome.

42 *Ibid.*, III, pp.51, 95, 107, 112, 191.

43 *Ibid.*, pp.27, 97, 261, 279, 282, 301.

Conclusion

By European standards, or even those of the later two major Jacobite incursions, the campaign in Scotland in 1689–1691 was on a small scale indeed. At most the Jacobite army never exceeded 5,000 men – far fewer than 'came out' in 1715 or in 1745. It was also geographically limited to the Scottish Highlands. Yet it lasted the longest of any of the Stuarts' attempts to restore the throne. Both of the later major efforts were over and done within the year; indeed within six months of raising the standard at Braemar, in 1715, the Jacobite leader, the Earl of Mar, had fled to France, his army about to disperse and by nine months from his arrival in 1745, Charles Edward Stuart was a man on the run, his army decisively defeated.

The longer duration of this campaign can be ascribed to its peripatetic nature and this was due to terrain, resources and logistics, making it as unlike conventional Continental warfare as it was possible to be. The Jacobites had no fixed base, which would have been a source of strength but also one of vulnerability. Although taking most of their strength from the western Highlands, there was no one place which was their headquarters. There was nowhere for the government to direct its forces to take, as there was to be in 1716 and 1746 (Perth and Inverness, respectively). The lack of supplies and manpower limited their opponents' ability to defeat them in the field if the Jacobites chose to – and were able to – avoid set piece battles, which they did after May 1690. The government was facing, in 1690–1, highly mobile enemies whom they could not wholly stamp out with the declining numbers of troops at their disposal.

By 1691, William's government had realised that a purely military solution was impossible in the short or even medium term. Their priority was the war in Europe and they wanted the maximum resources to be brought to bear there, against the French, who were always William's principal enemies. He had proposed indemnities since July 1689 to bring the conflict in Scotland to an end. These had been refused in 1689 and 1690. However, by 1691 the prospect of a French invasion and/or significant help from Ireland was increasingly unlikely. Negotiation made sense at this point as both sides realised that neither could gain an outright victory and prolonging the conflict would merely increase mutual impoverishment and deaths.

The Treaty of Achallader was the only time that the Jacobites and the government made a formal settlement in which none of the former were

Breastplate and helmet as worn by Viscount Dundee at the Battle of Killiecrankie. (Author, 2018)

formally punished and where the latter gave them a cash payout. This solution was discussed in October 1715 but never carried out and in 1746 was never even contemplated.

After the fighting at Cromdale a victory for the Jacobites was probably impossible. With activity of the Royal Navy and the new fort at Inverlochy as well as Mackay's garrisons and field forces it was impossible to field a sizable Jacobite army as it had been in 1689. It was still possible for the Jacobites to achieve local successes, but none were even remotely the stuff that topples governments. Yet for all the King's forces and all the King's men, they could not be hunted down and definitely beaten. The result was a compromise which suited both sides.

The Battlefields Today

Much of the geography of the battlefield of Killiecrankie remains today: the pass, the hills and the river. However, Roan Ruarrirdh, the house with the walled gardens mentioned by Mackay no longer exists as it was burnt down in the nineteenth century; a new house called Urrards now stands there, once the home of Sir William Gull, a royal surgeon. The A9 road runs right through the battlefield, parallel to the river, however, and is being made into a dual carriageway. There are also far more trees now than there were at the time of the fighting.

However at the pass of Killiecrankie can be seen the famous Soldier's Leap, allegedly made by private McBane, and this is marked by a plaque. Further along the trackway is the Balfour Stone, allegedly, although certainly incorrectly, where Brigadier Balfour was killed. There is also the National Trust for Scotland Visitor Centre, open from April to October; only two of the Scottish battlefields have such. There is a little about the battle there, though there are three swords of the time, one allegedly being that of Dundee. In the middle of the battle site, there is the Tomb Clavers or the Grave of the Officers, marking Ian Steward Fitzgerald Campbell the Younger, killed in the Malayan Emergency in 1950 as well as the battle of 1689. This is the focus of an annual commemoration. Finally, there is Dundee's grave and a plaque marking his remains in the former church of St. Bride's. A few miles away is Blair Castle, where Dundee's breastplate with bullet hole (made many years after the battle), is held, as is at least one of the three 'leather guns' used at the battle.

At Dunkeld, two of the houses still stand, though much modified; they are at the west end of Cathedral Road, to the north side and plaques denoted their survival. Then there is the church and the adjoining ruined cathedral. The church boasts a small museum, in an annexe, with a little information about the battle. There is also a plaque in the nave, erected in 1903 to Cleland, who is buried there: 'A noble soldier, a devoted patriot, A brave soldier, a pious Christian' by a later member of the same regiment. Another plaque nearby relates a concise account of the battle. Inside the ruined cathedral is a stone with the alleged initials of one of Cleland's men carved onto it. Outside the church, on the approach from the east, is a war memorial to all those killed in the battle. To the north of the church there is an information board about the battle.

Cromdale's surviving buildings are the old kirk by the river and Lethendry Castle/Tower, which is currently in a ruinous situation. There is also a plaque to the battle, declaring, not wholly correctly to this author's mind, 'This complete rout ended the first Jacobite war in the Highlands'.

Appendix

Jacobites engaged in the Campaign

Name	Remarks	Source
Sir Ewan Cameron		Thomson, *APS*, Appendix, IX, p.54.
John Cameron the Younger	Son of Sir Ewan Cameron	*Ibid.*, p.55.
Alexander MacDonald of Glengarry		*Ibid.*
Sir John MacLean	Aged 19	*Ibid.*
Captain Grant	Killed at Killiecrankie	*Ibid.*
Sir Archibald Kennedy		*Ibid.*
David Graham	Dundee's brother, quartermaster of King's Regiment of Horse, 1682	*Ibid.*
Lieutenant George Murray	Captain, Dumbarton's Foot, 1686	*Ibid.*
James Seton, Earl of Dunfermline	Ensign, Mar's Foot, 1687	*Ibid.*
James Galloway, Lord Dunkeld		*Ibid.*
Major James Middleton	Served in Wauchope's regiment, captain, Mar's Foot	*Ibid.*
Colin MacKenzie	Earl of Seaforth's brother, Captain, Mar's Foot, 1685	*Ibid.*
William Crawford of Ardmillan		*Ibid.*
James Crawford		*Ibid.*
Alexander Robertson of Struan		*Ibid.*
Sir David Ogilvie of Clova	Served, Airlie's Troop, 1667; lieutenant, independent Horse Troop, 1674	*Ibid.*
John Grant of Ballindalloch		*Ibid.*
John Clelland of Faskin	Quartermaster and cornet, King's Regiment of Horse	*Ibid.*
Captain Robert Charters		*Ibid.*
David Haliburton of Pitcur		*Ibid.*
Donald MacNeill of Gallachoille		*Ibid.*
John Stewart of Appin		*Ibid.*
Alastair MacDonald of Glencoe		*Ibid.*

Name	Remarks	Source
James Edmondstone of Newton		*Ibid.*
Hector MacLean of Lochbuie		*Ibid.*
MacLean of Ardgour	Aged 30-40, sister married to a Glengarry	*Ibid.*
John Cameron of Glendessarry		*Ibid.*
MacDonald of Auchterawe		*Ibid.*
Ronald MacDonald of Keppoch		*Ibid.*, p.56.
Patrick Stewart of Bellachin	Steward to the Marquis of Atholl	*Ibid.*, p.56.
Farquharson of Inveraray		*Ibid.*, p.56.
Kenneth MacKenzie of Dalemore		*Ibid.*, p.56.
Sir William Wallace of Craigie	Captain, King's Regiment of Horse, 1686	*Ibid.*, p.56.
Sir Alexander MacLean		*Ibid.*, p.56.
Laird of MacNaughton		*Ibid.*
Major William Graham of Boquhoppol		*Ibid.*
John MacNaughton		*Ibid.*
Robert Stewart		*Ibid.*
		Ibid.
Johnston		*Ibid.*
Laird of Strickmartin		*Ibid.*
William Erskine, Earl of Buchan		*Ibid.*
Lewis Crichton, Viscount of Fendraught	Lieutenant Colonel, Foot Guards.	*Ibid.*
Sir Archibald Kennedy of Culzean		*Ibid.*
Sir John Drummond of Machanie	'a tall man and large', Cornet in Scottish Horse, 1674, lieutenant, 1687	*Ibid.*
Iain Dubh MacNeachdain		*Ibid.*
William Charters	Captain, Foot Guards, 1685	*Ibid.*
Major Duncan Menzies	Ensign Mar's Foot, 1672, lieutenant, 1685, captain, Buchan's, 1688	*Ibid.*
Alexander Stewart of Ballachan		*Ibid.*, p.57.
Captain of Clanranald		*Ibid.*
Sir Donald MacDonald of Sleat		*Ibid.*, p.58.
Kinloch of Gourdie		*Ibid.*, p.59
Laird Menzies of Pitfodels	'a lusty black man'	*Ibid.*, p.59.
Dennis McSwyne		Grameid, p.105n.
Donald Glengarry	Killed at Killiecrankie	*Ibid.*, p.124n.
Allan MacDonald		*Ibid.*, p.125n.
Alexander Drummond of Balhaldy	Son-in-law to Sir Ewan Cameron	*Ibid.*, p.131n.
MacMartin		*Ibid.*, p.134n.
Alexander MacLean		*Ibid.*, p.138n.
MacNeill of Barra		*Ibid.*, p.144n.

Name	Remarks	Source
MacLeod of Raasay		*Ibid.*, p.145n.
William Fraser of Foyers	Captain, Mar's Foot, 1681	*Ibid.*, p148n.
Fraser of Culduthil		*Ibid.*, p.150n.
Alexander McAlister of Loupe		*Ibid.*, p.154n.
Lamont		*Ibid.*, p.155n.
Fullerton of Fullerton		*Ibid.*, p.158n.
Fenton of Ogil		*Ibid.*, p.159n.
Sir Alexander Innes of Coxton		*Ibid.*
James Kinnaird of Culbyn	Quartermaster, King's Regiment of Horse	*Ibid.*, p.161n.
Adamson		*Ibid.*, p.162n.
Scott		*Ibid.*
Reids		*Ibid.*, p.163n.
Gilbert Ramsay	Killed at Killiecrankie	*Ibid.*, p.163n.
Captain Andrew Bruce	Lieutenant, Graham's Troop, 1678	*Ibid.*, p.158n.
Alastair Dubh Macdonell of Glengarry		*Ibid.*, p.97n.
Angus Glengarry		*Ibid.*, p.123n.
Allan MacDonald of Clanranald		*Ibid.*, p.125n.
Tannachy		*Ibid.*, p.135n.
Turloisk		*Ibid.*, p.139n.

Irish officers

Name	Remarks
Colonel Lord Frederick Frederick	
Colonel Lord Bohan	
Colonel Sir William Wallis	
Colonel Charles Barkley	
Colonel Nicholas Purcell	
Lieutenant Colonel Fountaine	Captain, Douglas' Foot, 1678, Captain, Beaufort's Foot, 1685
Lieutenant Colonel Archibald Douglas	Captain, Dumbarton's Foot, 1679
Lieutenant Colonel Blair	
Lieutenant Colonel Robert Gordon	Lieutenant, Dumbarton's Foot, 1679
Lieutenant Colonel Charteris senior	*Ibid.*
Lieutenant Colonel Charteris junior	*Ibid.*

NRS, GD406/1/3535; Dalton, *Irish Army Lists, 1661–1685* (London, 1907), p.127.

Jacobite prisoners taken at Cromdale

Rank (if known)	Name
Captain	Allen MacLean
Captain	John MacLean
Captain	Colle
Captain	King
Captain	Hutchings
Captain	James Buchan
Captain	Brown
Lieutenant	John MacLean
Lieutenant	Middleton
Lieutenant	Scratzer
Lieutenant	Showan
Lieutenant	Alexander Haliburton
Lieutenant	Brawdie
Lieutenant	Sewell
Lieutenant	Drunmer
Ensign	John McNaughton
Ensign	David Dunbar
Ensign	John MacLean
Ensign	Ross
Cornet	Andrew Baird
Volunteer	Charles Cornwall
Officer	Patrick Roy
Officer	Henderson
Officer	Thomas Stewart/Paterson
Ranker	James Burnett
Ranker	John Campbell
Ranker	Edward Caffiedoe
Ranker	Denke Newlands
Ranker	Francis Beaton
Ranker	Peircie Sweetman
Ranker	Edward Dobie
Ranker	Murdoch Haddichan
Ranker	Patrick Burke
Ranker	David McDermount
Ranker	James Sumergrass
Ranker	Duncan MacDonald
Ranker	Michael Davidson
Ranker	Nicholas Bowrie
Ranker	Donald McLean
Ranker	Duncan Grame

RPCS, 15, p.304; *A True and Real Account.*

Government officer casualties: Killiecrankie

Unit	Rank	Name	Type
Balfour's	Brigadier	Barthold Balfour	Killed
Balfour's	Lieutenant	Chambers	Killed
Balfour's	Captain	Barthold Balfour	Prisoner
Balfour's	Captain	Thomas Erskine	Killed
Balfour's	Captain	William Manning	Killed
Balfour's	Captain	John Clerk	Killed
Balfour's	Captain	William Douglas	Killed
Balfour's	Captain	John Gibson	Killed
Balfour's	Captain	William Miln	Killed
Hastings'	Major	Jacob	Wounded
Hastings'	Lieutenant	Finch	Prisoner
Hastings'	Captain	Tom Stanley	Killed
Hastings'	Captain	Beverley Newcomen	Killed
Leven's	Major	Robert Bruce	Killed
Mackay's	Lieutenant Colonel	James Mackay	Killed
Mackay's	Captain	Angus Mackay	Killed
Mackay's	Captain	Alexander Lamy	Killed
Mackay's	Captain	Mackenzie	Killed
Mackay's	Captain	George Canocke	Killed
Mackay's	Lieutenant	Robert Mackay	Wounded
Mackay's	Lieutenant	Lammie	Prisoner
Ramsay's	Major	James Mackay	Killed
Ramsay's	Lieutenant	James Colt	Prisoner
Ramsay's	Captain lieutenant	Van Best	Prisoner
Kenmure's	Lieutenant Colonel	John Ferguson	Killed
Kenmure's	Captain	James Donaldson	Prisoner
Kenmure's	Lieutenant	John Nisbet	Prisoner
Kenmure's	Lieutenant	David Stewart	Prisoner
Unknown	Lieutenant	John Hay	Prisoner
Unknown	Lieutenant	Murray	Prisoner
Unknown	Lieutenant	Jacob Ferguson	Prisoner

Sources, Reid, *Last Scottish Army*, pp.26, 47–49.

Known Government rank and file casualties at Killiecrankie

Name	Rank	Unit	Nature of injury	Other
John McNaughton			Scar on left of lip	Born c.1667
John Dover			Shot in back of leg	Born c.1663
Walter McLaughlin			Cut with sword on left shoulder	Born c.16
David Joyner			Shot in left arm	Born c.1664
Andrew Lothian			Wounded in head and lost part of his skull	Born c.1660
Alexander Balsnott			Cut over nose and left shinbone	Born c.1661
Hennick			Killed	Married
James Fergusone		Balfour's regiment, Cunningham's company	Killed	Married
Alexander Pargill		Mackay's regiment, Lammy's company	Killed	Married
Alexander Milne		Mackay's regiment, Hackett's company	Killed	Married
William Stevenson		Mackay's regiment, Hackett's company	Killed	Married
Andrew Murray	Sergeant	Ramsay's regiment, Murray's company	Killed	Married
Thomas Windrame			Killed	Married
George Lausone	Sergeant	Beest's company	Killed	Married
Francis Opper		Leven's regiment	Killed	Married
William Menzies	Corporal	Annadale's Horse	Prisoner	
James Dewar		Mackay's regiment	Killed	Married
Hugh Ross		Mackay's regiment	Shot twice	
Richard Robertsone	Corporal	Kenmure's regiment, Donaldsone's company	Wounded 22 times	Married
Alexander Johnstone		Kerr's company	Prisoner	
Duncan McCawler		Kerr's company	Prisoner	
Robert Dowart		Kerr's company	Prisoner	
Daniel Campbell		Kerr's company	Prisoner	
Alexander Johnstone		Kerr's company	Prisoner	
Laflour				
Greenlands				
Stivensone				
Walker				
Addreoss				
Jackobs		Mackay's regiment		Married
Geilmans		Mackay's regiment		Married
McLauchlane		Mackay's regiment		Married
Michells		Mackay's regiment		Married
Fleck	Sergeant			Married
Francis Hopeteir	Master Hoyboy	Leven's battalion		Married and 5 children

RPCS 14, pp.38, 180, 256, 523 and 15, p.54–55, 123, 151, 181, 218, 228; WO116/1

Colour Plate Commentaries

Plate One

1. John Graham of Claverhouse, 1st Viscount Dundee (1648–1689), victor of Killiekrankie and one of its casualties. Claverhouse is dressed as a British general in a scarlet coat laced in gold. A fashionable laced cravat, back- and breastplate, crimson sash, with a blue vest and cavalry top, or 'jacked' boots. The blue cloth vest might easily be substituted with a leather version, equally popular, and the last vestige of the 'buff coat', so popular earlier in the century. The scalloped leather edging to his armour is there to provide protection from the edges of his armour for both himself and his expensive coat. There was no prescribed uniform for general officers in this period: generals wore the uniform of the regiment they were members of or had been previously, or more often a coat of scarlet or crimson decorated with gold or/and silver lace. Coloured cuffs were sometimes, but less often, worn. Officers of every rank, not just generals, perceived the 'King's coat' to be a form of livery, and this attitude persisted till the early part of the eighteenth century. The image is based on paintings of Claverhouse and pictures by Henri Gascars of a number of Scottish officers, including the Earl of Dumbarton.

2. General Hugh Mackay of Scourie (1640–1692), a long-serving officer in the Dutch army's Anglo-Scots Brigade. Scourie was killed in 1692 at Steenkirk during William III's campaigns in Flanders and Brabant. He carries a baton showing his status, and is wearing a fur-lined crimson riding coat over his scarlet frock coat. Like Claverhouse he wears the British Army's crimson sash, tied at the front. This sash was often worn by both sides during the Jacobite wars in their determination to claim legitimacy.

3. Colonel Cannon wears a senior officer's uniform of a French style. As an officer of the Queen Consort's Regiment of Dragoons he could also wear the regiment's yellow-faced coat, or a plain scarlet/red/crimson as was common.

4. A Government general officer/aide in the plain campaign dress of a red coat.

Plate Two

1. Pikeman, Purcell's Regiment. A poorly equipped Pikeman in a regular Jacobite regiment. Without a sword, and in a much-repaired old coat, he represents the difficulties Claverhouse's army had in obtaining equipment.

2. Trooper, Royal Regiment of Horse. The elements that remained loyal to James II were dressed identically to their Williamite counterparts, in this case in red-faced blue, for a Royal Regiment, and the buff crossbelts which distinguished cavalry from dragoons, who wore a waist belt.

3. Reformado officer. Often a serving officer whose regiment had joined William of Orange, or who had been dismissed because of his Catholicism. This man wears typical gentry dress, taken from the images on playing cards relating to the wars.

Plate Three

1. Based on John Michael Wright's portrait of Lord Mungo Murray c.1683, one of the few paintings of Highlanders made during the period. With a beautiful decorated collar of charges, a fine 'bollock' dagger and other exquisite accoutrements, Murray is the epitome of Highland gentry. For the picture his black befeathered bonnet was replaced by a plainer blue one. In the background of the original painting his ghillie can be seen, wearing trews.

2. Taken from the early-eighteenth century painting by Wait of Alastair Grant Mor, the Laird of Grant's ceremonial champion. Grant is armed with a sword and targe, and on the original painting, an elaborate fowling piece with a strange butt. Given the additional firearm, it may be that the positioning of the targe conceals bandoliers or a bullet bag of some sort.

3. With a 'Lochaber' axe and his plaid wrapped around him, this is what much of the Highland army must have looked like at Killiekrankie.

Plate Four

1. Based on a contemporary watercolour in the Royal Collection, as are the two other figures on this plate, this is a musketeer of Major General Hugh Mackay's Regiment.

2. A Musketeer of Colonel Bartholomew Balfour's Regiment in a red coat lined red, white vest, breeches and hose. C.C.P. Lawson lists their facings as yellow, but this seems unlikely. Balfour took over the regiment in 1684, and it passed to another member of the family on his death; it had originally been formed in 1603.

3. The final regiment of the Scots Brigade serving at Killiekrankie was Colonel George Ramsay's Regiment, with white linings and probably red vest.
1a. Probable colour for Balfour's Foot.
2a. Typical Scots colour of the period.
3a. Probable colour for Ramsay's Foot.
4a. Probable colour for Mackay's Foot.

Plate Five

1. There is some debate as to whether Scots regiments wore bonnets, at this time, with opinions divided on the subject. There is strong evidence that the long-established lowland regiments such as the Royal Scots wore hats, but it seems quite possible that the newly raised regiments wore bonnets. This is a musketeer of the Earl of Leven's Regiment with a collar of bandoliers and plug bayonet, which were used extensively at Killiekrankie.

2. Officer, the Earl of Leven's Regiment. In general, Scots officers' coats were less heavily decorated than their English counterparts. In addition there was also less prejudice against wearing the facing of the parent regiment. On this occasion, however, this officer has chosen to wear an unfaced coat in crimson, and a plain hat.

3. Pikeman of Lord Kenmure's Regiment in a red, lined red coat and a sword on his shoulder, rather than on a waist belt. Pikemen are sometimes depicted wearing a small plaid.

4. Possible flag types for these regiments. The first two are designs used by other Scottish units, the third being a possible reconstruction of a flag for the Earl of Leven's Regiment.

Plate Six

1. Musketeer of Colonel Ferdinando Hastings' Regiment. An English regiment, originally raised by the Earl of Huntingdon, it had red coats with yellow facings and breeches and hats turned up with white lace edging. The musketeer is equipped with a cartridge box, which is gradually replacing the bandoliers, and has a matchlock musket and plug bayonet.
1a. Colours of Hastings' Regiment, from left to right: the colonel's, lieutenant-colonel's and major's colours.

2. Trooper, Earl of Annandale's Horse. This regiment may have gone into action without their new uniforms, which were ordered to be red-faced red coats, with 96 buttons and hats with white tape. He wears the crossbelts which distinguish regiments of horse at this time.

3. Gunner, Scots Artillery. 'Gunners had suits of fine scarlet cloth, lined with serge and decorated with long silk loops, silver buttons, buff belts and silver buckles, fur caps, laced with gold gallon, and scarlet stockings'.

Plate Seven

1, 2, 3, 4. Musketeer, officer and pikeman and possible colour of the Cameronians. Previous comments regarding bonnets are also relevant here, though there is reference to the regiment throwing their bonnets in the air when the day had been won at Dunkeld. Sufferers from the vicious 'killing times', the Cameronians were the eventual nemesis of Dundee's rebellion.

Plate Eight

1. Trooper, Royal Regiment of Scots Dragoons, wearing the blue-lined red coat of a Royal Regiment, with blue breeches and vest. The whole regiment may have worn brown fur caps, or that might have been limited to the grenadier company.

2. Musketeer, James Leslie's Regiment, red coat lined red, grey breeches, white stockings.

3. Lord Colchester's Horse, red coat lined green, horse crossbelts and, on this occasion, back- and breastplates. There is some debate over armour in this period; certainly the armour issued to Marlborough's troopers in Flanders, from the middle years of the Spanish Succession Wars, was probably worn under the coat.

Bibliography

Primary Sources

Manuscript

Edinburgh University Archives
  Laing Mss, 338, f.88

The National Archives
  ADM8/2
  ADM51/3796.
  ADM4285/1.
  ADM51/389/4.
  ADM106/399
  ADM51/345.
  WO5/5.
  WO116/1.

National Archives of Scotland
  CH12/12/1717
  E100/13
  GD26/8/71
  GD26/9/4/3
  GD26/13/98
  GD77/189
  GD124/15/808
  GD406/1/3595, 3605-3609, 3644, 3647,

National Library of Scotland
  ADV13.1.8
  MS, 3738, 7026
  MS3740

Royal Archives
  Cumberland Papers, 1/17–24.

Printed

T. Thomson (ed.), *The Acts of the Parliaments of Scotland* (Edinburgh, 1814–1875)

John Addy, John Harrop and Peter MacNiven, 'The Diary of Henry Prescott, LLB, Deputy Registrar of the Diocese of Chester', Vol. III, *Record Society of Lancashire and Cheshire,* CXXXIII (1997)

James Allardyce, *Historical Papers relating to the Jacobite Period, 1689–1746*, I (Aberdeen: Spalding Club, 1895)

A True and Real account of the Defeat of General Buchan and Brigadier Cannon (London, 1690)

An Exact Narrative of the Conflict at Dunkeld (Edinburgh, 1689)

Anon., *Memoir of Lord Dundee* (London, 1711)

Anon., 'Gleanings from the Cluny Charter Chest', *Transactions of the Gaelic Society of Inverness*, XX (1894–1896)

Archaeological Metal Detecting Survey at Killiecrankie Battlefield (2015)

John Atholl, *Chronicles of the Atholl and Tullibardine Families*, 5 vols. (Edinburgh: privately printed, 1908)

Balcarres, Earl of, *Memoirs touching the Revolution in Scotland* (Edinburgh: Bannatyne Club, 1841)

Andrew Browning (ed.), *English Historical Documents*, VIII (London: Eyre and Spottiswoode, 1953)

Gilbert Burnet, *History of His Own Time* (London, 1883)

Robert Burns, *Complete Poems and Songs* (Glasgow, 1995)

Calendar of State Papers Domestic of the Reign of William III, Preserved in the Public Record Office, 1689–1690 (London: HMSO, 1913)

George Carleton, *The Military Memoirs of an English Officer* (London, 1728)

J.S. Clarke (ed.), *Life of James the Second*, II (London, 1816)

Andrew Crichton, *Life and Diary of Lt. Colonel John Blackadder* (Edinburgh: H.S. Baynes, 1825)

Charles Dalton, *English Army Lists and Commission Registers, 1660–1714*, 6 vols (London: Eyre and Spottiswoode, 1892–1904)

Charles Dalton,, *Scots Army, 1661–1688* (London: Eyre and Spottiswoode, 1909)

John Dalrymple, *Memoirs of Great Britain and Ireland*, II (Dublin: David Hey, 1773)

Dundee Letters: Letters of John Graham of Claverhouse, Viscount Dundee (Edinburgh: Bannantyne Club, 1826)

Lord Elcho, *Short Account of the Affairs of Scotland, 1744–1746* (Edinburgh: David Douglas, 1907)

John Evelyn, *Diary* (London: Everyman, 2006)

English Courant, 1688–1689

William Fraser, *Melvilles Earls of Melville and the Leslies Earls of Leven*, 3 vols. (Edinburgh, 1890)

James Grant (ed.), 'Seafield Correspondence', SHS, series 2, vol. 3 (1911)

Report on the Manuscripts of the Duke of Athole, and of the Earl of Home (London: HMSO, 1891)

Report on the Manuscripts of the Duke of Buccleuch and Queensberry preserved at Montagu House, Whitehall (London: HMSO, 1903), II

Report on the Manuscripts of S.H. Le Fleming, Esq. of Rydal Hall (London: HMSO, 1890)

Report on the Manuscripts of J.J Johnstone, Esq. of Annandale (London, HMSO, 1897)

Report on the The Manuscripts of the Duke of Hamilton (London: HMSO, 1887)

Report on the Manuscripts of F.W. Leyborne- Popham, Esq. of Littlecote, Co. Wilts (London: HMS, 1899)

Historical Manuscripts Commission, Sixth Report VI (London: HMSO, 1887)

Calendar of the Stuart Papers belonging to His Majesty the King Preserved at Windsor Castle, I (London: HMSO, 1902)

London Gazette, 1688–1692

Narcissus Luttrell, *A Brief relation of State Affairs, 1678–1714*, 6 vols. (Oxford: Oxford University Press, 1857)

Richard Kane, *The Campaigns of King William and Queen Anne* (London: J. Millan, 1745)

Duncan McBane, *The Expert Sword-Man's Companion* (Glasgow: Fallen Book Company, 2015)

Hugh Mackay, *Memoirs of the War carried on in Scotland and Ireland, 1689–1691* (Edinburgh: Bannatyne Club, 1833)

John Mackay, *Rules to be observed by the body of Infantry* (Edinburgh, 1693)

Annie M. Mackenzie (ed.), *Orain Iain Lunn, Songs of John MacDonald, Bard of Keppoch* (Edinburgh: Oliver and Boyd, 1964)

J. MacKnight (ed.), *Memoirs of Lochiel* (Glasgow: Maitland Club, 1842)

J. MacConechy, *Papers Illustrative of the Political Condition of the Highlands of Scotland from the years 1689 to 1696* (Glasgow: Maitland Club, 1845)

James MacPherson (ed.), *Original Papers, containing the Secret history of Great Britain* (London, 1775)

Evan Whyte Melville Balfour-Maitland (ed.) 'Estate Proceedings, An Account of the Proceedings of the Estates of Scotland, 1689-1690', *SHS*, series 4, vols. 46, 47 (1954–1955)

David George Mallan (ed.), 'Protestant Piety in Early Modern Scotland: Letters, Lives and Covenants, 1650–1712', *SHS*, series 5, Vol. 17 (2008)

A.H. Miller (ed.), 'Eye Witness Account of Killiecrankie', *Scottish History Review*, III (1905)
Thomas Morer, *A Short Account of Scotland* (London: T. Newborough, 1702)
Rev. Alexander Murdoch (ed.), 'The Grameid: an heroic poem on the Campaign of 1689', SHS I, Vol. 3 (1888)
Mark Napier, *Memorials and Letters of Dundee*, 3 vols. (Edinburgh and London, 1862)
G. Neil (ed.), 'Journal of a Soldier in the Earl of Eglington's Troop of Horse', *Transactions of the Glasgow Archaeological Society*, I (1868)
Roger Orrery, *A Treatise of the Art of War* (London, 1677)
John Patten, *The History of the Rebellion in the year 1715* (London: James Roberts, 1745)
Register of the Privy Council of Scotland, 3rd series, vols. 13–16, 1686–1691 (Edinburgh, 1932–1970).
Pat Rogers, *Daniel Defoe's Tour through the Whole Island of Great Britain* (Harmondsworth: Penguin, 1971)
Andrew Murray Scott (ed.), 'Letters of John Graham of Claverhouse', *SHS Miscellany 11*, 5th series, Vol. 3 (1990)
Walter Scott (ed.), *Memoirs of the Insurrection in Scotland in 1715* (Edinburgh: Abbotsford, 1858)
The Scotsman, 1932
G. Storey, *An Impartial History of Affairs of Ireland during the last two years* (London, 1691)
J. and D. Stewart, *The Stewarts of Appin* (Edinburgh: privately printed, 1880)
Extracts from the Council Registers of the Burgh of Aberdeen, 1643–1747 (Edinburgh, 1832)
Theatrum Scotiae (London, 1693)
Universal Intelligencer, 1688

Secondary Sources

Anon., *Dunkeld its Straths and Glens* (Dunkeld: A. MacLean and Son, 1865)
Anon., *The Killiecrankie Story* (National Trust for Scotland, 1978)
John Barratt, *Battles for the Three Kingdoms, 1689–92* (Stroud: Sutton Publishing, 2006)
Michael Barthorp, *The Jacobite Rebellions, 1689–1745* (London: Osprey Publishing, 1982)
David Blackmore, *Destructive and Formidable: British infantry Firepower, 1642–1765* (London, Frontline Books, 2014)
Lyndsey Bowditch, Benjamin Notley, Euan O'She and Louise Medine, *Killiecrankie* (National Trust for Scotland, 2015)
John Buchan, *The Massacre of Glencoe* (London: Peter Davies, 1934)
Thomas Carter, *Historical Records of the 26th or Cameronian Regiment* (London: Byfield, Stanford & Co., 1867)
David Chandler, *Marlborough as Military Commander* (London: Batsford, 1973)
David Chandler, *Oxford History of the British Army* (Oxford: Oxford University Press, 2003)
John Childs, *The Nine Years War and the British Army, 1688–1697* (Manchester: Manchester University Press, 1991)
John Childs, *James II, the Army and the Glorious Revolution* (Manchester: Manchester University Press, 1980)
John Childs, *The Williamite War in Ireland, 1688–1691* (London: Hambledon Continuum, 2007)
James Ferguson, 'Papers illustrating the History of the Scots Brigade in the service of the United Netherlands, I, 1572–1697', *SHS*, 1, Vol. 32 (1898)
Catriona Fforde, *A Summer in Lochaber* (Colonsay: House of Lochar, 2002)
Leo Gooch, *The Desperate Faction? The Jacobites of North East England, 1688–1745* (Hull University Press, 1995)
Charles Stewart Grant, *From Pike to Shot, 1685–1720* (Wargames Research Group, 1986)
James Michael Hill, *Celtic Warfare, 1595–1763* (Edinburgh: John Donald, 1986)
Tim Harris, *Revolution: The Great Crisis of the British Monarchy, 1685–1720* (London: Allen Books, 2006)
Paul Hopkins, *Glencoe and the end of the Highland War* (Edinburgh: John Donald, 1989)
John Kenyon, *The Stuarts* (Glasgow: Fontana, 1970)
Bruce Lenman, *The Jacobite Risings in Britain, 1689–1746* (London: Methuen, 1980)
Bruce Lenman, *The Jacobite Clans of the Great Glen, 1650–1784* (London: Methuen, 1984)
Magnus Linkwater and Christian Hesketh, *John Graham of Claverhouse, Bonnie Dundee: For King and Conscience* (Edinburgh: Cannongate, 1989)

Paul Monod, *Jacobitism and the English people, 1689–1788* (Cambridge: Cambridge University Press, 1989)
Oxford Companion to Scottish History (Oxford: Oxford University Press, 2007)
Oxford Dictionary of National Biography (Oxford: Oxford University Press, 2004)
Charles Petrie, *The Jacobite Movement* (London: Eyre and Spottiswoode, 1932)
Murray G. H. Pittock, *Jacobitism* (Macmillan, 1998)
Pollard, Anthony and Oliver, Neil, *Two Men in a Trench*, II (London: Michael Joseph, 2003)
John Prebble, *Glencoe: the story of the massacre* (London: Penguin, 1967)
Stuart Reid, *Killiecrankie* (Leigh on Sea: Partizan Press, 1989)
Stuart Reid, *The Last Scots Army, 1661–1714* (Leigh on Sea: Partizan Press, 2003)
Stuart Reid, *Sheriffmuir: Battle for Scotland* (Barnsley: History Press, 2014)
James Rennie, *In the Footsteps of the Clansmen* (London: Rich and Gowan, 1951)
Trevor Royle, *Civil War: The War of the Three Kingdoms* (London: Littlebrown, 2005)
John Sadler, *Glencoe: The Infamous Massacre* (Stroud: Amberley, 2008)
Andrew Scott, *Bonnie Dundee* (Edinburgh: John Donald, 2000)
David Stevenson, 'Scotland's Leather Guns', *History Scotland*, 2/6, Nov./Dec. 2002
Daniel Szechi, *The Jacobites: Britain and Europe, 1688–1788* (Manchester: Manchester University Press, 1994)
Alastair and Henrietta Tayler, *John Graham of Claverhouse* (London: Duckworth, 1938)

Electronic sources

<www.lochiel.net/archgives/arch173.html>
Paul Hopkins, 'Loup Hill. 16 May 1689. The First Battle of Dundee's Highland war', *Kintyre Antiquarian and Natural History Society*, web edition, 18 and 19 June 1998